CHICAGO SKETCHES

Chicago in 1779; inset: Jean Baptiste Pointe du Sable (c. 1745–1818). Aquatint by A. Ackermann and Sons, from an engraving by Rauol Varin (Chicago Historical Society, ICHi–05622). Du Sable was Chicago's first permanent settler. His trading post was located at the mouth of the Chicago River near what is now the Tribune Tower.

CHICAGO SKETCHES

URBAN TALES, STORIES, AND LEGENDS
FROM CHICAGO HISTORY

June Skinner Sawyers

 Wild Onion Books

an imprint of
Loyola Press
Chicago

∞

Wild Onion Books
an imprint of Loyola Press
3441 North Ashland Avenue
Chicago, Illinois 60657

Wild Onion Books publishes provocative titles on Chicago themes that offer diverse perspectives on the city and surrounding area, its history, its culture, and its religions. Wild onion is a common nickname for Chicago.

Cover design: Frederick Falkenberg and Nancy Gruenke
Cover photo collagé: Bob Masheris
Maps and interior design: Katie Hayden

Most of these selections appeared in the *Chicago Tribune* column "Way We Were" from July 1986 to October 1989 in slightly different form.

Wild Onion Books staff:
Editorial director: Joseph F. Downey, S.J.
Imprint editors: June Sawyers, Jeremy Langford
Production coordinator: Jill Mark Salyards

Library of Congress Cataloging-in-Publication data
Sawyers, June Skinner, 1957–
        Chicago sketches: urban tales, stories, and legends from
    Chicago history/June Skinner Sawyers
                p.   cm.
        Includes bibliographical references and index.
        ISBN 0-8294-0820-7 (alk. paper). —ISBN 0-8294-0819-3
    (pbk. : alk. paper)
        1. Chicago (Ill.)—History. I. Title.
    F548.35.S29 1995   94-40991
    977.3'11—dc20   CIP

To E. M. L. P.

CONTENTS

PHOTOGRAPHS

MAPS

 ACKNOWLEDGMENTS

A collection of this sort could not have been done without the cooperation of many people. In particular, I would like to thank Mary Ann Bamberger at the University of Illinois at Chicago; Mary Ann Johnson at Jane Addams's Hull-House Museum; the staff of the Chicago Historical Society, especially Eileen Flanagan in the Prints and Photographs department; the Newberry Library; and the *Chicago Tribune* library for their cooperation. At the *Tribune,* Steve Marino and Abby DeShane deserve special praise for their diligent research, patience, and unfailing good humor.

Wayne Rethford, director of the Scottish Home in North Riverside, and Bill Currie helped me with the section on the Illinois Saint Andrew Society and Scottish immigration to the United States, while Richard C. Bjorklund and Carl R. Hansen shared information on the *Viking*'s journey to the New World. Many others helped in countless ways. They include Les Orear, Norman Schwartz, Danny Newman, Irving Cutler, and Jacob Mark.

Thanks also to Kevin O'Donnell and Chris and Tom Kastle for granting permission to use the lyrics of their songs, "The Illinois and Michigan Canal" and "The *Eastland,*" respectively.

Throughout the editing process, Jane Samuelson gave generously of her time and considerable expertise. At Loyola Press, Sarah Downey did a lot of last-minute checking—a tedious task for which I am very grateful! Jeremy Langford perused the manuscript with his usual flair and attention to detail.

Finally, a personal word of appreciation to Bill Mañago, my editor at the *Chicago Tribune Sunday Magazine,* for his skill and expertise with a blue pencil; and to Beverly Godfrey for her persistence.

INTRODUCTION

Fifty-eight of the following seventy-two essays originally appeared in the *Chicago Tribune Sunday Magazine* in slightly different form. Fifteen are new essays.

There are various drawbacks to writing a weekly history column. With a deadline always looming, there never seems to be enough time to do the proper research. (One always wishes to do more, to check one more source.) Nor is there ever enough space to do as thorough a job as I would like.

This collection of essays allows me some latitude. I have taken advantage of the opportunity by adding, whenever possible, information to the previously published essays, while making the new essays a bit longer.

A book format also allows me to acknowledge the many historians who have set the groundwork for future generations of history students. Thus, the reader will find a rather extensive annotated bibliography and, when necessary, endnotes at the end of the particular chapters. Whenever possible, information on museums, organizations, and select historical sites has been added. I have included maps for a number of essays in order to give the reader a mental picture of the subject matter.

Although I have tried to cover as many topics as possible in this collection, *Chicago Sketches* makes no attempt to be comprehensive. There are already many books that admirably serve that purpose. Indeed, one could say my selections reveal a distinctive bias toward certain subjects. I admit forthrightly, for example, that I do have a soft spot in my heart for the offbeat, the unusual, the slighty skewed personalities who have walked through the pages of Chicago history books.

I have divided the essays according to subject and, within each category, something that I hope approaches vaguely chronological order. Thus, there are sections devoted to early Chicago, radicals and reformers, literary institutions, neighborhood life, law and disorder, spirituality, politics, disasters and events, the arts, visitors, and sports and recreation.

I have also included a chronology of major events in Chicago history, a list of Chicago's mayors, and an appendix of topics that didn't quite fit into the text proper.

The original columns were meant to offer glimpses into Chicago's past; signposts, if you will, into history. This collection of essays serves a similar function. I hope these modest sketches whet the appetite of readers and encourage them to dig deeper on their own and, perhaps in doing so, to find some personal meaning in the pages of dusty history books. For what is history if not a means of connecting with our past?

EARLY DAYS

Chicago River, circa 1915. Now the site of Illinois Center, which is
bounded roughly by the Chicago River, North Lake Shore Drive, North
Michigan Avenue, and East Lake Street.

THE LAST OF THE POTAWATOMI:
THE TREATY THAT GAVE IT ALL AWAY

In 1833 Chicago was little more than a sparse community of about 150 souls living in hastily erected houses. It barely deserved to be called a village. In August of that year more than eight thousand people—including as many as six thousand Potawatomi—flocked to the tiny settlement on the edge of Lake Michigan. The Potawatomi had come to sign a treaty that would give away the land that had been theirs for generations.[1] They were joined by thousands of con artists, salesmen, journalists, prostitutes, and various fly-by-night operators. Interested observers have described the meeting as part circus and part spectacle. Historian Milo Quaife, for example, called it "the last and greatest Indian council ever held at Chicago. . . . " It also happened to be a moment of enormous historical significance.

The Potawatomi chiefs reportedly signed the historic treaty in September of that year under an old elm tree that once stood at what is now the intersection of Rogers, Kilbourn, and Caldwell Avenues on the Northwest Side. A plaque, now tarnished, marks the spot.

The Chicago treaty stipulated, among other things, that the Potawatomi were to immediately leave their Illinois and Wisconsin lands and move to a reservation on the east bank of the Missouri River. (The mass upheaval did not actually begin, however, until 1835.) The following three commissioners were on hand to determine who would get what: George B. Porter, governor of the Michigan Territory; Thomas Owen, Indian agent; and William Weatherford, politician.

Surrounded by woodlands and prairie, a carnival atmosphere prevailed in the little village. Tents were propped up along the river. The Indians entertained themselves with conversation, gambling, and horse racing. They brought with them their squaws, ponies, and papooses. There were also land speculators, horse dealers—and horse thieves, for that matter—and Indian agents present. Traders and hangers-on also attended, further taxing the patience of the residents. Chicago had a few hotels at the time—primitive by today's standards. Those Indians who could afford it wore gaudy costumes with colorful sashes and shawls, their faces painted in blue, black, and white hues. Quaife describes the spectacle of fifty or so Indians, riding on horseback and followed by an additional thirty naked braves, dancing and shouting their way from Fort Dearborn to the foot of South Water Street.

The Native American leaders were no fools. On the contrary, they were shrewd negotiators. Pressured by the American government to give up their land and vastly outnumbered by an increasing stream of white settlers, they tried to make the best of an increasingly bad situation. President James Monroe and later Andrew Jackson pursued an aggressive government policy that promoted Indian removal from their ancestral home by promising them vast sums of money and the allure of expansive tracts of land in the West. The Indians were, notes historian James Clifton, "determined to secure the best possible bargain."

A leading figure in Chicago during that time was Billy Caldwell. Caldwell, the son of a British army officer and an Indian mother, was an influential trader and Indian expert. He was also a well-educated man who spoke French and English as well as several Indian languages and fought on the side of the Potawatomi during the War of 1812. After the war ended, he encouraged the white and Indian peoples to pursue a policy of peace. He even played a part in the Fort Dearborn Massacre, reportedly saving members of the Kinzie family from certain death.

Caldwell persuaded the Potawatomi to cede their remaining lands to the government. For his support of the treaty of 1833, he received ample perks from the government, including, according to one account, a lifetime annuity of six hundred dollars and a private reserve of two and one-half sections along the north branch of the

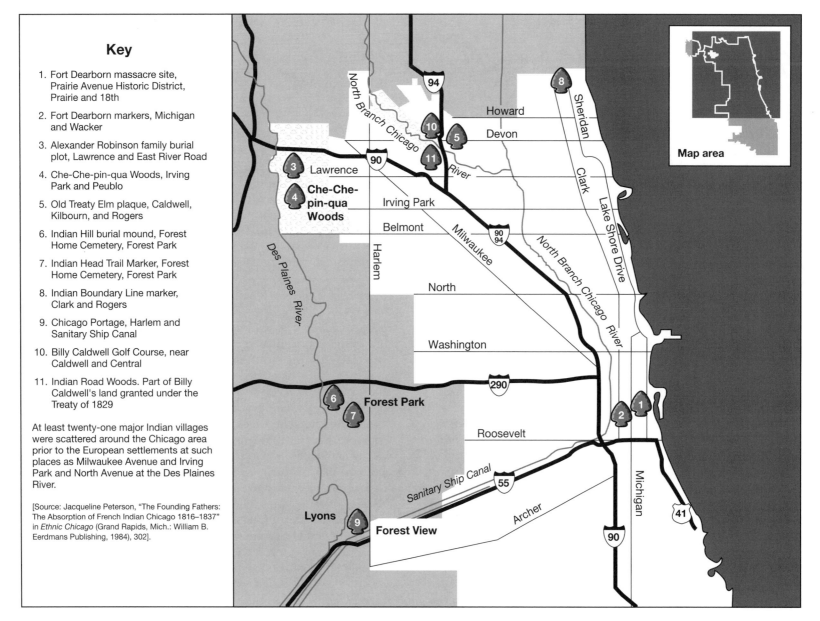

Key

1. Fort Dearborn massacre site, Prairie Avenue Historic District, Prairie and 18th

2. Fort Dearborn markers, Michigan and Wacker

3. Alexander Robinson family burial plot, Lawrence and East River Road

4. Che-Che-pin-qua Woods, Irving Park and Peublo

5. Old Treaty Elm plaque, Caldwell, Kilbourn, and Rogers

6. Indian Hill burial mound, Forest Home Cemetery, Forest Park

7. Indian Head Trail Marker, Forest Home Cemetery, Forest Park

8. Indian Boundary Line marker, Clark and Rogers

9. Chicago Portage, Harlem and Sanitary Ship Canal

10. Billy Caldwell Golf Course, near Caldwell and Central

11. Indian Road Woods. Part of Billy Caldwell's land granted under the Treaty of 1829

At least twenty-one major Indian villages were scattered around the Chicago area prior to the European settlements at such places as Milwaukee Avenue and Irving Park and North Avenue at the Des Plaines River.

[Source: Jacqueline Peterson, "The Founding Fathers: The Absorption of French Indian Chicago 1816–1837" in *Ethnic Chicago* (Grand Rapids, Mich.: William B. Eerdmans Publishing, 1984), 302].

Map 1 Indian Historic Sites

Chicago River.[2] The government also built a frame house for him at what is now the corner of Chicago and Wabash Avenues.[3] He lived there with his wife until 1836, when he traveled with his tribe to their reservation in Missouri and finally to another reservation near Council Bluffs, Iowa. Caldwell died on September 27, 1841.

Another important figure in early Chicago was Alexander Robinson, or Che-che-pin-qua (Winking Eye or Blinking Eye). The son of a Scottish trader and an Ottawa Indian mother, Robinson lived with the Potawatomi as a young man near St. Joseph, Michigan. In 1826 he married Catherine Chevalier, daughter of a Potawatomi chief. The marriage ceremony was reportedly performed by John Kinzie, one of the city's founding fathers. When Robinson's father-in-law died, Robinson became the chief.

Robinson moved to Chicago in 1814. He reportedly lived in a cabin at a place called Hardscrabble (the former name of Bridgeport) at Racine Avenue and the south branch of the Chicago River. He also worked as an interpreter for the Indian agent Alexander Wolcott. In 1830 he was given a license to open a tavern in Chicago, which stood at Canal and Lake Streets, at the fork of the Chicago River.

Robinson acted as an interpreter at Fort Dearborn and, like Caldwell, promoted peace. For this reason, the U.S. government awarded him two sections of land on the Des Plaines River near present-day Lawrence Avenue and later gave him a life annuity of two hundred dollars. The Chicago Treaty in September 1833 granted him an additional three hundred dollars for life. Robinson's Reserve consisted of about twelve hundred acres from south of what is now Irving Park to Foster Avenue on the north where the Des Plaines River ran through the property. Today this is mostly forest preserves and is called, appropriately, Che-che-pin-qua Woods, Robinson Woods, and Catherine Chevalier Woods, respectively.

Indian Head Trail Marker, Forest Home Cemetery, Forest Park (photo by June Skinner Sawyers). Erected in 1947 "to mark an old trail through woods and wild plum bushes along the river," the marker consists of the profile of an Indian head carved into a large boulder. In the same cemetery is the Indian Hill Marker, a seven-foot granite monument, erected in 1941, that commemorates what was once the center of a Potawatomi village and burial ground.

The Potawatomi essentially signed away everything they owned to the U.S. government. The treaty eventually sent them into exile in Iowa, Missouri, and Kansas. Others traveled north into the forests of Wisconsin; still others went east to the shores of Lake Huron in Canada. The last of the Potawatomi left Illinois in 1835. The "freedom" they purchased proved to be a short-lived and hollow promise.

Notes

1. The Potawatomi were not the only tribe involved. A united contingent of Potawatomi, Chippewa, and Ottawa tribes ceded all their land east of the Mississippi in exchange for some five million acres west of the Missouri. See Jacqueline Peterson, "The Founding Fathers: The Absorption of French-Indian Chicago 1816–1837," in *Ethnic Chicago,* edited by Melvin G. Holli and Peter d'A. Jones (Grand Rapids, Mich.: William B. Eerdmans Publishing Company, 1984), 329–30.
2. Other sources say he received an annuity of four hundred dollars, a six hundred dollar gift for his family, and a five thousand dollar bonus.
3. Other sources say his house was located at the corner of what is now State Street and Chicago Avenue.

Museums

- *Field Museum of Natural History.* Roosevelt Road at Lake Shore Drive, Chicago 60605; 312-922-9410. Hours: Daily, 9 A.M.–5 P.M. Closed New Year's Day, Thanksgiving, and Christmas. Admission: Adults, $3; children 2–7, senior citizens, and students, $2; families maximum, $10; children under 2, free; Thursday free. Indian costumes, weapons, and cultural artifacts in the Webber Resource Center.
- *Mitchell Indian Museum.* Kendall College, 2408 Orrington Avenue, Evanston, Illinois 60201; 708-866-1395. Hours: Monday–Friday, 9 A.M.–4 P.M.; Sunday, 1 P.M.–4 P.M.; Closed in August, on Saturday, and on Kendall College holidays. Admission: Free, but donations suggested. Art and artifacts of the native peoples of North America.
- *D'Arcy McNickle Center for the History of the American Indian.* Newberry Library, 60 West Walton Street, Chicago 60610; 312-943-9090. Hours: Tuesday–Thursday, 10 A.M.–6 P.M.; Friday–Saturday, 9 A.M.–5 P.M. Admission: Free. Seminars, conferences, workshops, adult education courses. The Edward E. Ayer and Everett D. Graff collections contain more than 150,000 volumes on American Indians.

- *Schingoethe Center for Native American Cultures.* Aurora University, 347 South Gladstone, Aurora, Illinois 60506; 708-844-5402. Hours: Monday, Tuesday, Thursday, and Friday, 10 A.M.–4:30 P.M.; Sunday, 1 P.M.–4 P.M.; Closed Wednesday, Saturday, and Aurora University holidays. Represents Southwest, Plains, Woodlands, Northwest Coast, and Northeast Woodlands Indian cultures.

Organizations

- *American Indian Center.* 1630 West Wilson Avenue, Chicago 60640; 312-275-5871. Hours: Monday–Friday, 8:30 A.M.–5 P.M. Admission: Free.
- *Native American Educational Services College (NAES).* 2838 West Peterson Avenue, Chicago 60659; 312-761-5000.

Select historical sites

(All sites are in Chicago unless otherwise indicated)

- *Fort Dearborn Massacre.* Pavement markers, corners of Michigan Avenue and Wacker Drive, commemorate the site of Fort Dearborn.
- *Fort Dearborn Massacre or the Potawatomi Rescue.* Sculpture, in the Prairie Avenue Historic District, honors where the actual attack took place reportedly at what is now Prairie Avenue and Eighteenth Street.
- *Old Indian Cemetery.* East River Road and Lawrence Avenue, marks the site of the family burial plot of Alexander Robinson.
- *Old Treaty Elm plaque.* Intersection of Caldwell, Kilbourn, and Rogers Avenues. Marks the spot where an old elm tree once stood, site of the northern boundary of the Fort Dearborn reservation and also where an Indian treaty ceding land to the government was signed in the 1830s.
- *Indian Hill Burial Mound.* Forest Home Cemetery, 863 Desplaines Avenue, Forest Park, Illinois 60610; 312-287-0772. Former site of a Potawatomi village. Nearby in a secluded corner of the cemetery is the Indian Head Trail Marker, which consists of a striking profile of a Native American brave carved into a boulder.
- *Indian Boundary Line marker.* Clark Street and Rogers Avenue. A marker on the side of a nondescript apartment building honors the boundary line of Indian territory.

(For a description of other prominent Indian sites as well as ancient Indian villages in Illinois, see the appendix.)

THE CANAL THAT BROUGHT THE WORLD TO CHICAGO

So, bid farewell to famine, it's off to Americay
To work as a navigator for 90 cents a day
And hope to dig a fortune by the time they reach LaSalle
On the Illinois and Michigan Canal

"The Illinois and Michigan Canal"
Kevin O'Donnell
(© 1987 Arranmore Music)[1]

Chicago was merely a frontier outpost surrounded by marshy swamplands at the edge of a great lake until a canal linking Lake Michigan to the Illinois River changed all that. Starting from the south branch of the Chicago River at what is now Ashland Avenue near Twenty-eighth Street in the Bridgeport neighborhood, the Illinois and Michigan Canal (I and M) ran along the south bank of the Des Plaines River, joining it at Joliet. From the Des Plaines River south of Joliet, it went along the north bank of the Illinois River until it hooked up with it in LaSalle-Peru, a journey of nearly one hundred miles. By being provided with a waterway that cut across the state and, through the Illinois River, led into the Mississippi River and on to New Orleans, the fledgling town took a giant stride toward becoming a commercial and industrial giant.

As far back as 1673, French explorers Louis Jolliet and Father Jacques Marquette had envisioned a waterway along a portage route between the Chicago and Des Plaines Rivers. In 1822 the state legislature authorized construction of the Illinois-Michigan Canal and appointed a canal commission to mark out the proposed route between Chicago and LaSalle-Peru.

The plan? To build a canal sixty feet wide and six feet deep along some ninety-six miles. The commissioners needed workers to dig the "old ditch"—men who were not afraid to work hard, who could do the back-breaking work without complaint. And work hard they did—fourteen hours, six days a week. Digging began, amid cheers and celebration, on July 4, 1836, in Bridgeport. The work crews were composed mostly of Irish immigrants, or "navvies," who moved with their families from their native land to seek a better life in the New World. These workers lived in shanties along the Des Plaines River. Many had already gained experience building the Erie Canal. Aware of the religious differences and regional rivalries that divided the Irishmen, crafty canal foremen would square off workmen from the north of Ireland against those from the south and challenge them to show who could do more work faster. A severe depression in 1837 interrupted construction for a while, but the canal was finally completed in April 1848, when the *General Fry* made the twenty-nine-mile journey from Lockport to Bridgeport.[2]

The earliest users of the canal were passenger and cargo boats towed by horses or mules at about six miles an hour. At four dollars a head (which included meals and a berth), excursion trips were always popular. Leaving Chicago or LaSalle three times a day, the excursionists made the round trip in just under twenty-four hours.

The "old ditch," as the I and M canal was called, brought a new level of prosperity to Chicago. Business expanded at a tremendous rate, and the population boomed. Boats carrying lumber, corn, grain, sugar, salt, and pork traveled up and down the busy waterway. Along with LaSalle-Peru at the canal's south end, other communities along its route blossomed, too—Lockport, Joliet, Seneca, and Ottawa.

After reaching its peak in 1882, canal traffic began to taper off and soon became an anachronism, largely because the train had come along as a faster, more comfortable, and more efficient means of commercial and personal transportation.

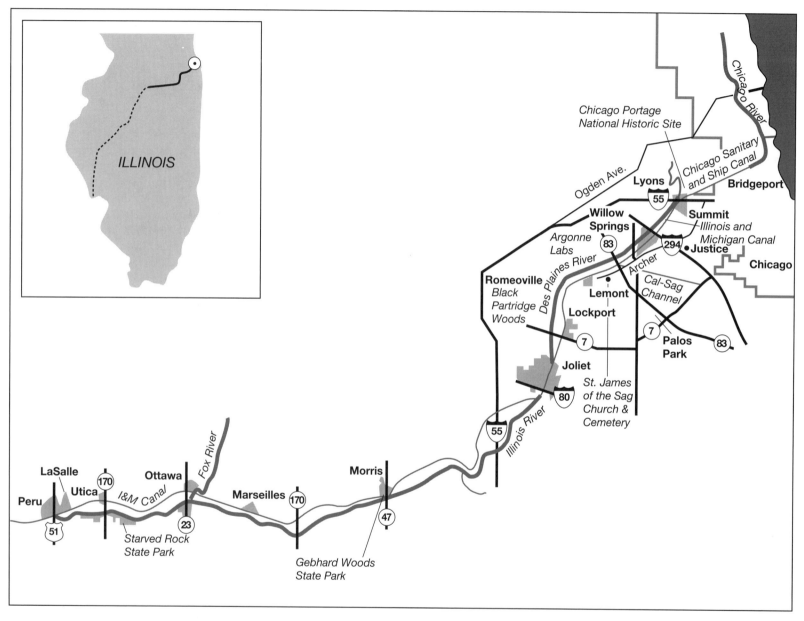

Map 2 Illinois and Michigan Canal

A direct competitor came in the form of the Illinois Sanitary and Ship Canal. Opened in 1900, the wider and deeper waterway, running parallel to the old canal between Chicago and Joliet, handled both waste disposal and barge traffic. By 1933 this section of the I & M had become a city refuse dump and breeding ground for mosquitoes, and in the 1940s there were various proposals to fill in this end of the canal and build a superhighway on or along it. The Stevenson Expressway, in fact, now covers portions of the old canal between Leavitt Street at Thirty-first Street in Chicago and the suburb of Summit.

In 1974 the sixty-mile stretch of the canal from Joliet to LaSalle was designated the Illinois and Michigan Canal State Trail. A decade later, in 1984, President Ronald Reagan signed a bill creating the Illinois and Michigan Canal Heritage Corridor as a model national park to preserve and utilize the historical, recreational, and industrial aspects of the I and M. Institutions such as the Illinois and Michigan Canal Civic Authority and the Illinois and Michigan Canal Museum in Lockport have helped to restore as much of the canal as possible. The canal between Joliet and LaSalle-Peru is still recognizable as such, and along the northern edge of the Palos Forest Preserve between Willow Springs and Illinois Highway 83, a portion of it has been preserved as a small memorial to the great role it once played in the growth of a great city.

Notes

1. "The Illinois and Michigan Canal" appears on *Island Home* by Arranmore (Arranmore Music).
2. According to local historian Kenan Heise, the *General Fry* sailed from Lockport to the Chicago River on April 10. Later, another ship, the *General Thornton,* made the entire trip along the canal, leaving LaSalle on April 19 and arriving in Chicago on April 23. See Kenan Heise and Michael Edgerton, *Chicago: Center for Enterprise,* 2 vols. (Woodland Hills, Calif.: Windsor Publications, 1982), 56.

Museums

- *Fitzpatrick House.* Illinois and Michigan Canal National Heritage Corridor Commission, 15701 South Independence Boulevard, Lockport, Illinois 60441; 815-740-2047. Hours: Monday–Friday, 8 A.M.–4:30 P.M. Named after Patrick Fitzpatrick, an Irishman who worked on the canal and prospered. Houses the Federal Commission for the Illinois and Michigan Canal National Heritage Corridor.
- *I and M Canal Visitor Center.* 200 West Eighth Street, Lockport, Illinois 60441; 815-838-4830. Hours: Daily 10 A.M.–5 P.M.; Closed Monday and Tuesday.
- *I and M Canal State Trail Headquarters—Gebhard Woods Access.* P.O. Box 272, Ottawa Street, Morris, Illinois 60450; 815-942-0796. Hours: Daily 10 A.M.–4 P.M.

Organizations

- *Heritage Corridor Visitor Bureau.* 81 North Chicago Street, Joliet, Illinois 60431; 815-727-2323 or 1-800-926-2262. Hours: Monday–Friday, 8 A.M.–4:30 P.M.

Select historical sites

- *Chicago Portage National Historic Site.* Forest Preserve District of Cook County, Cummings Square, 536 North Harlem Avenue, River Forest, Illinois 60305; 708-771-1330. Sculpture of Marquette and Jolliet and their Native American guide.
- *St. James of the Sag Church and Cemetery.* 10600 Archer Avenue, Lemont, Illinois 60439; 708-257-7000. Historic Catholic church built in the 1850s. Laborers, many of them Irish immigrants, who worked on the canal are buried here.

The Viking. Oil painting by Emil Bjorn (Chicago Historical Society, ICHi–02508). Artist's interpretation of the *Viking* on the open sea, en route to the World's Columbian Exposition of 1893 in Chicago.

ALONG THE VIKING TRAIL: MAGNUS ANDERSEN'S JOURNEY IN THE NEW WORLD

It must have been quite a sight. On July 12, 1893, a Viking longship entered Chicago harbor and was met by a flotilla of sailboats, tugboats, canoes, rowboats, and yachts, including steamers carrying various welcoming parties and Scandinavian societies. Crowds gathered on the shore and gave the twelve-man Norwegian crew a hearty welcome, including a twenty-one-gun salute. "Remember, Captain Andersen," Mayor Carter Harrison said in his opening remarks, "that the city of Chicago is the fourth largest Scandinavian city in the world . . . I welcome you in the name of your brother Northmen in Chicago."

Unlike their seafaring ancestors, these latter-day Vikings had come to the New World by invitation. Members of the planning committee of the World's Columbian Exposition had asked Norway to lend the Gokstad ship—a national treasure—to Chicago for the fair. Ultimately, the Norwegians turned down the request because they were concerned about the ship's fragile condition. But the idea of steering a Viking ship from Norway to America captured the imagination of Magnus Andersen, a merchant, newspaperman, and expert yachtsman. Performing such a feat, he reasoned, would prove to the world that a Viking ship had sailed to the New World as much as five hundred years before Columbus arrived. Initially, Andersen's plans were greeted with mixed reaction in his native Norway. The Norwegian government, for example, refused to fund the venture, while the business community, originally quite enthusiastic, dropped out. Many newspapers ridiculed Andersen's ambitious dream, and more than a few of his countrymen questioned his judgment and even his sanity.

Andersen persevered, however. As editor of the *Norwegian Shipping Journal* and an avid seaman, he was able to persuade many of Norway's finest seafarers to participate. The experienced twelve-man crew was chosen from among three hundred volunteers. Support came mostly from ordinary folk—some fifteen thousand, according to historian A. A. Dornfeld. The Scandinavian committee of the Chicago world's fair also assisted.

The ship, called the *Viking,* that sailed into Chicago harbor that July day was a replica of the famous Gokstad ship, a Viking ship built circa 900 A.D.[1] Andersen's *Viking* was constructed for a specific purpose: to cross the Atlantic like the Viking ships of old. Norwegian craftsmen built the ship using the same types of tools and techniques as the original. At 76 feet long, 17 feet wide, and 6½ feet high, the ship's measurements also duplicate those of the original. It was constructed of mostly black Norwegian oak. Each side of the *Viking* had 16 oarholes that held 32 pine oaks ranging from 16 to 18 feet in length. Above the oarholes hung 64 shields (32 alternating black and yellow shields on each side). A carved dragon head and tail decorated the bow and stern. Andersen had nothing but praise for the ship's sturdy construction. "[The] rudder must be regarded as one of the conclusive proofs of our forefathers' acumen and skill in shipbuilding and seamanship," he proclaimed. "The rudder is a work of genius . . . a man could steer with this tiller in all kinds of weather without the least discomfort."

With only a single sail and oars to power them, the crew left Bergen, Norway, at noon on April 30, 1893, on their journey across the Atlantic. Andersen tried to follow as much as possible the likely route of his Viking ancestors: north of Scotland past the Orkney and Shetland Islands and south of Iceland and Greenland, while enduring sleet, freezing temperatures, and fierce winds. Twenty-eight days later, on May 27, the crew sighted the coast of Newfoundland. The ship then turned south to New York, went up the Hudson River, through the Erie Canal, and into the Great Lakes, until it reached its destination of Chicago on July 12, 1893.

For the most part, the Norwegians were treated warmly in America.[2] The city certainly made every effort to make the Norwegians' stay in Chicago a pleasant one. The *Viking* was visited by thousands of Chicagoans as it lay docked at the Van Buren Street pier. Mayor Harrison presented Andersen and his crew with the freedom of the city. The following day Andersen and the officers of the *Viking* were given a tour of downtown and, in the evening, a reception was held in their honor at the old Central Music Hall.

After its appearance at the fair, the *Viking* passed through the Illinois and Michigan Canal, maneuvering expertly and gingerly through its narrow passageway. It reached the Illinois River and from there traveled along the Mississippi southward to New Orleans and into the Gulf of Mexico. Thus the *Viking* became the first ship both to cross the Atlantic and travel through the inland waterways of America.

The *Viking* then returned to Chicago and was presented as a gift to the city. For many years it was moored in the lagoon adjacent to the Field Columbian Museum (later the Museum of Science and Industry and then the Field Museum) until vandalism demanded that something be done to save the ship for posterity. In 1920 through the efforts of the Norwegian Women's Federation of Chicago and other groups, the *Viking* was renovated and moved to Lincoln Park Zoo and placed "temporarily" in an open shed.

Seventy years later, the *Viking* remained in its "temporary" home in a fenced-off section near the Duck Pond. In early December 1993, the Chicago Park District considered an offer from Vesterheim, a Norwegian-American museum in Decorah, Iowa, to purchase the ship. Several days before Christmas 1993, however, the Chicago Park District Board voted to sell the ship to the American Scandinavian Council for $1. Finally, in early 1994, the *Viking* was moved again and placed in temporary storage to make way for a new five million dollar Reptiles and Small Animals Building.

During the *Viking's* long hibernation in Lincoln Park, vandals made away with some of the ship's most precious jewels, including sixty-four Viking shields. Nature was just as cruel. Incessant exposure to the elements led to dry rot while decades of pigeon droppings accumulated, in some places, to as much as six inches thick. A massive and expensive clean-up job—the Chicago Park District reportedly spent $10,000 to rid the ship of the stubborn stains—was necessary before the *Viking* could be placed in storage.

One can only hope that the *Viking* will have a kinder future that is worthy of the proud ship that crossed the Atlantic, making possible the dream of a stubborn Norwegian sailor.

Notes

1. The Gokstad ship is on permanent display in the Viking Ship Museum, in Oslo, Norway. Excavated in 1880, the dig yielded the remains of a buried chieftain, three rowing boats, and various kitchen utensils.
2. The exception was New York, where, for some unfathomable reason, they were physically harassed, were forced to defend themselves, and ultimately were arrested. Andersen later said that he believed the harassment was a set-up by individuals who thought the Norwegians were trying to steal the thunder from Christopher Columbus. A *Chicago Tribune* editorial of July 13, 1893, commented on the behavior of the New Yorkers: "This is no Brooklyn, but a city abounding with Scandinavian merchants, manufacturers, and professional men and with Scandinavian policemen who will not maltreat their kinsfolk."

Museums

- *Swedish American Museum.* 5248 North Clark Street, Chicago 60640; 312-728-8111. Hours: Tuesday–Friday, 10 A.M.–4 P.M.; Saturday and Sunday, 10 A.M.–3 P.M. Admission: $2; senior citizens and students, $1; children under 12, $.50; members, free. Collects, restores, and displays artifacts relating to Swedish immigration to Chicago. Sponsors lectures, exhibits, and special events.

Organizations

- *American Scandinavian Council.* 2644 Dempster, Suite 201, Des Plaines, Illinois 60016; 708-635-1199. Established in 1987 to stimulate and perpetuate Scandinavian heritages and traditions through educational and cultural exchanges, special events, and celebrations.
- *Viking Ship Restoration Committee.* 518 Davis Street, Evanston, Illinois 60201; 708-492-1829. Organization dedicated to the preservation of the *Viking*.

Study centers

- *North Park College, Center for Scandinavian Studies.* 5125 North Spaulding Avenue, Chicago 60625; 312-583-2700. Houses the archives of the Swedish American Historical Society. Offers courses, lectures, and special programs on Scandinavian topics; facilitates the exchange of students and faculty, information, and understanding between Americans and Scandinavians; fosters and supports research and scholarship in Scandinavian-American history and culture.

YANKEES AND COPPERHEADS: THE REVOLT AT CAMP DOUGLAS

Chicago was on edge. Rumors circulated through the streets that a Southern conspiracy was brewing and that the Confederate prisoners confined at Camp Douglas, the Civil War prison camp located from Thirty-first to Thirty-third Streets and Giles to Cottage Grove, were poised for a mass breakout. Thousands of inmates had already died from cholera, typhus, and smallpox. In desperation, the survivors were ready to try anything to gain their freedom.

Civil War prison camps were overcrowded bastions of filth and disease. Southern prisons were the most notorious—at Camp Sumter in Andersonville, Georgia, almost thirteen thousand Union soldiers died from diseases, exposure, and starvation. But Northern camps were not much better. Camp Douglas, originally a training center for Union soldiers built on sixty acres of land donated to the government by Senator Stephen A. Douglas of Illinois, became a prison camp in February 1862, its first inmates the nine thousand Confederate soldiers who were captured at Fort Donelson, Tennessee.

Chicagoans, especially those originally from the South, were largely sympathetic to the plight of the prisoners, some of whom had relatives in the city (in 1864, two thousand Chicagoans belonged to the Sons of Liberty, a pro-Confederate group). Many made regular Sunday visits to the camp, bringing wagonloads of medicine, food, blankets, and clothing. Collections were taken at churches, and a Relief Committee of Citizens was organized. Others, however, agreed with the Board of Trade's official position that Chicagoans should "abstain" from visiting the barracks and trying "to make lions and distinguished visitors of any of the prisoners now among us."

By the summer of 1864, as conditions worsened considerably and Chicagoans grew uneasy—the prisoners vastly outnumbered their guards—the inmates had made several unsuccessful attempts to mount a mass uprising, including an ill-fated endeavor to disrupt the Democratic Convention, but the most elaborate scheme was the "Chicago Conspiracy," planned to coincide with the presidential election in November of that year. Its goal was to attack the camp from the outside with the help of the Copperheads, a secret organization sympathetic to the Confederacy. The prisoners, once freed, would then stuff ballot boxes to defeat Abraham Lincoln's bid for reelection, pillage the city, and rob its banks, sending the loot to Confederate President Jefferson Davis.

To carry out the scheme, Davis sent some of his best agents, who established their headquarters at the Richmond House at Michigan Avenue and Lake Street, then one of the city's most fashionable hotels. Rebel sympathizers, soldiers, escaped prisoners, and other "suspicious characters" swarmed into the city: some from as far away as Toronto, center of a vast Confederate network, others from Christian and Fayette Counties in downstate Illinois, long a hotbed of Copperhead activity.

Their leader was Captain Thomas H. Hines, a twenty-six-year-old master spy with vast guerrilla-warfare experience. According to the plan, the camp was to be attacked in four groups. John T. Shanks was to lead one party in an assault against the main gate. Copperheads Vincent Marmaduke, Benjamin Anderson, and Charles Walsh were each to lead three other forces in a simultaneous charge, break down the prison fence, free the prisoners, and force the Union garrison to surrender. Then small bands of rebels would slip into the night, cut the telegraph wires, and burn the railroad depots.

On the eve of the election, Union counterspies, abetted by double agent Shanks, foiled the plot and captured the ringleaders.[1] Hines, however, escaped by hiding in the mattress of a bed occupied by

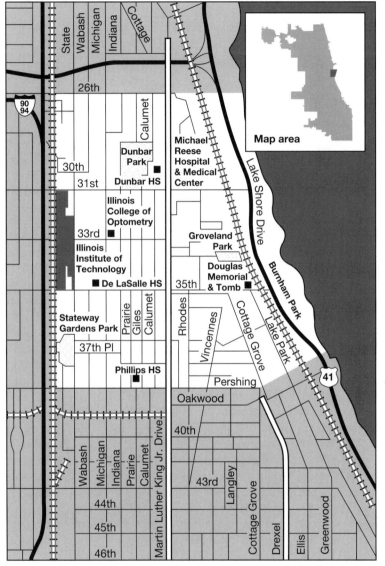

Map 3 Camp Douglas

The original site of Camp Douglas consists of open, flat prairie. The sixty-acre camp was situated between what is now 31st Street on the north, 33rd Street on the south, Cottage Grove on the east, and Giles Avenue on the west. (See Theodore J. Karamanski, *Rally 'Round the Flag*, 1993, 83).

the ailing wife of one of his cohorts. The next morning federal troops accompanied citizens to the polls.

After the Civil War ended in 1865, most of Camp Douglas's twelve thousand remaining prisoners swore allegiance to the federal government and were released. Housing projects now stand where death and pestilence once reigned. Nearby, at Thirty-fifth and Cottage Grove, is the Stephen A. Douglas memorial and tomb, and farther south, in Oak Woods Cemetery, a bronze portrait of a Confederate soldier watches over the unmarked graves of the six thousand Johnny Rebs who died at the camp.

Notes

1. More than 150 were arrested. Most were innocent. See Theodore S. Karamanski, *Rally 'Round the Flag: Chicago and the Civil War* (Chicago: Nelson-Hall Publishers, 1993), 221.

Museums

- *Chicago Historical Society.* Clark Street and North Avenue, 312-642-4600. Hours: Exhibition galleries—Monday–Saturday, 9:30 A.M.–4:30 P.M.; Sunday, noon to 5. Research collections—Tuesday–Saturday, 9:30 A.M.–4:30 P.M. Closed New Year's Day, Thanksgiving, and Christmas. Suggested admission: Adults, $3; students 17–22 and senior citizens, $2; children 6–17, $1. Monday, free. Civil War artifacts and exhibits. The research library contains extensive material on the Civil War.
- *Chicago Public Library.* Harold Washington Library Center, Special Collections Division, 400 South State Street, Chicago 60605; 312-747-4876. Hours: Monday, 9 A.M.–7 P.M.; Tuesday and Thursday, 11 A.M.–7 P.M.; Wednesday, Friday, and Saturday, 9 A.M.–5 P.M., Sunday 1 P.M.–5 P.M.
- *Newberry Library.* 60 West Walton Street, Chicago 60610; 312-943-9090. Hours: Tuesday–Thursday, 10 A.M.–6 P.M.; Friday and Saturday, 9 A.M.–5 P.M. Regimental histories, diaries, letters, and memoirs on the war.

Organizations

- *Civil War Round Table.* Chicago chapter, 410 South Michigan Avenue, Suite 841, Chicago 60605; 312-341-1865. Founded in 1940. Activities include monthly dinner meetings, annual battlefield tours, and monthly newsletter.

Confederate prisoners at Camp Douglas, 1864 (Chicago Historical Society, ICHi–22085).

Select historical sites

(All sites are in Chicago unless otherwise indicated)

- *Stephen Douglas tomb.* Douglas Tomb State Memorial Park, Thirty-fifth Street east of Cottage Grove Avenue. (1881) A bronze figure (measuring nine feet, nine inches tall) of Douglas, the famous Illinois senator of Scots descent who lost the presidential race to Abraham Lincoln, stands atop a column, nearly one hundred feet above the ground. Designed by Leonard Wells Volk, the memorial is located on land that once belonged to Douglas's estate, Oakenwald.
- *Oak Woods Cemetery.* 1035 East Sixty-seventh Street; 312-288-3800. Six thousand Confederate soldiers who died at the infamous Camp Douglas are buried here at the Confederate Mound Monument.
- *Rosehill Cemetery.* 5800 North Ravenswood; 312-561-5940. *Civil War Soldiers Memorial* is a pillar topped by the figure of a Union soldier.
- *St. Joseph Carondelet Child Care Center.* 739 East Thirty-fifth Street. Formerly the Chicago Soldiers' Home for disabled Civil War veterans. Now the property of the Archdiocese of Chicago.

SCOTIA'S CHILDREN:
SCOTTISH SOCIETIES IN CHICAGO

In 1845 several Scotsmen gathered together in downtown Chicago to eat, sing a few songs, and reminisce about the land they had left behind. But they had more on their minds than simple nostalgia. Like most emigrants, they had settled in the United States in search of a better life, but they also wished to help other Scots less fortunate than themselves, to look after their "ain folk." They did so by forming the Illinois Saint Andrew Society in 1846,[1] the oldest philanthropic organization in the state.

Details on the founding of the society are a bit sketchy, since many of the early documents were destroyed in the Great Chicago Fire of 1871. Most likely the decision to form the Illinois Saint Andrew Society was made at the Lake House on the north bank of the Chicago River between Rush Street and Lake Michigan on November 30, 1845. However, the first official meeting reportedly did not actually take place until either January 25 or 26, 1846, also at the Lake House. To further confuse the issue, the oldest existing records use 1846 as the founding date although the society later began using 1845.

The Lake House, a three-story brick building constructed in 1835, was considered one of the finest hotels in the city at the time. The Scots who met there apparently were specially invited. Seventeen reportedly attended the first meeting; of those, thirteen were elected as officers. It seems that the first constitution was not adopted until 1850; actually, incorporation did not occur until February 10, 1858.

The society's purpose was clear: "to aid the unfortunate among our countrymen." Further, it declared ". . . that no deserving Scot, seeking aid, would ever go hungry, homeless, without medical attention, or be buried in a potter's field." The society's motto was equally direct and just as generous: "Relieve the Distressed."

For many immigrant Scots with little means, the society proved a godsend. It provided assistance when life became too difficult or conditions in the New World became too hard to bear. A report of November 5, 1885, for example, informed its members that the society, among other things, helped pay railroad fare for thirty-six Scots, helped send seven elderly people in ill health back to Scotland, and assisted in burying five Scots.

From the beginning, society members were involved in the lifeblood of their adopted city. George Steele, the first president of the society, was born in Forfarshire, Scotland, and came to Chicago via Canada in 1837. He was a contractor on the Illinois and Michigan Canal and also served as president of the Chicago Board of Trade in 1852 and 1853. Robert Fergus, an early Chicago pioneer and the city's first printer, was a charter member of the society.

Other prominent members of the society, past and present, have included Civil War General George B. McClellan, businessman Philip Armour, merchant Cyrus McCormick, bibliophile John Crerar, and, more recently, the late Norman Maclean, author of *A River Runs Through It* and former professor at the University of Chicago.

For years members had considered operating a facility that would serve the medical needs of elderly Scots. The Scottish Home, an attractive residence for the elderly in North Riverside, is reportedly the only institution of its kind in North America. It was founded in 1901, however, under considerably more humble conditions in a rented house in the Douglas Park neighborhood on the South Side.

But the actual idea of building a home to care for Scottish immigrants who could not take care of themselves was much older, dating back to the 1860s. Members of the society had collected funds for this purpose and had even found a downtown lot. The devastating results of the Great Chicago Fire delayed their plans until the issue was raised again in the 1890s, when seven elderly people had no place to turn.

When the house in Douglas Park became too small to adequately address the needs of its residents, the society began looking

elsewhere for space. Dr. John A. McGill, a physician and a former president of the society, donated land that he owned in North Riverside for the construction of a new and bigger building. In 1910 this building burned down and a new building was constructed. The present building dates from 1917.

But the Illinois Saint Andrew Society was by no means the only Scottish organization in the city. By the late nineteenth century, others had been established.[2] The Caledonian Society of Chicago, for example, was organized on June 4, 1884. Its chief objects were the "cultivation of friendship and sociability among the natives of Scotland, and their children, resident in this locality; the encouragement of the Scottish national costume and games; and the perpetuation of Scottish music, history and poetry." The society sponsored monthly socials of a literary and musical nature. Business meetings were held on the second Thursday of each month at 45 East Randolph Street.

Another social group was the Orkney and Shetland Benevolent, Social, and Literary Society, which was organized on February 7, 1885, by a handful of Orcadians and Shetlanders at 199 South Clark Street. In addition to literary pursuits, they would sponsor an occasional special event, such as their version of the Up-Helly-Aa Viking fire festival. The society usually met once a month in a building at the corner of Clark and Washington Streets. Members had typical Orcadian and Shetlandic names like Leith, Seator, Driver, Tait, Isbister, Johnston, and Flaws. They even published a monthly journal, the *Orkney & Shetland American,* which was "devoted to the social and commercial interests of Orcadians and Shetlanders abroad."[3] The contents consisted mostly of local news, reports from overseas, and miscellaneous items. Occasionally, though, controversy erupted.

Illinois Saint Andrew Society headstone. Rosehill Cemetery, 5800 North Ravenswood Avenue (photo by June Skinner Sawyers). In 1858, one year before the actual cemetery dedication, the Illinois Saint Andrew Society purchased lots in Rosehill for the burial of "poor and friendless" Scots. More than two hundred Scots are buried here.

During a spirited exchange of letters, two writers debated the merits of national identity and commented, in particular, on the matter of whether a Shetlander could pass for a Scot. One virulent letter writer, for example, maintained that both Shetlanders and Orcadians were closer in spirit to Scandinavia than Scotland. "Orcadians and Shetlanders first, and Scandinavians second is what I say," wrote the incensed letter writer, "but never let us consider ourselves Scotch." The letter concluded with an unequivocal: "I am, SCANDINAVIAN." The whole identity issue seemed to be resolved, however, when members took a vote that "resulted in an overwhelming victory for the Scotchmen."

Most of the older societies and organizations no longer exist, discontinued through lack of interest and the rapid Americanization of Scottish emigrants. The overall decrease of emigration from Scotland to the States also played a role. Although Scots are among Chicago's oldest immigrant groups, they are also one of the most invisible, since, as English-speakers, they assimilated easily into the fabric of American society.[4]

Yet through the tug and pull of emigration, the Illinois Saint Andrew Society has proven to be one of the most durable Scottish institutions in the state. Today, its charitable work is now almost totally devoted to the perpetuation of the Scottish Home and the care of its sixty-two residents. The society shows its public face, though, at the annual Highland Games held in the third week of June and the "Feast of the Haggis" dinner in November. On these occasions, the spirit of Old Scotland comes alive.

Notes

1. There are approximately three hundred Saint Andrew societies, Caledonian clubs, and similar Scottish organizations in the United States and Canada, as well as an additional two hundred clan societies. See Catherine Aman, *The Scottish Americans* (New York: Chelsea House Publishers, 1991), 15.

2. There was even a hospital with a Scottish connection. In 1907 Scottish-American physicians founded Robert Burns Hospital, named in honor of the Scottish poet. The twenty-five-bed hospital, located at 3807 West Washington Boulevard, opened on July 15, 1907.

3. The Scottish press in the United States has traditionally maintained a low profile. The weekly *Scottish-American Journal* was founded in New York in 1857; after 1886 it shortened its name to the *Scottish-American* but ceased publication altogether in 1925. *The Highlander*, published in northwest suburban Barrington, is strictly a historical journal. See Rowland Berthoff, "Under the Kilt: Variations on the Scottish-American Ground," *Journal of American Ethnic History* 1, no. 2 (spring 1982): n. 49, p. 31. The leading Scottish-American newspaper in North America today is the *Scottish Banner,* which maintains offices in both the United States and Canada. *U.S. Scots,* a fairly new magazine based in Ohio, features articles on the contemporary Scottish-American experience and historical perspectives.

4. According to the 1980 census, less than 1 percent of the population, or 142,000 people, are foreign-born Scots. However, more than ten million in the United States can claim some Scottish ancestry. See Aman, *The Scottish Americans,* 13, 107.

Organizations

- *Illinois Saint Andrew Society.* Twenty-eighth and Des Plaines Avenue, North Riverside, Illinois 60546. The society, the oldest philanthropic organization in Illinois, operates the Scottish Home, a health care facility primarily for Scots-born or those of Scottish descent. The society sponsors the Saint Andrew Highland Games each year in mid-June and the "Feast of the Haggis" in November.

- *Scottish Cultural Society.* P.O. Box 486, Lombard, Illinois 60148. Established in 1977 by a dozen Scottish enthusiasts, the society sponsors meetings, lectures, and special events, such as the Annual Scottish Fair, a two-day indoor festival held each October.

Select historical sites

- *Robert Burns statue.* Garfield Park, Washington Boulevard between Central Park and Hamlin Boulevards. (1906) Scotland's national poet holds a copy of *Poems, Chiefly in the Scottish Dialect.* The bronze sculpture, unveiled in August 1906, as a gift of the Robert Burns Memorial Association, is the work of another Scot, W. Grant Stevenson.

- *"Early Scotch Settlement" historical marker, Argyle.* Site of an old Scots community situated in a rural area some eighty miles west of Chicago in Boone County. The first permanent settler was John Greenlee, a native of Argyllshire in Scotland, who came to the area in the late 1830s. The Willow Creek United Presbyterian Church was organized in 1844 and the original building erected in 1849. The present structure dates from 1877.

- *Graceland Cemetery*. Irving Park and Clark Street, Chicago 60613; 312-525-1105. Allan Pinkerton, the famous Glasgow-born detective, is buried here.
- *Charles H. Kerr House*. 566 Hillside, Glen Ellyn, Illinois 60137. Scottish-American socialist publisher and founder of the publishing house that bears his name lived in this house, which is now a private residence.
- *McGill Parc Apartments*. 4938 South Drexel Boulevard. Designed in 1890 by the noted architect Henry Ives Cobb in medieval French style, this imposing mansion was converted to apartments in 1982. Dr. John A. McGill served three successive terms as president of the Illinois Saint Andrew Society.
- *Rosehill Cemetery*. 5800 North Ravenswood Avenue, Chicago; 312-561-5940. In 1858 the Illinois Saint Andrew Society purchased lots for the burial of "poor and friendless Scots." More than two hundred Scots are buried here.
- *Scottish Hall of Fame*. Basement of the Scottish Home, Twenty-eighth and DesPlaines Avenue, North Riverside, Illinois 60546; 708-447-5092. Hours: Monday–Friday, 8 A.M.–5 P.M.; Saturday and Sunday, 9 A.M.–4 P.M. Located in the basement or "undercroft" of the Scottish Home in North Riverside is a little-known monument to famous Scots around the world. The exhibit consists of wall plaques that commemorate the achievements of two hundred Scots. A corner of the "undercroft" contains Robert Burns memorabilia.

RADICALS, REFORMERS, AND ECCENTRICS

Greenstone Church (Pullman United Methodist Church), Twelfth Street and St. Lawrence Avenue (photo by George Lane). Greenstone Church, completed and dedicated in 1882, was the only religious institution allowed in the Pullman community. Constructed of green serpentine rock from Pennsylvania, the church, like most of the buildings in Pullman, was designed by architect Solon S. Beman. The Methodists purchased the church in 1907.

FOLLOWING THE NORTH STAR:
DARE AND DOING ALONG THE UNDERGROUND RAILROAD

The legendary Underground Railroad was neither underground nor a railroad. It was a clandestine operation that helped fugitive slaves travel to freedom in the Northern free states and across the border into Canada during the years before the Civil War. It was carried out by an informal network of abolitionists and freedmen, by farmers, ministers, and others, many of whom assumed great personal risk for doing so.

Among the Chicagoans who took part in this heroic and historic endeavor were some prominent citizens like Allan Pinkerton of the Pinkerton Detective Agency and John Jones, founder of Olivet Baptist Church and, as a Cook County commissioner from 1871 to 1875, the first black man to hold public office in Illinois. But the real heroes were largely ordinary folk from the city and surrounding areas.

There are accounts of fugitives—"passengers" in railroad jargon—being moved from household to household by "conductors" and being hidden in basements, in an old brewery in Naperville, in a Congregational church, in an old tollhouse in Warrenville, in a mill in Oak Brook, in various storefronts in Dundee and Downers Grove, in haylofts, in the Quinn Chapel, which is now located at 2401 South Wabash Avenue. Wheaton historian Glennette Tilley Turner tells of "stationmaster" John S. Coe of Hinsdale, who hid many runaways under a tarpaulin and then led the fugitives north along the Des Plaines River. Other stories tell of runaways being hidden inside creaky covered wagons that traveled surreptitiously through the woods.

The underground routes usually followed the paths of rivers—the Fox, Du Page, Des Plaines, and, of course, the Mississippi. According to Turner, most of the slaves who fled to Illinois came to the state through Missouri, crossing the Mississippi either at Quincy or Alton. Plank roads from the old stagecoach days were another common route from the South.

Segments of the underground routes often followed rail lines, and some of the more daring fugitives would sometimes ride the trains. For this reason, according to at least one historian, train conductors usually kept no records of train schedules or passengers, presumably to avoid being accused of complicity in the escapes.

Dr. C.V. Dyer, who headed the Chicago, Burlington, and Quincy Railroad, reportedly arranged for slaves to ride in his boxcars, earning for his efforts the nickname of President of the Underground Railroad in Illinois. Many slaves hidden in produce-filled wagons were taken to the Tremont House station for transport farther north. And with other escapes being made also on other rail lines like the Chicago and North Western and the Galena and Chicago Union, the city became "the Illinois terminus of most Underground Railroad routes," writes Turner in *The Underground Railroad in Du Page County, Illinois.*

Under the Fugitive Slave Act of 1793, slaveowners were empowered to recover their runaways by merely showing proof of ownership. Going beyond this law, the Fugitive Slave Act of 1850 imposed a stiff fine of six months in jail for anyone found guilty of helping a slave escape or of impeding recovery of a slave by the authorities. The press called the law a boon to "professional slave-catchers."

The abolitionists, who promoted antislavery meetings, wrote petitions to Congress, and circulated tracts and pamphlets in their drive to put an end to slavery, played such a key role in the Underground Railroad that some slaveowners offered rewards for the capture of abolitionists themselves. Because Chicago was one of the leading centers of the abolitionist movement, the city, according to historian Larry Gara, was denounced as the headquarters of an organized system of "Negro stealing." To one downstate newspaper editor, Chicago was "a sinkhole of abolition."

There were some abolitionists, though, who opposed the Underground Railroad on grounds that it was doing more harm

than good to the antislavery cause. As a Chicago abolitionist newspaper put it, it might be better for the slave to remain a slave and be a martyr rather than to escape to one of the free states in the North or all the way to Canada.

Exactly how many slaves gained their freedom through the Underground Railroad is not known, but estimates range from forty thousand to sixty thousand. For many of them, Chicago was one of the stops on their way to the Promised Land.

Museums

- *Graue Mill and Museum.* York and Spring Roads, Oak Brook, Illinois 60521; 708-655-2090. Hours: mid-April to mid-November: daily, 10 A.M.–5 P.M. Admission: Adults, $1.50, children 3–5 and senior citizens, $.50; children under 3, free. Considered to be one of the few authentic Underground Railroad stations in Illinois.
- *Downers Grove Historical Museum.* 831 Maple Avenue, Downers Grove, Illinois 60515; 708-963-1309. Hours: Wednesday, 1 P.M.–4 P.M.; Sunday, 2 P.M.–4 P.M. Admission: Free. Occupies two buildings on property originally owned by early settlers, Israel and Avis Dodge Blodgett, who settled there in 1835.

A safe haven. Aurora Avenue, Naperville, Illinois (photo by June Skinner Sawyers). This elegant structure, built in 1847 by a James Wright for a Dr. Lilly, was reportedly a stop on the Underground Railroad. Formerly known as Willoway Manor, it now houses a tapas bar and restaurant.

Radicals, Reformers, and Eccentrics

PATRICK CRONIN AND THE CLAN-NA-GAEL

It was a great place for a murder—an old cottage in an open area in what was then suburban Lake View and is now the Uptown neighborhood. There, on the night of May 4, 1889, Dr. Patrick Henry Cronin, a forty-three-year-old prominent Chicago physician, was bludgeoned to death. His attackers were allegedly members of the Clan-na-Gael, a secret organization working for Irish independence, and for months the murder was the talk of the town.

The clan, according to historian Michael F. Funchion, was founded in New York in 1867 and established a branch in the Bridgeport neighborhood in 1869.[1] Its local head was a lawyer, Alexander Sullivan. Cronin's troubles with the clan began when he accused Sullivan and others of misappropriating clan funds and threatened to bring his charges to the press. Sullivan, in turn, accused Cronin of being a British spy.

In February of 1889, according to some reports, the Sullivan group concocted an elaborate plot to kill Cronin. On March 20 a man calling himself Frank Williams rented an old cottage in Lake View for twelve dollars a month. The cottage stood one block away from the offices of the O'Sullivan Ice Company. Its owner, Patrick O'Sullivan, was reportedly a Clan-na-Gael member who had recently hired Cronin as company physician. Williams told the owner of the cottage that his brother and invalid sister would be moving in with him shortly, and several days later a wagonload of cheap furniture, including a large trunk, was delivered to the cottage.

On May 4, Dan Coughlin, a detective from the Chicago Avenue police station, came to the stable of Patrick Dinan and told the liveryman that a friend of his would be needing a horse and buggy. "Say nothing to anyone about it," he warned. That evening Coughlin's friend picked up a two-seater buggy and a white horse.

Later that same evening Cronin, a bachelor, was entertaining friends in his flat at 468 North Clark Street when the doorbell rang.

At the door was a visibly agitated man who presented an O'Sullivan business card and said one of O'Sullivan's workers had been injured badly, that it was a matter of life and death, and asked if the doctor could come. "I've got a fast horse at your door," he added. Cronin said yes and quickly picked up a large black satchel. As he stepped outside, he ran into a fellow member of the Celto-American Society who reminded him about a meeting scheduled later that night. Cronin said he had an emergency to attend to but would try to stop by afterward.

A soft light glowed behind drawn blinds at the cottage when Cronin and his driver arrived. Rushing up the wooden steps, the doctor knocked on the door, which opened and immediately closed behind him. What happened next must have been a violent struggle. Two passersby later testified in court that they heard angry voices, furniture being broken, and a muffled cry, "Jesus."

On May 23 Cronin's nude body was found in a catch basin near Broadway and Foster Avenue. His neck had been broken, and a blunt instrument had apparently been used to strike him on his cheek and temple. A mile away a large bloodstained trunk was found, with a lock of Cronin's hair in it. In November his clothes, which apparently had been cut away from his body, were discovered in a manhole at Broadway and Buena Avenues.

Seven men were indicted for Cronin's murder, of whom four—Patrick O'Sullivan, Dan Coughlin, Martin Burke (alias Frank Williams), and John Kunze—were found guilty and given prison sentences. Burke and O'Sullivan died in prison. Coughlin was later acquitted in a second trial. Kunze, who served three years in jail, claimed innocence all along. No one ever confessed to committing or aiding in the crime, though some historians think the killing itself was done by Burke and Patrick "the Fox" Cooney, who fled the country.

As for Patrick Henry Cronin, an indirect victim of the struggle for Irish independence, he was given a hero's funeral and buried in Calvary Cemetery in Evanston.

Notes

1. Although the Clan-na-Gael had branches throughout the country, the Chicago unit was one of the most powerful. Some historians believe this was due, in no small part, to the support it received from local institutions, especially from the Irish-dominated Catholic Church hierarchy. Patrick Feehan, archbishop of Chicago and Father Maurice Dorney, pastor of Saint Gabriel's in the Stock Yard district, reportedly supported the Clan-na-Gael and its goal of an independent Ireland. There was also strength in numbers. At the time of the Cronin murder, 17 percent of the population was Irish. See Paul Luning, "Irish Blood," *Chicago History* 22, no. 3 (November 1993): 23, 27.

Museums

- *Irish American Heritage Center.* 4626 North Knox Avenue, Chicago 60630; 312-282-7035. Hours: Monday–Friday, 9 A.M.–11 P.M. Admission: Free. Sponsors Irish concerts, classes, dances, art gallery events, and related activities.

HAYMARKET

They had gathered on the evening of May 4, 1886, at Haymarket Square on Randolph Street between Desplaines and Halsted Streets to express a collective feeling of anger and frustration. When the night was over, a bomb had been thrown, seven police officers lay dead,[1] and more than one hundred civilians had been injured.

The Haymarket Affair,[2] as it is now called, is considered a pivotal moment in labor history in America. Workers went on strike demanding shorter hours and better working conditions, issues taken for granted in today's leisure-oriented society.

At the time of Haymarket, Chicago was considered America's most radical city. It was, after all, the home of the International Working People's Association (IWPA), the most radical organization in America during the nineteenth century. The city also had over half a dozen anarchist newspapers reaching some thirty thousand readers. Socialist parties in Chicago date back to the 1870s.[3]

Chicago was such fertile ground for anarchism for a number of reasons. From 1871 to 1886, the city had changed considerably from a commercial and transportation economy to an industrial base with a large proportion of the population—almost 50 percent toward the end of the nineteenth century, according to labor historian Bruce Nelson—engaged in manufacturing. This fairly rapid rise in industrialization coincided with several economic depressions in the 1870s and 1880s. In December 1873, for example, "bread riots" erupted in city streets when scores of unemployed workers demonstrated outside the LaSalle Street offices of the Relief and Aid Society, demanding that the organization release badly needed funds to relieve hunger.

Another reason for the strong radical element in the city was the large population of immigrants. Between 1870 and 1900, says Nelson, Chicago's foreign-born constituted at least 40 percent of the city's population. The Industrial Revolution transformed America. Massive factories were built, and jobs seemed plentiful. But the only people who enjoyed the fruits of production were the owners, not the workers. Consequently, it became increasingly difficult for working-class families to make ends meet—60 percent of their income was spent on food or rent, notes Nelson.

The central issue of the American labor movement was the passage of a nationwide eight-hour workday. Dissenters in Haymarket Square assembled to protest police brutality and the subsequent death of several strikers at the McCormick Harvester Works on the South Side the previous day. Those who gathered had no cause for worry, since Mayor Carter Harrison had proclaimed the meeting to be perfectly legal.

Haymarket Square could hold a vast number of people, as many as twenty thousand if necessary. Estimates of the crowd that night were much more modest: from twelve to thirteen hundred. Although scheduled to address the crowd at 7:30 P.M., the first speaker—August Spies—began an hour behind schedule. The speakers' "platform" was actually the bed of a wagon and was situated in front of the Crane Brothers factory on the east side of Desplaines Street. Albert Parsons spoke next, followed by Samuel Fielden. Minutes after Fielden began to speak, the sky opened up and a downpour flooded the streets. As the crowd had begun to disperse, a contingent of uniformed police officers suddenly marched toward the site. Apparently district commander John Bonfield, fearful of a violent outbreak, ordered 180 officers from the nearby Desplaines Street station to end the meeting. Fielden, however, offered no resistance. As he stepped down from the makeshift platform, a loud explosion popped. One officer, Mathias Degan, was instantly killed when a fragment of the incendiary device severed the main artery in his thigh; from sixty to seventy

Albert Parsons (courtesy Charles H. Kerr Publishing Company). Of the four Haymarket martyrs, Parsons (c. 1848–87) was the only one who was American-born.

police officers were injured—six of those later died.[4] Police instinctively opened fire on the crowd; three civilians were killed and scores more hurt, according to Nelson.

Throughout the city, thousands of known or suspected anarchists were arrested. Anarchist meetings were disrupted, and anyone with even the most tenuous of leftist connections was brought in, often without a warrant.

On May 27, 1886, the grand jury indicted ten men—one avoided trial by testifying for the state; the other left the country. The trial was held at the Cook County Court House at Hubbard and Dearborn Streets. Eight men eventually stood trial: Albert Parsons, August Spies, Samuel Fielden, George Engel, Louis Lingg, Adolph Fischer, Oscar Neebe, and Michael Schwab. Although all eight espoused the cause of anarchy, only four had actually attended the meeting that night in Haymarket Square.

The trial was swift—it began on June 21 and ended on August 20, 1886. It was also one of the most sensational trials in U.S. legal history. Any attempt at fairness was thrown out the window. Jury members, for example, made it clear they believed the defendants to be guilty. Questionable evidence was allowed.

Despite no physical evidence and based on the slimmest of circumstantial evidence, all eight men were found guilty. Seven were sentenced to death; Neebe was ordered to serve fifteen years in prison. Historians remind us that there was more at stake than just a simple matter of the guilt or innocence of the defendants; rather, it involved a fundamental difference between two societies—one capitalist, the other anarchist. The Haymarket martyrs were punished more for their beliefs than their deeds.

On November 11, 1887, a day that came to be known as "Black Friday," Parsons, Spies, Engel, and Fischer were executed in the alley behind the old Cook County Jail at Dearborn and Illinois Streets at 11:30 A.M. Nearly two hundred witnesses, including more than fifty reporters, were present.

In June 1893, Governor John Peter Altgeld pardoned Fielden, Neebe, and Schwab, the three remaining martyrs who escaped the same fate as their colleagues, and gave them long prison terms instead. Defending his decision on the basis of justice, Altgeld called the jury "packed" and the trial judge "prejudiced" against the defen-

Execution of Haymarket martyrs (Illinois Labor History Society). August Spies, Adolph Fischer, George Engel, and Albert Parsons were executed on November 11, 1887, a day that was remembered for many years as "Black Friday."

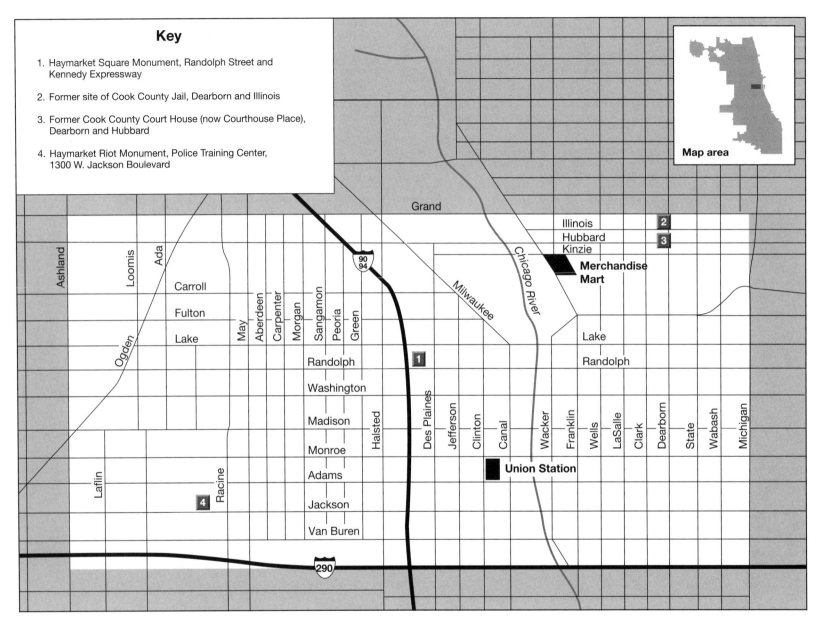

Key

1. Haymarket Square Monument, Randolph Street and Kennedy Expressway

2. Former site of Cook County Jail, Dearborn and Illinois

3. Former Cook County Court House (now Courthouse Place), Dearborn and Hubbard

4. Haymarket Riot Monument, Police Training Center, 1300 W. Jackson Boulevard

Map area

Grand

Illinois   2

Hubbard   3

Kinzie

Merchandise Mart

Ashland
Loomis
Ada
Carroll
Fulton
Lake
Ogden
May
Aberdeen
Carpenter
Morgan
Sangamon
Peoria
Green
Milwaukee
Chicago River
Lake
Randolph   1
Randolph
Washington
Halsted
Des Plaines
Jefferson
Clinton
Canal
Wacker
Franklin
Wells
LaSalle
Clark
Dearborn
State
Wabash
Michigan
Madison
Monroe
Union Station
Laflin
Racine
Adams
Jackson   4
Van Buren
290
90 94

Map 4 Haymarket Sites

dants. It was a tremendously brave act but one that veered on political suicide (Altgeld never won public office again and for weeks after his controversial decision his image was hanged in effigy).

All four men proclaimed their innocence until the end. To this day, no one knows for certain who threw the bomb.[5] All that remains is conjecture and the tragedy of justice gone awry.

Notes

1. The police officers were Mathias J. Degan, Timothy Flavin, John J. Barrett, Michael Sheehan, George Mueller, Nels Hansen, and Thomas Redden. Degan died instantly. See Bruce C. Nelson, *Beyond the Martyrs: A Social History of Chicago's Anarchists 1870–1900* (New Brunswick, N.J.: Rutgers University Press, 1988), 189.

2. The Haymarket martyrs were as follows: **Albert Parsons** (1848–87) Born: Montgomery, Alabama. Considered the leader of the anarchist movement in Chicago; **August Spies** (1855–87) Born: Germany. Editor of the German workers' newspaper, the *Arbeiter-Zeitung;* **Samuel Fielden** (1847–1922) Born: Todmorden, England. Began work at a textile mill at age eight, he came to Chicago in 1871 and worked as a laborer; **George Engel** (1836–87) Born: Cassel, Germany. Orphaned at age twelve, he helped organize the Socialistic Labor Party and in January 1886 he established the *Anarchist* newspaper. Engel advocated class warfare; **Louis Lingg** (1864–87) Born: Schwetzingen, Baden, Germany. A carpenter by training, he arrived in Chicago in 1885. He committed suicide in prison; **Adolph Fischer** (1858–87) Born: Bremen, Germany. Immigrated to America at age fifteen in 1873. In 1883 he moved to Chicago and became a printer at the *Arbeiter-Zeitung*. He and Engel founded the *Anarchist;* **Oscar Neebe** (1850–1916) Born: New York City but raised in Germany. He returned to the United States at fourteen and settled in Chicago in 1887; and **Michael Schwab** (1853–1898) Born: Bavaria. Orphaned at the age of twelve, he came to the United States in 1879.

3. By 1886, says Nelson, there were twenty-six anarchist groups in the Chicago area as well as eight newspapers in four languages: *The Alarm* in English, *Den Nye Tid* in Dano-Norwegian, *Budoucnost* and *Lampcka* in Czech, and *Arbeiter-Zeitung, Die Fackel, Vorbote,* and the *Anarchist* in German. See Nelson, "Anarchism: The Movement Behind the Martyrs," *Chicago History* 15, no. 2 (summer 1986): 11.

4. There seems to be a discrepancy as to the number of officers who died that night. Some say one died immediately and six later succumbed; others say seven, not six, died later.

5. The grand jury did indict Rudolph Schnaubelt but did not have enough evidence to convict. Other possible candidates have included George Schwab, a German shoemaker, and George Meng, a German anarchist. Nelson, *Beyond the Martyrs,* 189–90.

Select historical sites

- *Waldheim Jewish Cemeteries.* 1400 South Desplaines Avenue, Forest Park, Illinois 60130; 708-366-4541. Seven of the eight Haymarket martyrs are buried here: George Engel, Adolph Fischer, Louis Lingg, Oscar Neebe, Albert Parsons, Michael Schwab, and August Spies. Dedicated June 1893.

- *Haymarket Riot monument.* Police Training Center, 1300 West Jackson Boulevard, Chicago 60607; 312-746-8310. Bronze statue of a nineteenth-century Chicago policeman. Originally located in Haymarket Square, the sculpture was moved to Union Park on the Near West Side in 1928. During the turbulent sixties, it was defaced and blown up twice, prompting its removal in 1976 to its present location.

- *Haymarket Square monument.* In March 1992 the city council granted historic landmark status to the Haymarket Square area, a one-block stretch of urban concrete of Desplaines Street between Lake and Randolph.

- *John Peter Altgeld.* Lincoln Park, near Lake Shore Drive, south of Diversey Parkway, east of Cannon Drive. Sculpture by Gutzon Borglum of the Illinois governor who pardoned three of the Haymarket martyrs.

 THE ECCENTRIC "CAPTAIN" OF STREETERVILLE

Streeterville is now a posh lakefront area bounded by Lake Michigan to the north and east and, roughly, Michigan Avenue to the west and Erie Street to the south. But one hundred years ago, when it extended south to the Chicago River, it was a wasteland that gave rise to pitched battles and legal skirmishes between the authorities and the eccentric man who gave it its name, "Cap'n" George Wellington Streeter.

Streeter served a spell in the Civil War before embarking on a colorful career as showman, circus promoter, and Mississippi steamboat operator. Coming to Chicago in July 1886, he bought a rickety old schooner, called it the *Reutan,* and used it to make frequent excursions between the city and Milwaukee. During one of those trips, a fierce storm led his passengers to take the train instead of the *Reutan* back to Chicago, leaving Streeter; his wife, Maria; and several crew members to sail on through the storm until, late at night, the boat ran aground just north of Chicago Avenue.

At daybreak, the captain found himself on a sandy, barren stretch of shoreland. Judging it to be an ideal place, he and his wife decided to stay put, making their stranded boat their home and receiving permission from N. Kellogg Fairbank, the wealthy businessman who owned the land, to remain there until their boat was fixed.

At what is now the Northwestern University downtown campus, Streeter built a shack, naming the surrounding area the "Deestrict of Lake Michigan" and, from an office he opened in the Tremont Hotel at the corner of Lake and Dearborn Streets, sold parcels of it to gullible buyers. The area, he said, owed allegiance only to the federal government, basing his claim on an 1821 military survey, squatters' rights, and some dubious documents allegedly signed by President Grover Cleveland.

Offended by Streeter's shabby shack and his land-grabbing scheme, his lakeshore neighbors began to take steps to remove him

from the potentially valuable lakefront property. In July 1888 five constables arrived with an eviction notice but were driven off at gunpoint. The next month several officers in a surprise visit caught the rifle-toting Streeter off guard. "Now we gotcha," said one officer triumphantly. But just as they were about to lead him away, Maria emerged and threw boiling water from a kettle at the bluecoats. Streeter then grabbed his rifle and sent the lawmen fleeing.

Another time, Streeter's self-appointed "military governor," William Niles, fired several shots at the buggy of a police captain. The next day a contingent of five hundred officers came to arrest the old man once and for all, but the officers were met by an "army" of hobos and squatters who tried to repel the attack with rocks, stones, and clubs. Streeter was eventually arrested, but he was released the following day because, according to historian Emmett Dedmon, firing at a police officer was not then considered a crime.

Two years later Streeter was found guilty of killing John Kirk, a night watchman, for alleged trespassing. After serving his nine-month sentence in the Joliet penitentiary, Streeter went right back to his shanty, and the struggle to evict him began all over again.

By then Streeter's "Deestrict" had become a favorite watering hole for a number of Chicagoans to quench their thirst with booze supplied from his shack—even on Sundays. Invoking Sunday-closing laws, Mayor Bill Thompson ordered a raid that ended up with the police seizing hundreds of beer bottles and burning the shack to the ground. "This here is an outrage," said Streeter. "It's worse than the Kaiser ever did. I'll have the law on 'em."

Streeter then turned to the courts to win the legal recognition of his claims to his "Deestrict," continuing his struggle until he died of pneumonia, at age eighty-four, on January 24, 1921.

Picking up the fight, his second wife, Elma (Maria died in 1903), in 1924 filed a claim of a billion dollars against fifteen hundred lakeshore property owners for the loss of what by then had

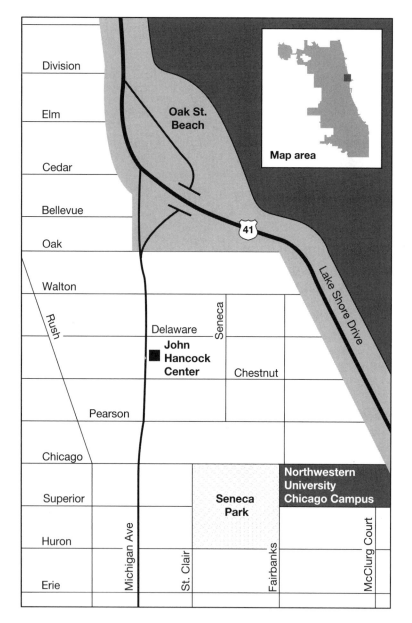

Map 5 Streeterville

become known as Streeterville. By the time she died in 1936, many other Streeter heirs had also submitted their own claims. Not until 1940 did Streeter's fight finally end, when the last of the claims were dismissed in federal court.

FRANCES WILLARD
AND THE BATTLE AGAINST "DEMON" ALCOHOL

Alcohol consumption rose sharply in Chicago in the years following the Civil War as thousands of war-weary men made their way back into town and became avid patrons of the city's saloons. Alarmed by this trend, the temperance movement, led by the Women's Christian Temperance Union (WCTU) and other similar groups, marshalled its forces, beginning a campaign that eventually led to Prohibition.

The movement was largely a woman's campaign, perhaps because women—as Frances Willard, founder and national president of the Evanston-based WCTU, then suggested—had reached a higher stage of moral development than men.

With no political clout to speak of, women took their campaign to the streets. The WCTU organized meetings in local churches, and Willard and others gave temperance speeches to anyone willing to listen. But it was more common to see bands of women praying outside—and sometimes inside—Chicago saloons. A brave few would actually implore saloonkeepers not to serve the demon alcohol or ask customers to abstain from drinking it.

Though often met with all kinds of abuse, including being spat upon with tobacco juice, the crusaders carried on, at one point collecting thousands of signatures and then marching to City Hall to demand enforcement of the largely ignored Sunday-closing ordinance. The city's response was to tell saloonkeepers to be more discreet on the Sabbath by keeping their doors closed and blinds drawn without actually closing down.

The temperance cause at first seemed hopeless. "There is no more use of these women launching themselves in praying bands against saloons than there would be of attempting to stop by similar means the flow of Niagara River," said one local newspaper. But the tide slowly began to turn. The Polyglot Petition, circulated in 1884 by Willard and the WCTU, made its way around the world, collecting nearly eight million signatures in support of temperance.

By the late 1880s, the WCTU had become the most influential women's organization in the world. Many of the nation's public schools, predating today's say-no-to-drugs campaigns, began exhorting students to abstain from alcohol. In 1889 Illinois passed a law requiring that instruction be given "with special reference to the effects of alcoholic beverages, stimulants and narcotics on the human system." Chicagoans formed abstinence societies, organized children's temperance groups, and attended lectures by reformers on the evils of alcohol. Physical exercise was touted as a healthy alternative to drink. Willard, who took up cycling in her fifties, encouraged young men to spend their leisure time pedaling a bike rather than imbibing liquor in a saloon.

No longer an object of ridicule, the WCTU began to be called the conscience of the nation and regarded as a potent political force. In addition to temperance, the group supported other causes, including prison reform, the eight-hour workday, and stiffer penalties for crimes against women. By 1890 it had nearly 150,000 members. In 1891 construction began on a new WCTU Chicago headquarters, a massive structure at the corner of LaSalle and Monroe Streets that was designed by John Wellborn Root, of the influential architectural firm Burnham & Root, and called the Woman's Temple. (It was demolished in 1926.) Willard herself, nicknamed "Saint Frances" and already somewhat of a folk hero, became a strong national figure and the most prominent woman of her day.

She died, however, in 1898, in a New York City hotel room, before she could see the greatest achievement of her life's labors—the passage, twenty-one years later, of the Eighteenth Amendment and the start of the "noble experiment" that was Prohibition.

The WCTU itself lives on. From its national headquarters, which stands behind the Frances Willard House, now a museum, at 1730 Chicago Avenue in Evanston, Illinois, the organization continues to

Frances Willard House, 1730 Chicago Avenue, Evanston, Illinois (photo by June Skinner Sawyers). The "Rest Cottage," as it was known, was the home of Frances Willard (1839–98) and the international headquarters of the Women's Christian Temperance Union (WCTU). In 1965 the Willard House was placed on the National Register of Historic Places.

work toward, among other goals, a society free from the evils and dangers of alcoholism.

Museums

- *Frances Willard House*. 1730 Chicago Avenue, Evanston, Illinois 60201; 708-864-1397. Hours: By appointment only. Museum dedicated to the life of Frances Willard and her work at the WCTU.

A TOWN CALLED PULLMAN

The Hotel Florence began life in 1881 as the centerpiece of a community called Pullman. After generations of attracting visitors with its elegance and charm, it still stands proudly on South Forrestville Avenue across the tracks from the Illinois Central 111th Street station as the "Grand Old Lady of 111th Street."

Pullman, the company town built during the early 1880s by railroad sleeping-car magnate George Pullman near Lake Calumet, was the nation's first planned industrial community.[1] It was a self-contained world with seventeen hundred housing units, its own plants, newspaper, three-story shopping mall, churches, schools, hospital, community stable, and 140-acre farm.

The living quarters followed along the company's organizational lines. Executives lived in houses with as many as ten rooms, managers in smaller frame houses, skilled laborers in tight row houses, and unskilled single men in crowded tenements and boardinghouses.

In class-conscious Pullman, workers were not allowed in the bar in the Hotel Florence, the town's only tavern, according to labor historian William Adelman. Instead, they had to venture to nearby "Schlitz Row," a two-block area of saloons and stables on South Front Avenue between 113th and 115th Streets.

The public face of Pullman was nothing if not impressive—the turreted Administration Building with its Clock Tower, the Gothic-inspired Greenstone Church, and the massive Arcade Building (now demolished) with its library, bank, post office, YMCA, one-thousand-seat theater, and some thirty shops. The most handsome of them all was the Hotel Florence, the social center of Pullman.

George Pullman insisted that the Hotel Florence, named for his favorite daughter, should be as luxurious as his famous sleeping cars, and there he played host to government leaders, vaudeville stars, and his many socialite friends. The four-story red-brick structure is a Victorian gem that originally had seventy guest rooms. The first-floor parlor had velvet-covered furniture, lovely stained glass windows, cherry-wood rocking chairs grouped around the fireplaces, and a high-ceilinged dining room that could seat fifty people. For male guests there was a fancy barber shop, and from the veranda, visitors had a view of the flower gardens of the Pullman and Arcade parks.

Although an international exposition in Prague in 1896 called Pullman "the most perfect town in the world," not everyone in it was happy. George Pullman was an uncompromising businessman who ran the community as a profitmaking enterprise. Complained one worker, "We are born in a Pullman house, fed from a Pullman shop, taught in a Pullman school, catechized in the Pullman church, and when we die, we shall be buried in the Pullman cemetery and go to a Pullman hell." To a magazine reporter, the town was a form of "benevolent feudalism."

Labor tensions plagued the town, which at its peak had twelve hundred residents. A devastating strike broke out in May 1894, when George Pullman laid off workers, cut salaries by as much as 50 percent, and refused to lower rents. The strike was eventually settled, but not until after federal troops were called in. Pullman died an embittered man in 1897 at age sixty-six. In 1898 the Illinois Supreme Court ruled that the company had to sell its property. Within a decade, the community of Pullman had been placed on the selling block.

A remnant of the grand experiment—the area, known as the South Pullman District, between 111th and 115th Streets and South Cottage Grove and Langley Avenues—has been designated both a national and a Chicago landmark. In late 1990 Governor James Thompson announced plans to convert the Pullman Works factory at 111th Street and Cottage Grove Avenue to a transportation museum. Pullman today is a vibrant community rooted in the past.

Notes

1. Pullman was not the only planned community in the Midwest, however. New Harmony, Indiana, perhaps the most famous, was originally founded by George Rapp, a German immigrant seeking religious freedom in the New World. In late 1824 Rapp sold New Harmony to Robert Owen. Owen, an Ango-Welsh entrepreneur with utopian tendencies, viewed New Harmony as a continuation of his work in the factory town of New Lanark, Scotland, a planned community known for its enlightened labor policies and humanitarian working conditions. For a discussion of Robert Owen and New Harmony, see D.F. Carmony and Josephine M. Elliot, "New Harmony, Indiana: Robert Owen's Seedbed for Utopia," *Indiana Magazine of History* 76 (September 1980): 161–261.

   Planned communities with religious roots in Illinois include Nauvoo, Bishop Hill, and Zion.

Select historical sites

- *Hotel Florence.* 111th Street and Forrestville Avenue. Built by the Pullman Company as a showplace for visitors, the imposing four-story building with the expansive veranda contains many Pullman memorabilia. Be sure to see the room where George slept. A special suite was reserved for Pullman on those nights when he didn't feel up to returning to his Prairie Street mansion. A sumptuous brunch is served at the hotel on Sunday.
- *Pullman United Methodist Church (Greenstone Church).* 112th Street and St. Lawrence Avenue. Dedicated in 1882 by Dr. James M. Pullman, a minister and the brother of George Pullman. Gothic-style structure and the only religious institution allowed in the town.
- *Pullman Administration Building and Clock Tower.* South Cottage Grove Avenue near East 111th Street. A Pullman landmark since 1880.

Pullman Administration Building and Clock Tower, 11101 South Cottage Grove Avenue (1880) (photo by June Skinner Sawyers). George Pullman's office was located in this imposing building, which once fronted the three-acre Lake Vista. Layers of concrete replaced the man-made lake when Cottage Grove was extended. Plans are currently under way to convert the historic structure into a transportation and labor history museum.

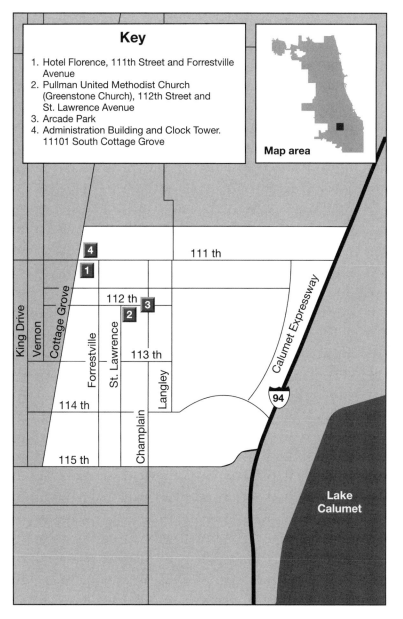

Key

1. Hotel Florence, 111th Street and Forrestville Avenue
2. Pullman United Methodist Church (Greenstone Church), 112th Street and St. Lawrence Avenue
3. Arcade Park
4. Administration Building and Clock Tower. 11101 South Cottage Grove

Map area

111 th

King Drive

Vernon

Cottage Grove

112 th

Forrestville

St. Lawrence

113 th

Langley

Calumet Expressway

94

114 th

Champlain

115 th

Lake Calumet

Map 6 Pullman Historic District

In addition, many of the original nineteenth-century buildings designed by Pullman architect Solon S. Beman are still standing. They include the former Pullman stables at 11201 South Cottage Grove Avenue, the Market Hall and Colonnade Apartments and Townhouses at East 112th Street and South Champlain Avenue, the Arcade row houses at 533–35 East 112th Street as well as other examples of Pullman company–era block houses, flats, and cottages.

JANE ADDAMS:
ACTIVIST, REFORMER, PACIFIST

To immigrants, children, and the poor, she was a friend, but to many newspaper editors, ward bosses, and businessmen, she was the enemy. Jane Addams is now generally revered as the pioneering social worker who founded Hull-House and the Women's International League for Peace and Freedom, wrote twelve books and hundreds of articles, received fourteen honorary degrees, and won the Nobel Peace Prize in 1931. But in her day she was regarded by many as "the most dangerous woman in America."

Hull-House was a haven for unpopular movements and new ideas. Modeled after Toynbee Hall in the Whitechapel district of London, Chicago's first settlement house, or community welfare center, welcomed the nonconformist and the eccentric, the revolutionary and the radical along with the poor and the outcast of society. English socialists Sidney and Beatrice Webb and novelist H. G. Wells visited, architect Frank Lloyd Wright lectured, and educator John Dewey discussed Greek philosophy. In such a heady atmosphere, Hull-House was an easy target for those who saw visions of communist conspiracies. Denounced as a "hotbed of anarchism," it was at one time called the key link in an elaborate network of "red" subversives.

Although no arrests were ever made at Hull-House, police were often assigned to keep an eye on its meetings. One night when a group of immigrants were passionately discussing political theory, a club-twirling police officer reportedly reprimanded resident Alice Hamilton: "Lady, you people oughtn't to let bums like these come here. If I had my way, they'd all be lined up against a wall at sunrise and shot."

Staffers became wary of newspaper reporters, who, on the prowl for a "good story," would often twist whatever they saw into something sensational.

Bitter opposition against Addams first surfaced in 1892, when her staff, shocked by conditions they saw in clothing-industry sweatshops, urged the passage of factory and child-labor legislation. When the state a year later passed a law forbidding the employment of children under fourteen and limiting women to an eight-hour workday, Addams and her cohorts were branded as radicals. Manufacturers, many of whom relied on cheap immigrant labor, denounced the law, calling it the way to ruin and a threat to the very foundation of free enterprise. Contemporary accounts reported one unhappy businessman as saying, "Jane Addams ought to be hanged to the nearest lamppost." (Two years later, in 1895, the law was declared unconstitutional by the Illinois Supreme Court.)

Addams served as labor arbitrator in the 1894 Pullman strike, the 1905 teamsters strike, and the 1910 garment workers strike. Her pro-union stance in these and other assignments prompted one merchant to write in 1916 that Hull-House "has been so thoroughly unionized that it has lost its usefulness and has become a detriment to the community as a whole."

Neighbors were suspicious, too, of her settlement house, especially in its infant days. Located in a dilapidated Near West Side area of crowded tenements, unpaved alleys and side streets, and small family-run shops, the house was surrounded by as many as nineteen different immigrant groups, among them Italians, Germans, Poles, Russian Jews, Irish, and French-Canadians. Most lived there not by choice but only because they had to; so why, they asked, did this strange woman choose to settle among them in that blighted neighborhood?

It was Addams's pacifism, however, that aroused the most malicious criticisms. When she traveled during World War I to The Hague in the Netherlands to urge world leaders to end hostilities through arbitration, she was quickly ridiculed for her idealism and naïveté.

An early shot of Jane Addams's Hull-House (courtesy Jane Addams's Memorial Collection, University Library, University of Illinois at Chicago). Jane Addams (1860–1935) was founder and director of Hull-House, Chicago's first settlement house. Other reform-minded individuals soon established their own facilities, including Graham Taylor's Chicago Commons and Mary McDowell's University of Chicago Settlement. In 1963 many of the original Hull-House buildings were demolished to make way for the University of Illinois at Chicago Circle campus. The 1856 Charles Hull mansion and the 1905 residents' dining hall are all that remain of the original thirteen-building complex.

Newspapers across the country launched bitter attacks against her. At one point several members of the American Legion labeled her "pro-German." Others condemned her as a pacifist traitor.

Jane Addams, who died in 1935, certainly felt much pain from these attacks on herself and her work. But her critics have long been silenced, their opposition an almost-forgotten aspect of her life. Today the Hull-House Museum, at 800 South Halsted Street on the University of Illinois at Chicago campus, is an honored memorial to Jane Addams's work and accomplishments on the urban frontier.

Museums

- *Jane Addams Hull-House Museum.* 800 South Halsted Street, Chicago 60607; 312-413-5353. Hours: Summer—Monday–Friday, 10 A.M..–4 P.M.; Sunday, 12 P.M.–5 P.M. Winter—Monday–Friday, 10 A.M.–4 P.M. Closed holidays. Admission: Free. Artifacts, memorabilia, furniture, and documents relating to Addams's life and work.

LEND ME YOUR EARS:
THE ORATORS OF BUGHOUSE SQUARE

For decades, Washington Square Park on the Near North Side was known as "Bughouse Square."[1] This small patch of greenery served as the meeting ground for various soapbox orators interested in engaging one another in political, social, and religious debate. All subjects were fair game, and any given Sunday night during the 1920s people could be heard heatedly discussing such matters as communism versus capitalism, atheism versus the existence of an omnipotent God, or whatever topic seemed most appropriate to the moment. Frank Beck, an author well versed in the milieu of the city's bohemian life, called Bughouse Square a "pocket edition of Greenwich Village."

Washington Square is bounded by Delaware Place and Dearborn, Walton, and Clark Streets. Washington Square Park was established in 1842. It is Chicago's second park and the oldest surviving park today, according to the Commission on Chicago Landmarks. The park was donated to the city in 1842 by Orasmus Bushnell and is, quite possibly, named after the famous square of the same name in New York. The block on the north side of the park was bought by Mahlon D. Ogden, brother of Chicago's first mayor, William B. Ogden. The house that Ogden built stood here until 1892, when it was demolished and replaced by the Newberry Library.

As early as the 1840s, the area began to attract people. Houses and churches were built and the semblance of a genuine community began to emerge. By the 1890s the park became known as Bughouse Square. Anyone and everyone who had something to say about anything came to Washington Square to voice an opinion. Many of the finer residences were converted to rooming houses. Nearby Clark Street, however, became a seedy center of vice. Artists and others attracted to the alternative lifestyle lived in nearby studios, while weekend bohemians visited the area and congregated around the park in an effort to savor the heady atmos-phere. Indeed, by the 1930s Washington Park was so known as the hub of the city's bohemian life that tourist buses traveled up and down the neighborhood streets giving the visitors a taste of big-city life. Canny entrepreneurs were more than willing to play the role of the eccentric avant-garde artist for a fee, even if it meant opening up their studios to reveal how the "other side" lived.

Sometimes thousands would gather in the park. Other times only three or four smaller groups would meet there. Whatever the size, groups were attracted to Bughouse Square because it offered a unique setting where petty crooks and thieves could mix with professors and editors. For those living a hand-to-mouth existence, soapbox oratory was also a way of picking up much-needed income. Some of the more enterprising could make well over fifty dollars a weekend.

Popular topics at the Square included women's issues, Freud, politics, and the relations between the sexes. Some of Bughouse Square's more colorful orators included Morris Levin, a blind man who quoted Shakespeare and just as easily could blurt out the Cubs and White Sox players' latest batting averages; James Sheridan, a bricklayer by profession, who recited poetry and discussed Marxian politics; a bulky Norwegian with the unlikely name of Triphammer Johnson, who was able to recall entire plays by Strindberg and Ibsen; and Frank Midney, who earned the nickname of the Mayor of Bughouse Square. The title of best orator belonged to John Loughman, a big, stocky Irishman whose sharp mind matched his rapier wit.

The person most at home on a soapbox, however, was the incomparable Ben Reitman, con man, physician, friend to prostitutes, hobo, bum, and founder of the Hobo College.[2] "Artists, trade unionists, socialists, prohibitionists, single-taxers, Druids, geologists who had proven the world flat, geologists who had proven that the earth's surface was inside a hollow sphere, atheists, suffragists, and people who had been in communication with inhabitants of Mars—they all congregated in the Square," writes historian and Reitman's biographer Roger Bruns.

The area along North Clark Street near Washington Square also attracted many homeless men. Indeed, Chicago in the early years of this century was considered the hobo capital of the country. Harvey Zorbaugh in *The Gold Coast and the Slum* estimated that between three hundred thousand to five hundred thousand hoboes passed through the city in a typical year.[3] The combination of artists and hoboes living closely together earned the area the nickname of "hobohemia." Bughouse Square, in particular, attracted the intellectual element of these men. They could find cheap lodging at the boarding rooms and flophouses of the neighborhood. There were many stores along Clark Street that catered to the homeless—resale shops and secondhand stores, especially near Clark Street and Chicago Avenue. There were also cheap places to eat. If a hobo wanted to hear what was going on, he would simply stop by one of the barbershops in the neighborhood to hear the news on the hobo grapevine.

During the day, especially on warm summer days, many of these homeless men could be seen sitting on benches in the park, reading newspapers. During the evening as many as a hundred or so would congregate there, listening intently to the soapbox speaker or congregating at the Radical Book Store at 817½ North Clark Street, a hangout for hobohemia where Communists and writers frequently mingled.

Another reason so many hoboes came to Chicago was that by then the city had earned a reputation as the "Wobbly" capital of America. It was, after all, the official headquarters of the Industrial Workers of the World (IWW). Many radicals and IWW sympathizers made their way here. Not surprisingly, their favorite gathering place was Bughouse Square, where they would set up their soapboxes and begin their evening's oration. After stepping down off the soapbox, the speakers would often pass the hat, hoping to earn some money by having impressed the listeners with their eloquence and oratory skills. Since anyone with the guts and the nerve to voice an opinion could speak—that is, if they could stomach the perpetual heckling—the open-door forum at Bughouse Square was an utterly democratic method of blowing off steam.

Bughouse wasn't the only outlet for debates. During the days before radio and television dominated America's interest, public forums in churches, in theaters, or out in the open formed a principal source of entertainment. These public forums offered free platforms of self-expression.

Just off Washington Square Park was the infamous Dill Pickle Club, the city's most notorious hangout. The club was founded by an irrepressible roustabout named Jack Jones, one of the most flamboyant inhabitants of Chicago's bohemia. Jones had worked many odd jobs over the years, from railroad worker to printer, before settling in Chicago. Since he missed the company of the people he met on the road—the street corner prophets and poets, the union organizers, and school dropouts-turned-philosophers—he decided to start his own club where everyone would be welcome, any idea encouraged.

Initially Jones opened a modest coffeehouse on Locust Street, patronized mostly by labor leaders. In 1916 he moved to larger quarters at 18 Tooker Place, within hailing distance of Bughouse Square. Starving artists, poets, labor organizers, reds and capitalists, writers and poets, the intelligentsia and philosophers, thieves and hoboes, working-class and assorted misfits all came to Jones's club. When they tired of being inside, they could, in good weather, saunter over to Bughouse Square to continue their conversations.

Speakers at the Dill Pickle Club included evangelist Aimee Semple McPherson, anarchist Emma Goldman, labor leaders Eugene Debs and "Big" Bill Haywood, and lawyer Clarence Darrow as well as celebrated literary figures such as Sherwood Anderson, Theodore Dreiser, Ring Lardner, Vachel Lindsay, Charles MacArthur, Edgar Lee Masters, Carl Sandburg, and the editor of *Poetry* magazine, Harriet Monroe. Ben Hecht's one-act play, appropriately titled *Dregs,* was presented there to an apparently appreciative audience. As always, Ben Reitman was a frequent visitor.

Discussions were held in the large lecture hall. Like the Bughouse Square sessions, topics were diverse and freewheeling. Most of the time the speakers were assaulted by verbal attacks from the audience. Many in the crowd, after all, had honed their oratory skills at

"Bughouse Square," circa 1909 (Chicago Historical Society, ICHi–22449, *Daily News* collection). Men and boys in dark suits and hats recall a different era at the North Side bohemian hangout. Little has changed in the immediate area surrounding the park, however. A fountain (not shown) was replaced in 1985 by a raised concrete platform. Otherwise, public institutions still dominate the area. The Newberry Library (1890–93; addition 1981) is on the left. Behind the trees looking east is the Scottish Rite Cathedral (1867; 1873; 1882).

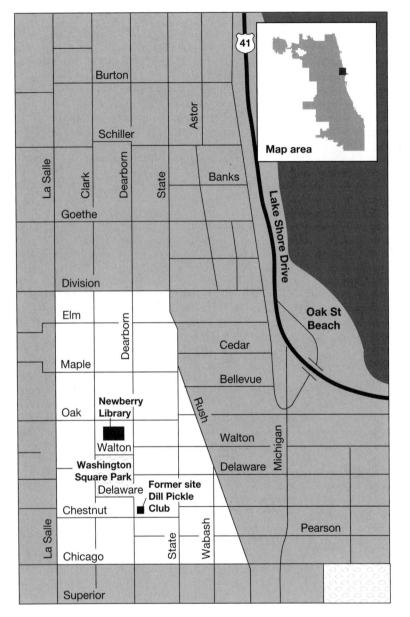

Map 7 Bughouse Square

Bughouse Square and had no qualms about letting their displeasure be known. Hecklers would throw barb after barb or taunt the speaker mercilessly with insults and sarcasm. Chicago journalist Vincent Starrett was an occasional visitor. "Geniuses with dirty necks read their poems, atheists denounced God, and wild-eyed pianists played their latest compositions," he recalled in his autobiography *Born in a Bookshop*. "Rarely, I think, were ideas expressed which, by any stretch if the imagination, could be called moderate. Everybody and everything was *anti*."

The Dill Pickle Club closed in the early 1930s. Jones himself died in 1940. Others tried to follow in its footsteps, such as the Cheese Box, the Mary Garden Forum, the Temple of Wisdom, the Intellectual Inferno, Seven Arts, and, in our own day, the College of Complexes.[4] But none captured the mood of the Dill Pickle Club.

With the Dill Pickle Club gone, the area around Bughouse Square was never quite the same either. Today, the voices have been all but extinguished, with the exception each summer of the Bughouse Square Debates hosted by the Newberry Library.

Notes

1. *Bughouse* was slang for insane asylum.
2. In 1913–14, James Eads How, the son of a prominent St. Louis family, opened the first Hobo College. Originally located at Congress Street near Wabash Avenue, the "college" offered lectures, discussions, readings, and courses on diverse subjects and even attracted some well-respected names such as opera singer Mary Garden. The ubiquitous Ben Reitman was the college's director. See Frank Beck, *Hobohemia* (West Rindge, N.H.: Richard R. Smith Publishers, 1956), 73–77.
3. Frank Beck also called Chicago "with its 60,000 or more homeless men" the hobo capital of America. See Beck, *Hobohemia*, 73–77.
4. The College of Complexes has had many lives. Slim Brundage, a housepainter and natural-born rabble-rouser, founded the first incarnation of the college in the early 1930s after the Dill Pickle Club closed (Brundage had been a bartender there). It resurfaced in the 1950s.

   During its peripatetic existence, the college has held fort in many locales: North Clark Street, North State Street, West Grand Avenue, North Wells Street, and in recent years, at what was formerly Hogen's restaurant (4560 North Lincoln Avenue), then at Ricky's Restaurant at the corner of

Belmont and Broadway, Cafe Classico on North Broadway, and El Pacifico on West Belmont Avenue.

During its heyday, the college featured "speakers, debates, folk singing, sword fights, chess tournaments, book reviews and piano recitals," according to Kenan Heise in the *Chicago Tribune*. Brundage died on October 18, 1990, in El Centro, California, at the age of eighty-six.

TOWERTOWN:
BOHEMIA ON THE PRAIRIE

Bohemia is a state of mind, a fluid land without boundaries that appeals to people during different phases of their life. From the Latin Quarter and Greenwich Village to Carmel and North Beach, the "kingdom of Bohemia" is a colorful place that has existed in one form or another throughout history.

Chicago has had its share of bohemias over the years—the Jackson Park artists' colony along Fifty-seventh Street and Stony Island Avenue in the teens,[1] Old Town in the 1960s,[2] and, in our own day, Wicker Park. Before World War I, Chicago's North Side bohemia was located in the shadow of the historic Water Tower, earning it the nickname of "Towertown." Towertown was a half-world of furnished rooms and walk-up apartments. But behind the garish facade, one could discover quirky restaurants, tearooms, arty shops, and the stables and garrets of would-be artists.

The residents of Towertown were varied. They included artists, students, the intelligentsia, slummers, and weekend bohemians; that is, professional men and women who dabbled in art and wanted to be part of the bohemian lifestyle. Towertown was also populated by people on the fringe of society, gays and lesbians, nonconformists and iconoclasts of every religious, social, and sexual persuasion. Some had come from Midwest farm towns, from nearby suburbs, or from farther afield to realize their dreams of living in blissful anonymity. Towertown also had a considerable number of little theaters, such as the Jack and Jill Players, the Impertinent Players, or the Studio Players, that gave a theatrical touch to the area.

A high proportion of the bohemians populating Towertown were young women. They were the ones most likely "to open most of the studios, run most of the tearooms and restaurants, most of the little art shops and book stalls, manage the exhibits and little theaters, dominate the life of the bohemias of American cities," writes Harvey Zorbaugh in *The Gold Coast and the Slum*.

As with most bohemias, Towertown also had its radical element. Some were Wobblies, some socialists, communists, or out-and-out anarchists. They congregated at places such as the Dill Pickle Club or Ye Black Cat Club and especially at the aptly named Radical Book Shop. Many of these so-called radicals would discuss the issues of the day at the Dill Pickle Club or, placing themselves on a soapbox, at Bughouse Square in Washington Park, across from the Newberry Library. Any topic was open to discussion, from "taboo" subjects such as sex and free love to Freud's interpretation of dreams—a hot topic at the time—to government and the rise of socialism.

The heyday of Towertown was during the years before World War I. At that time the compact neighborhood served as the headquarters of painters, artists, and writers, including such well-known wordsmiths as Carl Sandburg, Sherwood Anderson, Alfred Kreymborg, Floyd Dell, Edgar Lee Masters, and Ben Hecht.

But bohemia properly belonged to the unknown, anonymous artists who gave the neighborhood atmosphere and color. Some toiled at perfectly "proper" jobs during the day (at bookshops or at a newspaper) and composed their verses and prose at night over a typewriter. They attended poetry events around town, such as the gatherings sponsored by Harriet Moody at Au Petit Gourmet, a local literary cafe.[3]

After the war, Towertown deteriorated. The posers vastly outnumbered legitimate artists and a pervasive commercialism enveloped the little tightly knit community. Entrepreneurs, eager to make a fast buck, conducted bohemian tours of tearooms and studios for the outwardly curious. Towertown's seedy nightclubs also played up the bohemian connection. Anyone could be an artist by putting up a rickety sign, dabbing a few layers of paint over it, and calling it a studio. People desperately trying to be bohemian for a day camouflaged their vacuity under a guise of self-expression.

Seekers of pleasure and hangers-on became the bane of the community until the very notion of bohemia collapsed under the weight of all the sham.

High rents and rising land values forced the true bohemians of Towertown to seek shelter elsewhere. The studios and tearooms were replaced by more profit-making ventures. Bohemia was both a transient lifestyle and a transient community. As with bohemias everywhere, the residents were searching for a dream, a dream so elusive that it remained forever out of their grasp.

Notes

1. In the early years of the twentieth century, artists began moving into the abandoned storefronts that had sprung up during the Columbian Exposition of 1893 and turned the old quarters into living spaces, often quite primitive—usually little more than a potbellied stove and an outhouse. But the buildings did have their strong points, including ample light, high ceilings, and large backyards for social gatherings. Better yet, the rent was cheap and Lake Michigan was a few short blocks away. The Swedish painter B. J. O. Nordfeldt is credited with starting the movement toward the South Side; others soon followed him there. The Jackson Park art colony included editor and Chicago's prototypical bohemian Floyd Dell; his teacher wife, Margery Currey; and a coterie of friends and acquaintances, including Sherwood Anderson, George Cram Cook, Susan Glaspell, Llewellyn Jones, Ben Hecht, Margaret Anderson and her lover, Jane Heap, and Carl Sandburg. It was at one of Dell's gatherings where Anderson announced her plan to start *The Little Review*, a new literary magazine.

2. Old Town is remembered today as the center of Chicago's counterculture in the 1960s, but the community's bohemian origins are much older. In 1927 a group of artists, led by Sol Kogen and Edgar Miller, began converting Old Town's tumbledown flats and Victorian houses into lively expressions of their own idiosyncratic visions. Their work

---

Floyd Dell (1887–1969), king of the bohemians (courtesy Newberry Library). As editor of the *Friday Literary Review*, Dell was one of the most influential figures during the Chicago literary renaissance of the late nineteenth and early twentieth centuries.

Radicals, Reformers, and Eccentrics

can be seen today on streets such as West Burton Place and North Wells Street. For a description of Kogen-Miller buildings, see *AIA Guide to Chicago*, edited by Alice Sinkevitch (San Diego, Calif: Harcourt Brace and Company, 1993), 168–70, 173.

3. Harriet Moody, wife of poet William Vaughn Moody, opened the Au Petit Gourmet restaurant at 615 North Michigan Avenue in 1920. Her Sunday evening poetry readings attracted some of the finest poets in the country—including Carl Sandburg, Vachel Lindsay, Robert Frost, Padraic Colum, Maxwell Bodenheim, Countee Cullen, Amy Lowell, Edna St. Vincent Millay, and Harriet Monroe. See Olivia Howard Dunbar, *A House in Chicago* (Chicago: University of Chicago Press, 1947), 175–76. From 1913 to 1928, Moody's three-story red brick house on South Groveland Avenue (now South Ellis) was the city's premier literary salon. Here she played the gracious host to poets, artists, and musicians, offering an intoxicating mix of conversation, good food, and inspiration.

THE LITERARY BEAT

Encyclopaedia Britannica headquarters, Britannica Centre, 310 South Michigan Avenue (courtesy *Encyclopaedia Britannica*). Britannica has moved a number of times over the years: the Sears plant on the West Side, the Civic Opera Building, the now-demolished Mandel Building on the north bank of the Chicago River, and, most recently, the Britannica Centre. Note the glass beehive on the building's pyramidlike roof.

DEADLINES AND COFFINS:
THE NOT-SO-DISCREET CHARM OF THE WHITECHAPEL CLUB

Humor in Chicago journalism has a long and prestigious pedigree. As early as the 1840s, local readers enjoyed the biting wit of the comic writer's inventive mind. The tradition reached its zenith during the 1880s and 1890s, when the likes of Eugene Field, George Ade, and Finley Peter Dunne established Chicago's reputation as a vibrant literary and journalistic town.

The golden age of Chicago journalism found expression in the many drinking establishments and social clubs of the day. One of the most notorious was the Whitechapel Club, a newsmen's hangout off an alley near the newspaper offices on North Wells Street.

The origin of the club's name is the stuff of journalistic legend. One day when the group was gathered in the back room of Henry Koster's saloon at 173 West Calhoun Place, a newsboy dashed in yelling, "All about the latest Whitechapel murder!" Inspired by that reference to the grisly crimes of London's Jack the Ripper, Charles Goodyear Seymour, a *Chronicle of Chicago* reporter and the club's first president, reportedly raised his stein of beer and chortled: "Here's to the Whitechapel Club! That's the name for our club!"

In its life span of less than six years (1889–94), the club—even during its heyday—never had more than ninety members. Dunne, whose fictional Mr. Dooley raised the eyebrows and social consciousness of the *Evening Post*'s readers, was an early member. Field, the city's first nationally known humorist, was an occasional visitor. Newsmen from the city's eleven newspapers made up most of the membership, but there were also lawyers, doctors, musicians, politicians, and a clergyman or two.

The Whitechapel was most renowned for its gleefully morbid obsession with death. Skulls and a hangman's noose adorned the club's walls and ceilings. A huge coffin-shaped dining table, its lid embellished with large brass nails that each bore a member's

name, dominated the main assembly room. "Leave Everything Behind, Ye Who Go Hence" was the club motto.

Both members and guests were required to adhere to a code of honor. "Brains, honor, courage and humor were the necessary qualifications for membership," recalled reporter William Hay Williamson in a 1929 article in the *Chronicle of Chicago*. One steadfast rule of the club was that "a gentleman never gets drunk."

The club "roasted" members and visitors alike, poked fun at the inflated personalities of the day, and staged outrageous pranks like the one that welcomed the visiting members of the Clover Club of Philadelphia, who were invited ostensibly to advise their hosts on the formation of a similar club in Chicago. When some fifty Cloverites showed up one hot midsummer night resplendent, as was their wont, in formal evening attire, they were surprised to see that the Whitechapel men, seemingly more concerned with comfort than decorum, were all coatless. The surprise turned into alarm when suddenly, after a furious pounding on the door, uniformed policemen burst in announcing, "You're all under arrest!" Every man *not* in his shirtsleeves was hauled into police wagons, which then drove away through the bumpiest cobblestoned streets of what is now the Loop. The alarm, in turn, changed into embarrassment when the Philadelphians were dropped off not at a prison door but at the main entrance of their hotel.

Another notable event involved the bizarre funeral rite held in honor of Morris Allen Collins, who had taken his own life to show he had no fear of death. Seeing in Collins a kindred spirit and complying with his last wish, the Whitechapel men made plans to cremate him. Late on the night of July 16, 1892, thirteen members took Collins by train to Miller's Station, Indiana, and then by wagon to the dunes on the shore of Lake Michigan. There, as the aurora borealis danced against the black sky, Collins's Grecian-robed corpse was cremated. For five and one-half hours the pyre burned while Shelley's poetry filled the air. It was the Whitechapel Club's finest moment.

But the club's glory was short-lived, its life snuffed out by one of its own members. A "brilliant and courageous" man, that member turned out to be a crook who robbed the club "blind" and "plunged it into debt." Rather than borrowing funds to pay off the debt, the Whitechapel men paid it off themselves and "with laughter and jests" decided to call it quits, thereby ending a unique chapter of Chicago history.

Several years ago a group of Chicago-area poets, led by Marc Smith, staged a number of performances at the Green Mill, a noted jazz club and former speakeasy, dedicated to the memory of the original Whitechapel Club.

CLIFF DWELLERS CLUB:
LOWBROW AND HIGHBROW MEET ON MICHIGAN AVENUE

Hardly noticeable among the stores and buildings along a section of South Michigan Avenue downtown is a curious sign at the entrance to Orchestra Hall. It reads "Cliff Dwellers Club."[1] The club itself is on the ninth floor, reached by an elevator ride to the eighth floor of Orchestra Hall and up a steep flight of stairs. Founded in 1909 by a group headed by novelist Hamlin Garland as an all-male social club for the city's literary elite, the club became a center for patrons of the arts and was once renowned as the most erudite place in town. Here members and guests would gather for fine food and relaxed conversation amidst the soothing influences of book-lined walls, plush leather chairs, and original paintings.

In earlier days, though, the Cliff Dwellers were known to discard their Apollonian reserve for memorable moments of Dionysian merrymaking.

One of those happy events was their annual dunes barbeque celebration near Michigan City, Indiana. At midnight preceding the barbeque, the club's head chef and assistants would travel to the site, dig a deep barbeque pit, erect tables and tents, cut firewood, and get everything else ready for the evening's supper. By 2:00 P.M. the Cliff Dwellers arrived, ready to imbibe alcoholic beverages, play ball games, hike, or swim. At the end of an afternoon of hardworking fun, they were rewarded by a huge feast of steak, chicken, potatoes, and salad, followed by entertainment.

One time several Cliff Dwellers dreamed up a rather elaborate treasure hunt. The "prizes" included bottles of scotch, boxes of cigars, and, hidden inside a six-by-two-foot corrugated-carton box, a young model wearing nothing more than a pair of slippers, a girdle, and a wreath of flowers in her hair. During the hunt, two elderly and tiring Cliff Dwellers came upon the carton, half-buried in the ground, and thought it a perfect spot to rest. No sooner had

they set their haunches down on it when a muffled but loud scream pierced the air, sending them scurrying down the dunes as fast as their tired legs could carry them.

The barbeque usually concluded with a ritual fire by the lake, around which the happily inebriated Cliff Dwellers would prance to the beat of an Indian drum, chanting weird medleys, and calling upon the spirits of their dead Cliff Dweller brothers to awaken them from their graves and rejoin them.

The invocation was answered, after a fashion, for those members who thought themselves spiritual cousins of the cliff-dwelling Indians of the Southwest when one day some twenty Hopi and Navajo Indians in full ceremonial regalia suddenly appeared in Chicago. Led by John Collier of the Santa Fe Indian Welfare Society, the group was en route to Washington, D.C., to protest the Indians' harsh living conditions and was stopping briefly in the city to solicit contributions from friends, among them Cliff Dwellers Ralph Fletcher Seymour and Carter Harrison II, who had made a recent visit to the Southwest.

Seymour was at first stunned to see the Indians appear unexpectedly at his downtown studio, but he quickly regained his composure and insisted that the delegation accompany him to the club. So they all marched up North Michigan Avenue, their impromptu parade blocking traffic and generally creating a midday urban commotion. By the time they arrived at the club, word had spread that a tribe of Hopi and Navajo Indians had invaded Orchestra Hall.

The Cliff Dwellers welcomed their exotic friends warmly. After they had broken bread over a sumptuous meal, one of the Indians produced a drum, and soon the group was chanting in unison and stomping about in a ritualized Corn Dance. In the joyous pandemonium that followed, the usually reserved Cliff Dwellers jumped on their chairs and howled excitedly. As Collier made an appeal for money, Seymour passed the hat and collected hundreds of dollars. With that auspicious beginning, Collier and friends became instant media darlings, and during their brief stay in town, they were much sought after as luncheon guests. Seymour himself became a self-appointed expert on Indian affairs, speaking on local radio on behalf of his visiting friends.

Today's Cliff Dwellers, 350 or so writers, architects, musicians, and other devotees of the arts, have settled down to more typically quiet ways, all the more so, perhaps, because in 1984 the club opened its once all-male bastion to women members. The future of the club is precarious, however. In 1994 the Orchestra Association, which owns Orchestra Hall, began a proposed three-year, $95.5-million renovation project that threatens to remove the elite club from its much-sought-after space. Only time will tell the fate of the Cliff Dwellers.

Notes

1. Another important literary institution is the Caxton Club. In January 1895 fifteen bibliophiles founded the club to encourage "the literary study and promotion of the arts pertaining to the production of books." The club has published sixty books, including historical works, the history of printing and bookbinding, book collecting, poetry, literary works, plays, and an opera. See Frank J. Piehl, *The Caxton Club 1895–1995: Celebrating a Century of the Book in Chicago* (Chicago: Caxton Club, 1995).

ENCYCLOPAEDIA BRITANNICA:
THE ORIGINS OF A CHICAGO INSTITUTION

*E*ncyclopaedia Britannica is considered the oldest and most comprehensive reference work in the English language. It is known throughout the world for its scholarly writing and thoughtful editing. What is less known, however, is the reference giant's strong Chicago connection.

The story of *Britannica* began several centuries ago and thousands of miles away across the ocean in Edinburgh, Scotland, when three prominent men—printer Colin Macfarquhar, engraver Andrew Bell, and editor William Smellie—became determined to publish the best reference book on the market. In December 1768 the first of the three-volume encyclopedia appeared.

The topics of the original volume reflected the tenor of the time, such as medical advice for common maladies and midwifery. The cost of the three-volume set was £12. Smellie chose not to continue his involvement with *Britannica* after the first edition; Macfarquhar took over the editorial reins until his death in 1793. Bell died in 1809. Various publishers then assumed control during the company's early years—Archibald Constable in 1812 and Edinburgh bookseller Adam Black in the early 1830s.

Throughout its history, several editions have had major historical significance. The ninth edition, for example, made some historic firsts: the choice of *Britannica's* first non-Scottish editor, the English-born scholar Thomas Spencer Baynes; the first edition to contain bibliographies; and the first to appear in an authorized printing in the United States.

As the company expanded, it grew further and further away from its Scottish roots; so much so that by the turn of the century, two Americans—book promoter Horace Everett Hooper and publisher Walter Montgomery Jackson—bought *Britannica* from the Black family and moved operations to London. In 1902 an American division was formed simultaneously.

Over the years various organizations from the *Times* of London to Cambridge University to the University of Chicago had significant ties with *Britannica*. At one point, the *Times* accepted orders for the company with Cambridge University serving in an advisory capacity. Simultaneously, Sears, Roebuck, and Company promoted and sold *Britannica* through its mail order firm. Indeed, beginning in 1920, Sears held ownership rights to *Britannica* off and on for a number of years.

By the mid-1930s, Chicago had become the company headquarters. Sears offered *Britannica* to the University of Chicago but was turned down twice. Some university trustees apparently thought it was not in the university's best interest to own a "commercial enterprise." In 1942, however, William Benton, a University of Chicago vice president and cofounder of the Benton and Bowles advertising agency, agreed to put up his own money when Sears president General Robert E. Wood offered $100,000 of the company's inventory as a gift. It was too good to pass up. Thus, the university received a one-third interest and royalties as well as the right to use the university imprimatur.

Britannica has maintained several headquarters over the years: the Sears plant on Arthington Street on the West Side and the Civic Opera Building on Wacker Drive. In 1951 corporate headquarters moved again, this time to the now-demolished Mandel Building on the north bank of the Chicago River.

Another significant event in *Britannica* history occurred in 1952 with the publication of the fifty-four-volume *Great Books of the Western World,* which brought to public attention the classic literature of the West. A landmark achievement, the series was nine years in the making and was edited by William Benton, University of Chicago president Robert Maynard Hutchins, and philosopher Mortimer Adler. In the 1980s, the *Great Books* series was updated and revised.

Words of the wise (courtesy *Encylopaedia Britannica*). In 1952 *Britannica* published the fifty-four-volume *Great Books of the Western World,* which attempted to bring the classic literature of the Western world to a broader audience. The series was updated and revised in the 1980s, and today consists of sixty volumes. Throughout the changes, the familiar symbol of the Scottish thistle has remained constant.

In 1961 *Britannica* bought the F. E. Compton Company, publisher of Compton's Pictured Encyclopedia, and in 1964 acquired G. & C. Merriam Company (now Merriam-Webster), the dictionary publisher.

The massive fifteenth edition, otherwise known as *Britannica 3,* was hailed by many educators as a monumental achievement. Created at a staggering cost of $32 million, it consisted of 30 volumes and 43 million words, 30,000 pages, 20,000 color and black-and-white photographs, and 4,000 contributors from more than 130 countries.

Throughout its history, *Britannica* has prided itself on the quality of its writing and the caliber of its authors. Some of the more prominent contributors over the years have included Sir Walter Scott on chivalry and romance; Edward Everett, president of Harvard, who wrote a forty-thousand-word essay on George Washington; Leon Trotsky on Lenin; Thomas Babington Macaulay on Samuel Johnson and Oliver Goldsmith; Algernon Charles Swinburne on Mary, Queen of Scots and John Keats; George Bernard Shaw on socialism; and General George C. Marshall on World War II. Others have included Thomas Henry Huxley, Matthew Arnold, Robert Louis Stevenson, Alfred North Whitehead, Harry Houdini, Marie Curie, Albert Einstein, H. L. Mencken, and Sigmund Freud.

In 1983 company headquarters moved from the Mandel Building to the Britannica Centre at Michigan Avenue and Jackson Boulevard, where it occupies nine floors. The lower level houses the company's cafeteria named, appropriately enough, given its Scottish origins, the Thistle Club.

Today, the company that got its modest start on the rain-slicked streets of Edinburgh has more than 250 offices worldwide operating in 17 countries and distributors in some 130 countries. In addition to the encyclopedia, *Britannica* is also involved in film, videotape, computer software, and learning services. It can truly be called a world-class organization.

THE GOLDEN TONGUE OF MR. DOOLEY

Easily one of the most quoted and most influential persons in the city and country in the 1890s was an aging, acid-tongued Irish saloonkeeper from the South Side named Martin Dooley. Every week in the pages of the Chicago *Evening Post* his astute observations were assiduously devoured by readers of all classes.

Dooley, the philosophical barkeep of "Archey Road" (actually Archer Avenue in the Bridgeport neighborhood), was the creation of Finley Peter Dunne, a Chicago newsman who had worked for most of the Chicago dailies. The Dooley essays, for which he got an extra $10 a week, did not carry his byline, so only a few fellow journalists in town knew that Mr. Dooley was, in fact, Finley Peter Dunne.

Dooley was first modeled after an amiable Irish saloonkeeper named James McGarry, whose downtown bar on Dearborn Street was a favorite spot for politicians, judges, actors, and reporters. McGarry was "stout, rosy-faced, blue-eyed," an intelligent and dignified host who always wore a neat white vest and had an opinion on just about everything. One day in 1892 Dunne overheard a conversation between McGarry and a customer about the death of an important financier and was so impressed with the proprietor's caustic yet funny remarks that he quickly dashed off the first of what was to become a series of pieces featuring a wisecracking Irish saloonkeeper with the thickest Irish brogue.

The fictional saloonkeeper was named Colonel Malachi McNeery, but everybody within drinking distance of McGarry's saloon knew his true identity. Although a good friend of Dunne's, McGarry grew tired of his notoriety and nine months later asked the *Post*'s publisher, John R. Walsh, for some relief. Dunne then turned Colonel McNeery, the strapping ex-war veteran, into Martin Dooley, the cracker-barrel old sage of Bridgeport.

Dooley's saloon was "forninst th' gas house and beyond Healey's slough and not far from the polis station." Having Dooley denounce local evils in a thick Irish brogue allowed Dunne greater freedom of expression—something he could not do in the pages of the then-conservative Chicago press.

Every great conversationalist needs an equally great listener. Initially, Dooley's foil was John J. McKenna, a real-life Republican politician in the heavily Democratic Sixth Ward. He was later replaced by the fictional Mr. Hennessy, a day laborer with a large family.

Most of the Dooley essays were humorous and droll commentaries on contemporary American life, full of wicked satiric twists and delicious ironic turns. Occasionally, he wrote of tragedy, such as his portrayal of a quiet boy from a pious family turned by bone-wearying poverty into a criminal—"Sometimes I think they'se poison in th' life iv a big city." So moving was the tale that it was read annually for some years in one of the city's Catholic churches.

When Dunne moved to the *Chicago Journal* in 1898, his Dooley column gained even wider readership. Then the Spanish-American War catapulted Dooley to national attention. Dunne's piece on Admiral George Dewey's naval victory at Manila Bay, blithely equating American imperialism with the ring of the cash register, suited the cynical mood of the general public; it was a perfect expression of what many people in the country then felt.

In 1900 Dunne left Chicago to work as editor of the *New York Morning Telegraph*. There he continued to write his Dooley columns, for a total of some seven hundred. Of these, it is the first three hundred in which he so graphically captured contemporary life set against an ethnic neighborhood on Chicago's South Side, and which are considered his crowning glory. And though Finley Peter Dunne died virtually unknown in 1936 at age sixty-eight in New York, his fame continues to live on in the words of his alter ego, Martin Dooley, the neighborhood philosopher from the Archey Road in Bridgeport, Chicago.

SCHLOGL'S:
CHICAGO'S LITERARY ROUND TABLE

In 1916 Henry Blackman Sell, a former furniture salesman who had a passion for books, made an offer to the *Chicago Daily News:* Let him be editor of a new book review section, and the paper's reporters could have free lunches at Schlogl's Restaurant & Saloon nearby at 37 North Wells Street. The deal was struck, and the newsmen began meeting at a round walnut table in a corner of the restaurant. Thus was born the Round Table that soon became the talk of the town—an almost-daily gathering of literate souls who discussed books, life, and the world at large while they partook of German-style dishes well washed down with wine.

Lunches at Schlogl's were known sometimes to last longer than three hours. It was the kind of place that encouraged rambling conversations over endless cups of coffee. Part Viennese inn and part English men's drinking club (women were allowed only in the upstairs dining room), it had brass-plated umbrella stands, a long black walnut bar, an old pendulum clock, and hunting prints and oil paintings of hooded friars and rotund tavernkeepers on its walls. The once-white ceiling had blackened over the years from the incessant smoke of countless pipes, cigars, and cigarettes. A one-pound block of unsalted butter was on each table, and the menu included such unusual fare as eel in aspic, roast venison, partridges and mallards in season, and "owls to order."

Round Table regulars included such notable *Daily News* staffers as Henry Justin Smith, Keith Preston, Harry Hansen, Carl Sandburg, Eunice Tietjens, Vincent Starrett, John Gunther, and Ben (*The Front Page*) Hecht. Among those who joined them regularly were historian Lloyd Lewis, authors Sherwood Anderson and Theodore Dreiser, poets Edgar Lee Masters and Maxwell Bodenheim, journalists and editors Samuel Putnam, Llewellyn Jones, Charles Collins, Charles MacArthur, and the *Chicago Tribune's* editorial cartoonist, John T. McCutcheon. Visitors included Sinclair Lewis, Upton Sinclair, D. W. Griffith, and Louis Untermeyer. Throughout the comings and goings, however, Richard Schneider, the reassuring waiter, remained a stable presence.

Aware that it was Sell who had opened the doors of Schlogl's to them, the newsmen did not just eat, drink, and talk at the restaurant; they actually wrote most of their reviews for Sell's book section there.

As book editor, Sell was quite unorthodox. On one occasion he traveled to New York to interview English writer John Galsworthy, but instead of profiling the author and discussing his work, he chose to devote virtually his entire article to Galsworthy's rather pointed ears. He often had books reviewed more than once. *White Shadows in the South Seas,* for example, was reviewed twenty-six times, according to Alson J. Smith in *Chicago's Left Bank.* Sell even allowed authors to review their own books, and he had very flexible deadlines, if he had any at all. Sandburg once was supposedly given a copy of a book he was assigned to review; four months later he returned the book to Sell with no review but with the cheery message: "That was an interesting book about farmers you gave me. Thanks a lot. How are things going?"

Smith was an editor's editor. Fortunately, for the sake of Chicago literature, he also was an editor who encouraged his staffers to experiment with fiction. Indeed, Smith was one of the great figures of Chicago's Front Page era. A bit rough around the edges perhaps, undeniably brusque and stern, but also staunchly loyal and supportive of his talented staff. It is no exaggeration to say that some of the finest writing in Chicago literary history emerged from the able pens of journalists.[1]

Where writers gather, cynicism and irreverence often abound, and such was the case at the Round Table. One day an English lecturer who was researching the psyche of the American female was

invited to speak to the group. After dessert, he took out his note-book and cautiously began: "Now, we are all men here . . . So let me ask your opinion, that is to say, the sum of your own personal experience. Is it true that the American girl permits . . . ah, er . . . certain liberties with her person?" After a brief silence, Hecht took up the challenge, and with a wicked smile flashing on his impish face, proceeded to cover the subject in such minute detail that the Englishman was left both exhausted and red faced.

Nourished by Schlogl's good food and the participants' free spirits, the Round Table flourished as a Chicago literary institu-tion—the Midwestern equivalent of New York's Algonquin Round Table—until the 1930s. By then the sayings and exploits of the newspapermen who started it all had become almost as legendary as the deeds of their Arthurian counterparts.

Notes

1. Chicago has a long history of great bookshops and great book collec-tors. The leading antiquarian bookseller during the time of the literary renaissance was Walter Hill. Another important literary haunt was Ben Abramson's Argus Bookshop overlooking Lake Michigan. Ben Hecht and Maxwell Bodenheim were regulars at Covici and McGee's book-shop. Fanny Butcher, the literary editor of the *Chicago Tribune,* also ran a small bookshop. For many years A. C. McClurg's Bookstore at 218 South Wabash Avenue was a local literary landmark and gathering spot.

   Chicago's place as the country's foremost literary center was short-lived. In 1919 H. L. Mencken had uttered his famous line about Chicago being the literary capital of the United States in London's *The Nation.* At that time the movers and shakers of the movement were in their full glory. Their most prominent members included Sherwood Anderson, Carl Sandburg, Edgar Lee Masters, Ben Hecht, Theodore Dreiser, and Vachel Lindsay. In 1926 Mencken convinced journalist Samuel Putnam

---

Ben Hecht (1893–1964), journalist, screenwriter, and literary toast of the town. In 1928, Hecht and cowriter Charles MacArthur portrayed the care-free, irreverent, anything-goes world of Chicago journalism in their play *The Front Page,* which has spawned numerous film adaptations.

to sound the official death knell of the movement. See Samuel Putnam, "Chicago: An Obituary," *American Mercury,* August 1926.

The renaissance also produced a number of important publications. In addition to Harriet Monroe's *Poetry: A Magazine of Verse,* they included Margaret Anderson's *The Little Review; Friday Literary Review,* a literary supplement of the *Chicago Evening Post* that actually made its debut a decade earlier in 1909; Ben Hecht's irreverent *Chicago Literary Times;* and Vincent Starrett's *Wave. The Chapbook,* which originated in New England, moved its headquarters to Chicago in 1894. Various social events, including teas and book shows, were held at the magazine's offices on South Dearborn Street until it published its last issue in 1898 and merged with *The Dial. The Dial,* which became the leading literary magazine in the country, was founded in Chicago in 1880 by Francis Browne. It moved to New York in 1918, where it survived until 1929.

THE SEED:
VOICE OF THE FLOWER CHILDREN GENERATION

The whole world is watching!" That was what the demonstrators chanted over and over outside the Conrad Hilton Hotel, their angry voices reverberating up and down Michigan Avenue that hot and humid night in August 1968.[1] The Democratic National Convention had come to town, but not everyone who greeted the conventioneers was friendly. Clashes between demonstrators and the police took place. Rocks were thrown, nightsticks swung and guns fired, and Grant and Lincoln Parks became bloody battlefields.

It was a high point in a political-cultural revolution that marched to the rhythm of the Beatles, sang "All You Need Is Love" as its anthem, and held "Don't Trust Anybody over 30" as its motto. Embracing drugs and flaunting long hair, Sergeant Pepper frock coats, and bell-bottom pants, young adherents found a common cause in opposing the Vietnam War and a common means of expression in the underground press.

From 1967 to 1973, the underground press consisted of a loose network of some five hundred newspapers. Among the better-known papers were the *L.A. Free Press* and the *Berkeley Barb* in California, the *Rat* in New York, and the *Seed* in Chicago.

The *Seed,* originally *The Chicago Seed,* was published every two or three weeks from May 1967 until it petered out in late 1973 or early 1974. It carried a mix of neighborhood news, hippie wisdom, nature lore, cartoons, and colorful graphics. Thriving on subscription and ad revenues, the paper claimed during its heyday to have some forty thousand readers in forty-eight states and thirteen countries, including GIs in South Vietnam. It was founded by Don Lewis, a local artist, and Earl Segal, a poster shop owner, as a voice for the flower children who had flocked to the Old Town area.

As opposition to the Vietnam War—and the Establishment as a whole—escalated into violence on the streets and confrontations on college campuses, the *Seed* became more strident in its political views. Earlier exhortations to readers to "get their heads on straight" and vague hopes that humanity would evolve into a noncompetitive and nonviolent world later hardened into more combative editorial positions. From seeking permits to hold free concerts, the *Seed* championed student protests, black causes, resistance to the draft, and strikes and boycotts against grape growers. Its editor, Abe Peck, later a journalism professor at Northwestern University, then writing under the pen name of Abraham Yippie, at one point said he wondered whether he should carry a flower or a gun.

There was never any doubt about which side of the issues the *Seed* was on. During the Democratic Convention the four Chicago dailies ran stories about the Democrats' plans for the country; the *Seed* carried the demonstrators' agenda. While the dailies warned against the dangers of violence, the *Seed* ran an article entitled "What To Do in Case of Arrest."

Staying out of jail was always a concern of the underground press editor. Peck and reporter Michael Abrahams were arrested on an obscenity charge stemming from a Christmas 1968 issue of the *Seed* that had a centerfold featuring a composite photograph of a nude woman and of Mayor Richard J. Daley. Though the charges were later dropped, City Hall clearly was not pleased.

It was a time of one sensational story after another—the "Chicago 7" trial, the court martial of Lieutenant William Calley, the Charles Manson murders, the assassinations of Martin Luther King, Jr., and Robert F. Kennedy, the Woodstock phenomenon—and the *Seed* was right in the thick of it.

Not surprisingly, there were those who did not take kindly to the *Seed.* Allegations of police spying on its staff were not uncommon. One evening a bullet fired by two leather-jacketed teenagers shattered the front window of the paper's office at 837 North

LaSalle Street. Nobody was hurt, but Peck and another editor, Marshall Rosenthal, confronted the offenders and made a futile attempt to show them the errors of their antihippie ways.

In his book *Uncovering the 60s: The Life & Times of the Underground Press,* Peck writes, "The [underground] papers changed minds and lives and showed people they could fight City Hall. They ran the news that didn't fit when nobody else would."

But the youthful vigor and idealism (some would say blind naïveté) that were hallmarks of the underground press later deteriorated into bitter infighting among the editors. And when the Vietnam War came to an end and Richard Nixon resigned from the presidency, the *Seed* and its sister papers lost their sense of urgency and their very reason for being. The revolution was over; it was time to go home.

Notes

1. The violence culminated on Wednesday, August 28, 1968, as armed police and as many as seven thousand protesters clashed at the intersection of Michigan Avenue and Balbo Drive. The confrontation became known as the "Battle on Michigan Avenue." By the time the violence had subsided, almost seven hundred people had been arrested. See the editor's remarks to David Farber, "Welcome to Chicago," *Chicago History* 17, nos. 1 and 2 (spring and summer 1988): 62.

Select historical sites

- *Vietnam Survivors Memorial.* 815 South Oakley Boulevard, Chicago. Offbeat folk art by Vietnam veteran and preservationist William S. Lavicka commemorating his fellow veterans. The memorial's lead designer, Derrick Sudduth, died in 1990 at the age of thirty-two.

"The whole world is watching" (Chicago Historical Society, ICHi–20781). General John Logan Memorial in Grant Park, Michigan Avenue at Ninth Street, 1968. Demonstrators and police clash during the Democratic National Convention.

LIFE IN THE NEIGHBORHOODS

Chicago Commons, maypole party at day nursery (Chicago Historical Society, ICHi–03796).

BACK STREETS AND ALLEYS:
URBAN PLAYGROUNDS TO A GENERATION

Unlike New York, Boston, and other major American cities, Chicago from its earliest days has had alleys—their purpose to keep such mundane services as garbage collection, produce and milk deliveries, and utility lines from cluttering up the main streets. But to the children of another generation, they were urban playgrounds, and there they would play until dusk came and hunger pangs told them it was time to go home.

But it was there, too, that the children first learned they were but a small part of a larger social order. And as adults, they would look upon the alley as just another part of a hard life from which they would hope someday to escape.

During the early days of the city, rear tenements were regarded as "the worst possible dwellings for human beings." Lack of space forced the construction of two buildings to a single lot, one facing the main street, the other the alley. Into these congested back lot buildings poured the flood of immigrants who provided cheap labor for the city's burgeoning industries and gave ample opportunities for unscrupulous landlords to turn handsome profits.

By the turn of the century, back-street life became a favorite target of social reformers concerned about the filth and squalor, the high death rate, and the constant threat of epidemics that they saw there. And they knew what they were complaining about from firsthand experience because the easiest way into many rear buildings was from the alleys, and it was through the alleys that members, say, of the Visiting Nurses Association, a private health care group, would drive their horse-drawn wagons to tend to the needy and the bedridden.

But the children, unaware of their deprived status, thoroughly enjoyed the simple pleasures that the alleys provided. Poking through alleys in search of milk bottles might bring a nickel refund at the neighborhood grocery store. Two milk bottles got you into the Saturday afternoon movie matinee. And there were the games, many enlivened by playground rhymes. Kick the can. Hopscotch. Double dutch. Jack be nimble, Jack be quick. Tag. Cops and robbers. Cowboys and Indians. Simon says. One, two, three, red light. Marbles. Pitching pennies. Cracking the whip. Roly Poly.

The most popular game was hide-and-seek. In one variation, someone kicked a can, and the child who was "it" chased the can while everyone else hid. When flushed out of hiding, you had to outrace the "it" to the designated "home." If you were tagged, you were the next "it," and all the others still in hiding were brought in with shouts of "Ole Ole Olsen, all in free," "Ollie Ollie Oxen, free free free," or "Ollie Ollie Ocean free." The phrase, some say, came to Chicago with the early Norwegian settlers, who played a similar game back home called *gjemmespill.*

Rougher games attracted a more rambunctious crowd. In "buck buck," the biggest player would bend at the waist and grab a firm object like a utility pole to act as an anchor. The next player on his team would then lean over and grab him by the waist, and so on until a human chain was formed. The opposing team would then jump on their backs until the chain collapsed.

Interrupting the games was a constant stream of tradesmen pushing their creaky carts or driving their horse-drawn wagons as they announced their wares and services at the tops of their voices. "Rags and old iron, rags and old iron!" cried the ragpickers. And there were also the watermelon peddlers, junk buyers, icemen, knife and scissors sharpeners, and those who picked up goose, duck, and chicken feathers to feed a thriving business of pillow making.

Through the years Chicago's alleys underwent many improvements, mainly through paving and lighting. One of the biggest facelifts came in 1967, when some 51,000 sodium-vapor lamps were installed along 2,300 miles of alleys at a cost of $10.5 million. Some citizens complained that the brighter lights kept them from sleeping at night, but most welcomed the action. Owners of clubs and restaurants found it easier to park the cars of their evening customers. One city official claimed the garbage put out by residents on the well-lit alleys "definitely was neater." And in 1969 Police Superintendant James Conlisk, Jr., credited the lights with reducing "major crimes committed in alleys by 30.3 percent."

But the alley continues in one way or another to be a playground. Many now use it to host private parties and hold neighborhood fairs and festivals. And in contrast to its humble beginnings, the alley in certain sections of the city has become a fashionable place to live, as coach houses and back lot apartments are renovated and modernized and offered to an upscale crowd, many of whom are quite willing to pay goodly sums to live on "those things between streets."

GOING TO THE BATHS

Chicago's neighborhood bathhouses were worlds unto themselves, places to ease the aches and pains of everyday living, ersatz country clubs where customers rubbed each other down and ate and drank together. Through the doors of these bathhouses passed the poor and the wealthy, the powerful and the powerless. Ward bosses flashing their money, gamblers talking loudly of betting odds, housewives by themselves or with their young children, clergy and gangsters, politicians, jockeys and prizefighters, brokers and merchants—all came to the baths.

Few Chicagoans at the turn of the century had private bathing facilities. Possession of a bathtub or shower was considered a tremendous achievement, and data gathered at the time indicate only one bathtub for every four Chicagoans. There were, in fact, more automobiles than bathtubs per capita nationwide.

The first free public baths in Chicago, hardly more than a primitive shower really, reportedly opened in January of 1894, at 192 Mather (now West Lexington) Street. Free soap and a towel were handed out to each bather, who was allowed twenty minutes.

But bathhouses were not at all popular at first. In 1903 police officers had to be stationed day and night outside the half-finished Kosciuszko Bathhouse, 1444–46 North Holt (now Greenview) Avenue, to protect it from angry residents who threatened to storm the place. The people's anger subsided only after they were assured that a bathhouse in the neighborhood did not mean they would be forced to take baths.

Those early reservations about bathhouses soon disappeared, however. "Good health is priceless—cleanliness gives health," said a sign on the wall of one bathhouse, and Chicagoans heartily agreed. Soon some fifty public bathhouses were flourishing in the city, and by 1910, their peak year, they averaged some thirty thousand patrons a year. They were most popular especially during the summer months, when long lines of customers, from young children to senior citizens and from all levels of society, formed outside.

For many working-class Chicagoans, going to the baths was a special occasion. Tired housewives saw it as a reprieve from their daily chores and a welcome change from the bathing-and-washing routine at home. In most homes, a big tub, used for both bathing and clothes washing, was filled with water, and usually the eldest child went in first, washed up, and stepped out. Then, if they were lucky, the mother would empty the tub, pour in a fresh bucket of water for the next child, and repeat the process until every child had his or her turn.

Often a laborer would stop by the public baths for a quick shower before heading home. Patrons stayed in a waiting room until the attendant called their name. Each bather then entered a tiny cubicle, and as a bell sounded, water came gushing down—cold at first but eventually warming up. This "luxury" cost a nickel. The park district and the city's settlement houses had similar facilities with separate hours for men and women.

Bathhouses were built originally in areas with large concentrations of rooming houses and cold-water flats. Many considered a trip to the bathhouse on Sunday the social highlight of the week. Jewish men from the Maxwell Street district, for example, met their friends there on weekends, eating lox, herring, and black bread, and drinking homemade wine, according to author Ira Berkow. Wearing sandals and draped in sheets, they played cards and had endless conversations. For Orthodox Jewish women, the bathhouses were the place to do *mikvah,* the ritual purification bath taken at the end of the menstrual cycle.

Most bathhouses had a steam room and a pool. Customers would lather each other up with soapy warm water, using thick brushes of dried oak leaves. Fires from brick ovens would heat the room to a scalding 250 degrees. After taking the heat, patrons doused themselves with cold water, took a quick shower, and received a rubdown from a masseur.[1]

The finest bathhouse in the city was said to be in the Palmer House, where wainscoted bath cubicles and a small pool deep enough for swimming attracted the rich and powerful from across the country. A bath and scrubdown at the Palmer House followed by a wild night on the town was considered a luxury of the highest order. It was at the Palmer House that one of the city's most powerful—and most colorful—politicians of this century, First Ward Alderman John "Bathhouse John" Coughlin, got his start.

When a bathroom, even multiple bathrooms, became a standard element of private homes, public baths gradually faded into the past. Today only one park district bathhouse remains in operation, at 3225 South Racine Avenue, in Bridgeport. Actually it is little more than a community center with a few shower stalls—hardly worthy of the appellation. The tradition, however, is still very much alive, carried on by today's health centers and exercise facilities with their whirlpools and saunas, where, as in days of old, people go to relax, recoup, and recharge.

Notes

1. Harold Tannenbaum used to visit the Kedzie Bathhouse, a fixture of the Lawndale neighborhood, on a weekly basis. The elaborate bathhouse ritual or *shvitz* took place in a square room that contained three tiers. He offers the following description: "In one corner of the room was a brick oven, heated underneath by a gas burner. Granite stones were placed in the oven and made red hot. Then hot water was poured over the red hot stones, creating a steam. Your partner poured a bucket of cold water over your head to cool you off. Then a bucket of soapy water was placed on the floor next to you, and a broom-like utensil (twigs and oak leaves tied together in a bundle) was dipped into the soapy water and used to massage the whole body. After the *shvitz* we would wrap ourselves in sheets and go down to the dining room, where we would be served herrings, schnapps, black bread—and, if we wanted, a steak. In another room, the men would play cards until two or three o'clock in the morning. Then we would go up to the sleeping rooms, where we spent the rest of the night." See Beatrice Michaels Shapiro, *Memories of Lawndale* (Chicago: Chicago Jewish Historical Society, 1991), 49–50.

CHINATOWN

Exotic, enigmatic, inscrutable. That, to many Americans, is China. And to many Chicagoans, that, too, is the area in the city known as Chinatown.

Bounded roughly by Archer Avenue at its north end, Twenty-sixth Street on the south, the Dan Ryan Expressway on the east, and Canal Street on the west, Chinatown is deceptively small; it is only a few square blocks, but within it is the largest Chinese community in the Midwest.[1]

The city's first permanent Chinese resident, according to historian Ting C. Fan, was one T. C. Moy, who settled on the West Side in the late 1870s.[2] Feeling at ease in a city where immigrants formed a large portion of the population, Moy wrote to his friends in San Francisco and encouraged them to come here.

Soon there was a small Chinese community clustered around Clark and Van Buren Streets. By 1912, however, anti-Chinese sentiment and higher rents forced many of the Chinese residents to move farther south to Cermak and Wentworth Avenues.

As victims of widespread discrimination, the Chinese in Chicago and across the nation were forced to keep to themselves and engage only in those businesses allowed them by the dominant culture—namely, restaurants and laundry shops. Chicago's first chop suey house, King Joy Lo, was at Randolph and Dearborn Streets, according to historian Fan, and the first Chinese laundry, says historian Margaret Gibbons Wilson, was at the rear of 167 West Madison Street.

According to statistical records, close to 75 percent of all Chinese laborers in Chicago worked in a laundry setting in 1920. That setting, as described at the turn of the century by columnist George Ade, was typically three tiny and unbearably hot and uncomfortable rooms: one for washing, ironing, and cooking; one for drying the clothes; and one—"a small stuffy closet"—for sleeping.

During their early years here, the Chinese gained an unsavory reputation as criminals and wrongdoers, most of it unfounded and largely based on cultural prejudices. Of those who were arrested from 1915 to 1925, says Fan, the vast majority were charged with disorderly conduct, which meant anything from sitting in a vacant flat to walking the streets alone at night or sleeping in an alley.

Another problem, the result of exclusion laws that prohibited Chinese women from entering the United States legally, was the shockingly small number of women in American Chinese communities. Chicago's Chinatown in 1910 consisted largely of bachelors—some 1,179 males and only 65 females. Lacking female companionship, the men turned to cheap dance halls and nickel theaters for entertainment. Gambling, too, was a popular pastime. "If you didn't gamble, you didn't have a social life," says Dr. John Y. Ing, former president of the Chinese Consolidated Benevolent Association.

Under such conditions, the Chinese formed strong community organizations. Family societies met regularly in neighborhood assembly halls. There were exclusively Chinese churches, Chinese YMCAs, Chinese athletic clubs, and Chinese theaters. After their classes in public schools, Chinese youngsters also attended Chinese schools to study Chinese language, philosophy, and morals.

Of all these groups, none were more mysterious—and misunderstood—than the tongs. Essentially fraternal organizations whose origins go back thousands of years, the tongs in America helped the new immigrants adapt to their adopted land, but they also ran gambling dens, houses of prostitution, and other underworld activities. In Chicago the first known tongs were organized around 1905: On Leong, in Chinatown; and the Hip Sing, in what was left of the original South Loop community. Aside from a few police raids, though, Chicago's Chinese have been relatively free of the kind of tong wars that have plagued other cities.

Chinatown, looking north on Wentworth Avenue at Cermak Road, 1952 (photo by J. Sherwin Murphy. Chicago Historical Society). The extravagant On Leong building, Chinatown's "city hall," dominates the street.

More recently, a severe housing shortage in Chinatown has forced many of its residents to move elsewhere, mainly in the Uptown community along Argyle Street from Broadway to Sheridan Road to form a sort of Chinatown North or New Chinatown. Others have chosen to stay. For them, Chinatown—with its neat storefronts, family-run restaurants, and sense of community—will always be home.

The most enduring symbol of Chinatown remains the fanciful On Leong Merchants Association building at 2216 South Wentworth Avenue, a Midwestern version of a Chinese temple. Completed in 1928, the building has a rich history in its own right. For a dozen years or so, the building reportedly housed a gambling casino that brought in almost $2 million in profits. In February 1993 the Chinese Union Church of Chicago bought the building from the federal government for $1.4 million. Despite its controversial past, the City Council's Committee on Historical Landmarks recommended landmark status for the building long known as the "Chinese City Hall."

Notes

1. According to Harry Ying Cheng Kiang, Chinatown extends north to Eighteenth Street, east to Federal Street, west to Halsted Street, and south to Thirty-first Street. It covers an area of approximately six hundred acres and, as of 1990, has a population of 9,194, of which 6,376 are Chinese. See Kiang, *Chicago's Chinatown* (Lincolnwood, Ill.: Institute of Chinese Studies, 1992), 6.

2. Kiang claims that the first Chinese arrived in Chicago in 1870. See Kiang, *Chicago's Chinatown*, 4. According to Richard Lindberg, eight Chinese laundry workers lived in Chicago in 1870, but the Great Chicago Fire destroyed any record of their existence. See Lindberg, *Passport's Guide to Ethnic Chicago* (Lincolnwood, Ill.: Passport Books, 1993), 286.

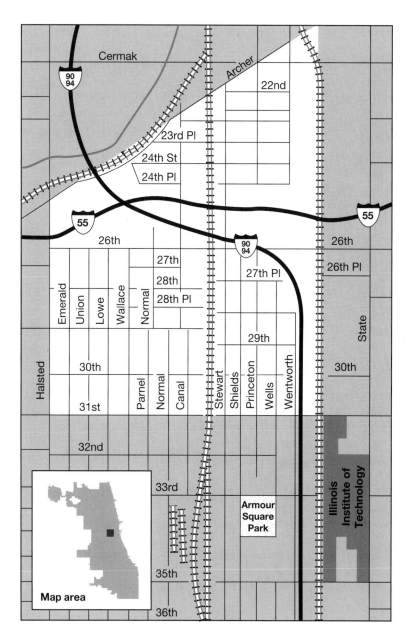

Map 8 Chinatown

 OPIUM DENS

Drug addiction is hardly a new problem in Chicago. In the 1880s the city experienced one of the worst epidemics of narcotic addiction in its history. The victims, however, were generally law-abiding citizens who, despite their drug use—or abuse—remained on good terms with the law. Their drug of choice was opium, which during those years was a perfectly legal substance.

Opium was billed then as a panacea for all of humankind's aches and pains. Available without prescription from drugstores, department stores, tobacco shops, bookstores, and mail-order firms, opiates were, along with alcohol, the only commonly known painkillers, and some of the most respected physicians believed that opium could cure asthma, cancer, cholera, diabetes, gonorrhea, emphysema, heart disease, hysteria, and even insanity.

Among the opium addicts were those who originally turned to it to ease their sufferings, among them an elderly couple who needed it to kill pain from rheumatism. Many others, however, used it for pleasure. "Young men use opium on the tips of their cigars to flavor the tobacco," said an article in the *Chicago Daily News*. "Young women cannot go to a ball without taking a dose of morphine (an opium extract) to nerve them and make them bright and agreeable. Young men chew opium with their tobacco. Young women take morphine in their coffee and tea."

Morphine was especially popular in underworld circles and among prostitutes. Already high on morphine mixed with beer or champagne, the addicts among them would gather in neighborhood drugstores and openly inject the substance into their arms for the entertainment of those present. But the narcotic also found its way into "legitimate" society. "Boys, especially messengers and newsboys, are apt to experiment with it, and many young men acquire the habit," wrote one reporter in 1907.

Opium was also smoked, usually in two-foot-long bamboo pipes in dimly lit opium dens, or "hop joints." Perhaps, because it was an alien practice brought to the United States by Chinese immigrants, this particular use of opium was looked upon as a hateful vice and denounced as "vile" by civic leaders. Consequently, the largest concentration of opium dens were in the city's Chinatown. "Every basement on Clark Street between Van Buren and Harrison," wrote Charles Washburn in his book, *Come Into My Parlor,* "was a hop joint." The back rooms of Chinese laundries, lit only by flickering kerosene lamps, also served as opium dens, each of them frequented on a daily basis by an estimated fifteen to twenty Chicagoans, including many prominent citizens.

Chinatown was then in the First Ward, which also encompassed the red light district. Although its alderman, John "Bathhouse" Coughlin, tolerated—and profited from—almost every other vice known to man, he said he "couldn't stomach" opium smokers, or "pipe hitters," and threatened to raid the dens himself if necessary.

During one raid on Clark Street, scores of Chinese were taken into custody, but not one of them would or could identify the den's owner. At the suggestion of a reporter, police officers then made use of a common belief that a Chinese person could be made to tell the truth if he was first forced to dip his fingers in the blood of a freshly killed chicken.

So an officer was dispatched to the South Water Street market to procure a live chicken, and Sam Moy, at that time the "mayor" of Chinatown, agreed to perform the ritual in front of a judge. While the suspected keeper of the den, a Chinese man, stood at the witness stand, Moy, assisted by a policeman, beheaded the hapless chicken. The suspect's fingers were dipped in its blood, and with Moy as interpreter he was asked, "Are you the keeper of the resort?"

Thereupon the suspect let loose with a flurry of words in his native tongue that went on and on. Finally he came to an abrupt stop, and the judge asked Moy, "What did he say?"

"He said no," came Moy's deadpan reply, sending the courtroom into a fit of loud laughter.

Under the pressure of constant raids and harassment by the police, the keepers found it increasingly difficult to continue operating their opium dens. In 1894 the city passed an anti-opium ordinance, and by late 1895 the last of the dens had shut down.

Soon thereafter a series of national and international laws prohibiting the use of opium for smoking and restricting over-the-counter sales of opiates gradually ended opium addiction, but not until after it had exacted a heavy personal and social toll from a generation of Chicagoans.

IN THE BLINK OF A CAMERA'S EYE

At the turn of the century a familiar sight on Chicago's streets was the roving photographer, in those days most certainly a man, who lugged around his heavy view camera, bulky tripod, and a box full of other equipment to capture on his film plates the people, the scenes, and the major events of his city.

Photography was then still in its infancy, but already the commercial market for these urban graphics was well established.

Enterprising photographers found the city an ideal area for scenic views or distinctive buildings. Some specialized in parades, fairs, and public celebrations, turning out prints soon after the events occurred. Others photographed tourists who wanted mementos of their visits to the city. Still others would snap informal portraits of unsuspecting passersby, hand their subjects an envelope for print orders, and ask them where they wanted the pictures sent—a common practice that declined after World War II but until recently was still carried out occasionally by their modern counterparts with more advanced equipment.

Disasters were especially popular events to photograph. A series of "stereographs," pictures composed of two superimposed images that took on a three-dimensional effect when observed through a viewing machine or "stereoscope," were made of the Great Chicago Fire, for example, with one side offering a "before" photo and the reverse side an "after" shot.

From the 1860s until the early 1930s these double-sided stereographs were all the rage, with perhaps as many as six thousand stereophotographers operating in the United States and another fifteen hundred in Europe. Chicago-based John Carbutt sold them locally to neighborhood bookshops, news agencies, and department stores. Millions of these double images were produced for the thousands of consumers who eagerly collected them at twenty-five to thirty-five cents each.

As the city's industrial base expanded and public tastes grew more sophisticated, commercial photographers found new economic avenues to pursue. Photographs were made into picture postcards and sold in bookstores, at newsstands, and by door-to-door peddlers.

One of the city's most innovative commercial photographers was George R. Lawrence, who in 1896 opened his first studio on Sixty-third Street. Lawrence, often called "the father of flashlight photography" because he invented a new flash lighting system designed for large indoor shots, was a pioneer in early aerial and panoramic photography, according to *Chicago History*. He used extension ladders to shoot pictures of Washington Park, for example, and a hot air balloon to take panoramic views of the Chicago metropolitan area from as high as two thousand feet.

Balloon photography, however, had its hazards. During Lawrence's first flight, over the Union Stockyards in 1901, the gas bag burst. Fortunately for the photo pioneer, the balloon struck some wires as it plummeted 230 feet to the ground, saving him from a sure death.

Undaunted, Lawrence created a "captive airship"—a contraption with a camera mounted in it that he sent aloft suspended from a kite to take pictures as "the eagle and the wild goose see." Using this "kite camera," he took the first airborne pictures of Fort Sheridan, Chicago Heights, and Waukegan. Another one of his creations was the world's largest camera. Weighing fourteen hundred pounds, it used eight- by four-foot film plates and needed fifteen able-bodied men to operate it.

But it was left to the mostly unknown neighborhood photographers to record the face of the city seldom seen by outsiders—not the public face of fashionable residences and architectural splendor but the inner city of workers on their lunch hours and solemnly dressed families skating together in the parks.

One of these unknown photographers was Henry R. Koopman II, who recorded the events—confirmations, graduations, weddings, funerals—and the nuances of daily life in the Roseland community on Chicago's South Side, and whose name has come down to us because he donated his photographs, diary, and other papers to the Calumet Historical Society.

Difficult working conditions made the photographer's life unpredictable at best. Outdoors, sudden weather changes often ruined precious chemicals; indoors, in studios lacking modern lighting systems, portraits could be taken only during the day. But those pioneers persevered, and their legacy remains—images of a bygone era captured forever in the blink of a camera's eye.

BLACK HEARSES AND WHITE HORSES:
THE ROLE OF THE UNDERTAKER

The popular stereotype is of a dark, sinister figure—sullen, stoop-shouldered, and ashen-faced, always dressed in black. Wherever he goes, gloom and despair follow. Yet for some Chicago ethnic groups, the undertaker was the last vital link between the bereaved and the beloved, between the Old World left behind and the new spread out before them.

The funeral business has usually been a family affair handed down through the generations—from father to son to grandson. In early days, starting a firm required little more than a storefront. Many undertakers began as operators of liveries where horses and carriages could be rented.

A neighborhood fixture, each funeral firm had its own clientele, oftentimes serving specific ethnic enclaves. Burial grounds, too, were segregated by nationality: the Irish in Mount Olivet and the Lithuanians in Saint Casimir on the Southwest Side; the Germans in Saint Mary's in Evergreen Park; and the Poles, Slovaks, and Bohemians in Resurrection in Justice.

Rites of passage—baptisms, confirmations, first communions, weddings—were momentous occasions among the city's ethnic groups. But for some, the funeral was the most elaborate ritual because it not only honored a departed member of the insular community but also reflected his or her status within that community. The cost of the funeral may have been an indication of affluence, but the number of people in attendance revealed the person's standing.

The undertaker's main duty was to prepare the body for burial, a chore usually done in the home. Among the Lithuanians of the Back of the Yards neighborhood on the South Side, certain traditions were honored. Inside, the woman of the house covered all the mirrors, stopped the clock, and turned off the radio. Songs and prayers from a special prayer book, a *kontichka,* were read. Candlesticks, rented from the undertaker, glowed in the living room. On the front door hung ribbons and flowers.

The funeral ceremony lasted two days, the wake virtually going on around the clock. Gender roles were clearly defined. The men talked and played cards. The women attended to the needs of the family—preparing the food, cleaning the house, watching the children. "Most of all, they cried, thus providing the proper atmosphere," writes Back of the Yards historian Robert A. Slayton.

At the formal service, there were seven pallbearers—three on either side of the coffin and one in front. Each wore a badge indicating his lodge or affiliation, since the social clubs paid their members a standard fee to participate in such events.

The most lavish demonstration of private grief was reserved for the funeral procession. Gaily decorated horses, with colorful plumes for the corners of the wagon carrying the body, passed by the modest homes. Most coffins were made of pine and lined with white silk. (One Back of the Yards undertaker, after buying his first *oak* casket, proudly displayed it in the window of his funeral parlor.) A one-carriage funeral cost $16.60, while a sixteen-carriage extravaganza could reach as high as $300.00.

The mode of transportation to the burial site was deeply symbolic. Thus, the colors of the hearse, carriage, and horse had to match: white for youth, gray for middle age, and black for elderly. As a result, undertakers kept a stable of at least six horses available at all times. A band of usually three instruments—drum, trumpet, and tuba—led the procession to the final resting place.

The trip to the cemetery could be an all-day affair. Back of the Yards residents had to travel to the Far Southwest Side, a three-hour journey in the best of weather. Opposite the gravesite was a tavern where the family gathered for a meal and drinks, all arranged by the undertaker. The long journey home was usually made in darkness.

Today, wakes are no longer held in homes, and prices have skyrocketed into the thousands of dollars, but such familiar names as Blake-Lamb, A. V. Furman, John M. Pedersen & Sons, John V. May, and many others still serve their community and continue a family tradition.

AN ISLAND CALLED "LITTLE HELL"

It is a forbidding place, even on a bright day. Grimy smokestacks, cluttered railroad yards, and mud-encrusted trucks crisscross its roughhewn face, where illicit whiskey stills and taverns once stood. It is called Goose Island, a largely forgotten, ugly, and forlorn patch of land on the fringes of downtown that nonetheless has played a big role in the city's growth as an industrial center.

Set in the north branch of the Chicago River, the oval-shaped island starts roughly at Chicago Avenue at Halsted Street and stretches northwest with the river to just below North Avenue at Magnolia Avenue. It is connected to the mainland by east and west bridges on Division Street, which cuts across its middle; two bridges on Halsted Street, which runs north and south across its southeastern tip; and the Cherry Avenue railroad bridge that leads from it into North Avenue.

Since the 1850s the 160-acre natural island, which William B. Ogden, Chicago's first mayor, acquired for the city in 1853 for six hundred dollars, has been an industrial area. Tanneries, soap factories, and lumberyards flourished. In the 1860s, when flames from the large coal plant that the Peoples Gas, Light, and Coke Company operated there cast an unearthly glow on the night sky, the island—and, indeed, the surrounding neighborhood—was nicknamed "Little Hell."

Among its first inhabitants were Irish immigrants who had been evicted from their Kilgubbin,[1] County Cork, farms at the height of the 1840s potato famine. Living in crude shacks, they kept cows and raised chickens, keeping to themselves and rarely venturing onto the mainland except to attend early Mass on Sundays. They also raised geese, which roamed the river channels by the hundreds and gave the island its name. After the Great Chicago Fire of 1871, the island became a temporary haven for thousands of refugees.

In the 1870s, after the Chicago and Pacific Railroad built a terminal at its south end, new businesses moved to the island. Among them were the tanneries, their rawhides coming by rail or water from the burgeoning South Side stockyards.

The plants provided plentiful but demanding jobs. The island's workers toiled from 6 A.M. to 6 P.M. six days a week hauling hides, lumber, and coal or working inside the factories. With the hard work came hard drinking. On Saturday nights, weary workers would sit on the stoops of their cottages drinking beer from buckets—"shooting the pail," as it was called—at a nickel a throw. Often enough, punches were thrown and brawls would erupt.

The new plants, however, kept pushing the islanders, already isolated from the mainland, farther north, and when several violent mob incidents broke out on the island during a period of labor unrest in the 1870s, it earned a reputation as a breeding ground of thieves and thugs.

Different ethnic groups moved into Little Hell and the surrounding areas over the years. The neighborhood even contained middle-class enclaves. As early as the 1870s, for example, the area was a port of entry for Swedish immigrants and earned the nickname of Swede Town. The Swedes established churches and businesses and became homeowners.[2]

As the Swedes moved north they were replaced by Irish and later Italian settlers so that by the turn of the century a population that was mostly Sicilian dominated the area. This was the age of the Black Hand, Sicilian thugs who terrorized neighborhood residents. The violence became so extreme that the corner of Oak and Cambridge Streets became known as Death Corner.[3]

At the turn of the century the island became a battleground for the so-called grain wars waged by speculators seeking to corner the grain market. In the 1890s Chicago entrepreneur Philip D. Armour, seeking quickly to store and move vast quantities of western wheat destined for eastern markets, had grain elevators built on the island in record time. On several occasions hundreds of carpenters worked around the clock for days at a time, completing elevators just as the wheat came pouring onto the island, and thereby contributing not a little to the success of Armour's ventures.

When, after Armour's death in 1901 his company was taken over by eastern bankers, Chicago ceased to be a grain-trading center, and the grain elevators on the island were torn down (the last one was destroyed in a fire in 1930). Then as the stockyards disappeared from the South Side, the tanneries closed down or moved away along with other industries and many island residents. By 1937 newspaper reports claimed only about thirty families, and by 1974 no more than six persons, still lived on the island.

Almost no one lives there anymore, but about thirty businesses still remain, and some developers have proposed that Goose Island be turned into a modern multimillion-dollar industrial park. In 1988 the city established Goose Island as one of three Planned Manufacturing Districts. (In 1934 politician George Gillmeister proposed that it be used as an airport.) Other developers want to convert its industrial buildings into residential lofts for artists and upscale professionals. Already the city is home to Goose Island Brewery; its symbol? A goose, of course.

If developers have their way, Goose Island could well become a gentrified area with gleaming new plants, sleek loft apartments, and well-groomed yuppies strolling in and out of fancy bars—a far cry, indeed, from its old days as "Little Hell."

Notes

1. Originally, Kilgubbin was located along Market Street (Orleans) between Kinzie and Erie. See Dominic A. Pacyga and Ellen Skerrett, *Chicago: City of Neighborhoods* (Chicago: Loyola University Press, 1986), 38.

2. Later the Swedes moved farther north to the Belmont and Sheffield area and, eventually, to Clark and Foster—the present-day Andersonville. For a history of the Swedes in Chicago, see Philip J. Anderson and Dag Blanck, eds., *Swedish-American Life in Chicago: Cultural and Urban Aspects of an Immigrant People, 1850–1930* (Urbana, Ill.: University of Illinois Press, 1992).

3. Other historians say the intersection of Oak and Milton (now Cleveland) was Death Corner. See Pacyga and Skerrett, *Chicago: City of Neighborhoods*, 49.

DAYS AND NIGHTS IN "BRONZEVILLE"

New York may have had its Harlem Renaissance, but in Chicago the center of African-American literary and cultural achievement was an area in the heart of the Black Belt called "Bronzeville."[1] At its peak Bronzeville had a population of three hundred thousand. Over the years, many prominent African Americans have lived there, including Richard Wright, Arna Bontemps, Katherine Dunham, Horace Cayton, and St. Clair Drake. Later, one of Bronzeville's most famous residents, poet Gwendolyn Brooks, would write down her reflections of the neighborhood in *A Place Called Bronzeville*.

Bronzeville was surprisingly small—only three and one-half square miles. Sociologists Horace Cayton and St. Clair Drake described it as "a narrow tongue of land, seven miles in length and one and one-half miles in width, where more than 300,000 Negroes are packed solidly . . ." It was bounded by State Street on the west, Cottage Grove on the east, Twenty-eighth Street on the north, and Sixty-third Street on the south.

Bronzeville was a vibrant community where black intellectuals worked and lived during the 1930s and 1940s. They would meet at places such as the Parkway Community Center at Fifty-second Street and South Parkway (now Martin Luther King, Jr. Drive) or the Abraham Lincoln Center at Oakwood and South Parkway (now Northeastern Illinois University Center for Inner City Studies).[2]

Forty-seventh Street and South Parkway functioned as the black downtown, harboring a diverse community of African Americans from all occupational and economic backgrounds: politicians, doctors, dentists, lawyers, teachers, civic leaders, writers, and musicians as well as the common working man and woman. There were also various newspapers (in addition to the *Defender*, other papers included the *Chicago Bee*, the *Chicago World, News-Ledger,* and *Metropolitan Post*) as well as restaurants and department stores, settlement houses and social organizations.

Bronzeville did not consist only of cultural institutions, however. The neighborhood also contained numerous underworld hangouts and dance halls frequented by the so-called lower classes as well as bridge clubs and scores of social clubs. Many of these clubs sponsored dances, dinners, teas, and other events. The popularity of the social groups is evident in the numbers: In the late 1930s some eight hundred social clubs existed with a combined total of ten thousand to eleven thousand members, according to Cayton and Drake.

In 1930 a newspaper editor at the *Chicago Bee* sponsored a contest to elect the so-called Mayor of Bronzeville. The Mayor acted as a sort of quasi ambassador to Bronzeville. This annual "election" soon blossomed into a major community event and became a great cause for neighborhood pride. The residents were encouraged to participate and they did so wholeheartedly, casting their "ballots" from corner stores, barbershops, and poolrooms. The inauguration of the Mayor usually culminated in a ceremony and a ball.

East Forty-seventh Street was the Magnificent Mile of Chicago's black community in the late 1920s, and the undisputed queen just off that jazzy boulevard was the Spanish-baroque Regal Theater at 4719 South Parkway. From its grand opening in 1928 through its golden days of the 1930s and into the 1940s and 1950s, no other theater in the area came close to matching its glamour.

Virtually every great black entertainer played the Regal: Duke Ellington, Count Basie, Ella Fitzgerald, Sarah Vaughan, Billie Holliday, the Mills Brothers, Billy Eckstine, Ethel Waters, Lena Horne. And many youngsters went wide eyed in wonder as they walked past the elegant marble staircase in the lobby, settled into the plush red seats, and gazed at the stars that twinkled off and on in the ceiling.

The Regal wasn't the only attraction in the neighborhood. In the same complex was the Savoy Ballroom,[3] where big bands played and neighborhood youths attended boxing and wrestling

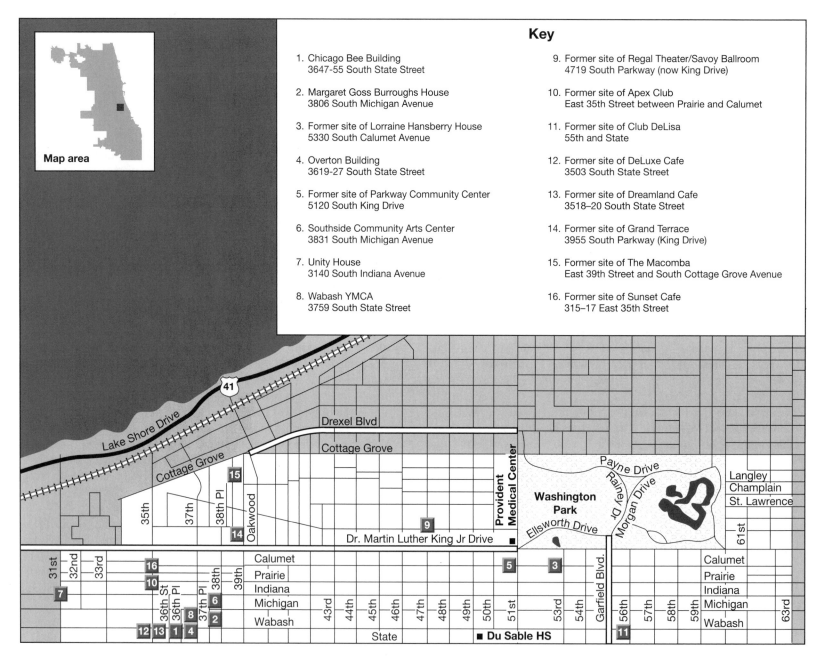

Key

1. Chicago Bee Building
   3647-55 South State Street

2. Margaret Goss Burroughs House
   3806 South Michigan Avenue

3. Former site of Lorraine Hansberry House
   5330 South Calumet Avenue

4. Overton Building
   3619-27 South State Street

5. Former site of Parkway Community Center
   5120 South King Drive

6. Southside Community Arts Center
   3831 South Michigan Avenue

7. Unity House
   3140 South Indiana Avenue

8. Wabash YMCA
   3759 South State Street

9. Former site of Regal Theater/Savoy Ballroom
   4719 South Parkway (now King Drive)

10. Former site of Apex Club
    East 35th Street between Prairie and Calumet

11. Former site of Club DeLisa
    55th and State

12. Former site of DeLuxe Cafe
    3503 South State Street

13. Former site of Dreamland Cafe
    3518–20 South State Street

14. Former site of Grand Terrace
    3955 South Parkway (King Drive)

15. Former site of The Macomba
    East 39th Street and South Cottage Grove Avenue

16. Former site of Sunset Cafe
    315–17 East 35th Street

Map 9 Bronzeville

matches and basketball games. On the corner stood the Metropolitan Theatre, a movie house where Saturday matinees could be enjoyed for a dime. And there were all kinds of variety stores, restaurants, and taverns.

On Saturday afternoons a carnival atmosphere pervaded the area, with sword swallowers, blues singers, and guitar players vying for pennies. Ministers preached as cool jazz wafted from speakers outside the shops and police detectives in their black fedoras sauntered through the crowd.

Between 1917 and 1921 many musicians came north from New Orleans and made Chicago the jazz capital of the world. All along South State Street from Thirty-first to Thirty-fifth Streets and on nearby boulevards clubs such as the Elite Cafe, the Sunset Cafe, the Pekin Inn, Dreamland, the Royal Garden, the Grand Terrace, and the Plantation—to name just a few—produced a wonderland of music. Joe "King" Oliver, Johnny and Baby Dodds, Jelly Roll Morton, Cab Calloway, Earl Hines, and the greatest of them all, Louis Armstrong, all at one time played in Bronzeville or on its northern fringes.[4]

The renaissance ended in the late 1940s, when many middle-class residents left. Changing social conditions in the form of poverty, urban renewal, and rising crime rates undermined the stability and the fragile infrastructure of the African-American community.

In 1973 the Regal, the once-elegant showpiece, was demolished, and the site was turned into a parking lot. In August 1986 the Avalon, another movie palace from the 1920s, located farther south at Seventy-ninth Street and Stony Island Avenue, reopened as the New Regal Theater. Today, the area once known as Bronzeville is one of the poorest, most economically deprived, and crime-ridden neighborhoods in the city.

But not all the news is bad. Among the bleak public housing highrises and vacant lots, hope has resurfaced at last. In June 1994 the Mid-South Planning and Development Commission with the aid of city government announced a long-term plan to revitalize the battered community. Tentative plans include the creation of a Muddy Waters Blues District and an African-style marketplace. Further, some of the area's historic buildings, including the Overton Hygienic/Douglass National Bank Building, the *Chicago Bee*

Jesse Binga (courtesy Urban Research Institute). Binga (1865–1950) was Chicago's leading African-American entrepreneur during the 1920s. He built the Arcade building in 1929.

Building, the Wabash Avenue YMCA, the Eighth Regiment Armory, Victory Sculpture, the *Chicago Defender* Building, Supreme Life Insurance Building, and Unity Hall, are to receive major facelifts.

Arcade and Old Binga
building, Thirty-fifth
and State Streets, 1951
(photo by Tedward A.
Dumetz, Jr. Chicago
Historical Society).

Finally, the planners have recommended the construction of a major four-hundred-room hotel and entertainment center and a forty-thousand-seat assembly hall to attract visitors to the area.

Notes

1. The Harlem Renaissance refers to the vibrant period of cultural activity in the 1920s among African Americans in Harlem, a black enclave of New York City, where writers, artists, and musicians lived and worked. The movement's most prominent members included poets Countee Cullen, Claude McKay, Langston Hughes, and Jean Toomer. For a full-scale treatment of the renaissance, see Nathan Irvin Huggins, *Harlem Renaissance* (New York: Oxford University Press, 1971). See also *Classic Fiction of the Harlem Renaissance,* edited by William L. Andrews (New York: Oxford University Press, 1994).

2. Originally the Abraham Lincoln Center was a social center founded by Jenkin Lloyd Jones, uncle of the famous architect Frank Lloyd Wright. Lloyd Jones was pastor of the nearby All Souls Unitarian Church (now demolished).

3. The Regal Theater opened on February 4, 1928, in the Savoy Ballroom complex. The Savoy, however, had opened three months earlier on Thanksgiving night 1927. See William Howland Kenney, *Chicago Jazz: A Cultural History,* 1904–1930 (New York: Oxford University Press, 1993), 162.

4. The focal point of South Side entertainment changed over the years. During the World War I era, African-American nightlife centered on South State Street, just north of Bronzeville, in the old Levee or red-light district in an area nicknamed "The Stroll." During the 1920s the activity moved further south near Thirty-fifth and State. By the end of the decade, Forty-seventh and State—the heart of Bronzeville—became the new center. See Kenney, *Chicago Jazz,* 14–15.

Museums

- *DuSable Museum of African American History.* 740 East Fifty-sixth Place, Chicago 60637; 312-947-0600. Hours: Monday–Friday, 9 A.M.–5 P.M.; Saturday, noon–5 P.M. Closed New Year's Day, Easter, and Christmas. Admission: Adults, $1; children and students, $.50. Thursday, free. Oldest African-American museum in the United States. Permanent exhibits include "Blacks in Early Illinois" as well as collections of African sculpture, masks, drums, and dolls. Exhibits, lectures, classes, films, publications, and special events. Also contains a library with extensive files on African-American history and culture.

- *Carter G. Woodson Regional Library.* 9525 South Halsted Street, Chicago 60628. Hours: Monday–Thursday, 9 A.M.–9 P.M.; Friday and Saturday, 9 A.M.–5 P.M. Houses the Vivian G. Harsh Collection, which contains more than seventy thousand books and original manuscripts on the African-American experience and is reportedly the largest black studies collection in the Midwest.

Select historical sites

- *Chicago Bee Building.* 3647–55 South State Street, Chicago 60609. Constructed from 1929 to 1933 by Anthony Overton, an African-American entrepreneur who founded the *Chicago Bee* newspaper.

- *Margaret Goss Burroughs House.* 3806 South Michigan Avenue, Chicago 60653. Original home of the DuSable Museum.

- *Former site of Lorraine Hansberry House.* 5330 South Calumet Avenue, Chicago 60615. The African-American playwright, author of *To Be Young, Gifted, and Black* and other plays, once lived here. It is now a vacant lot.

- *Overton Building.* 3619–27 South State Street, Chicago 60609. Another building affiliated with African-American entrepreneur Anthony Overton.

- *Former site of Parkway Community Center.* 5120 South King Drive, Chicago 60615. Home at various times of Richard Wright, poet Langston Hughes, and sociologist Horace R. Cayton. Cayton was the director of the center from 1940 to the 1950s. Hughes lived there in 1941–42, when he was director of the Skyloft Players, a local theater group. Wright lived there in 1941, when he was writing *12 Million Black Voices,* a pictorial history of African Americans in America.

- *Southside Community Arts Center.* 3831 South Michigan Avenue, Chicago 60653; 312-373-1026. Hours: Monday and Tuesday, closed; Wednesday–Friday, noon–5 P.M.; Saturday, 9 A.M.–5 P.M.; Sunday, 1 P.M.–5 P.M. Important culture center during the heyday of Bronzeville.

- *Unity House.* 3140 South Indiana Avenue, Chicago 60616. Former headquarters of Oscar DePriest's Peoples Movement Club, the first major African-American political organization in Chicago.

- *Wabash YMCA.* 3759 South State Street, Chicago 60609. Many African Americans turned to the Wabash YMCA, a Bronzeville institution, for sustenance and shelter.

(See the appendix for other African-American historical sites in Chicago.)

IN EVERY DREAM A BUNGALOW

For many, many Chicagoans of the 1920s, the bungalow was what made it possible to realize the American Dream of home ownership. From the Far South Side to the fringes of Jefferson Park, clusters of these brick single-family homes proliferated during the building boom of that decade, enabling countless citizens to enjoy the comforts of good urban living.

Surprisingly enough, the bungalow, which has come to symbolize the typical Chicago home, is not indigenous to the city. The original was a one-story cottage of India—"bungalow" comes from the Hindi *bangla,* meaning "of Bengal"—consisting of a family room surrounded by small sleeping quarters. When the British went to India, they were reportedly so taken by the cottage's design that they took it with them to many other parts of their colonial empire.

Admired for its simplicity, the efficient use of space, and low construction cost, the bungalow eventually found its way to the United States, becoming popular first in southern California and from there quickly spreading to the Midwest.

The typical "Chicago bungalow"—a hip-roofed brick house with a living room, a dining room, two bedrooms, a bath and a kitchen on the main floor, a full basement, and an attic, and compact enough to fit on a twenty-five-foot-wide city lot—was, more directly, an offshoot of the Chicago cottage, a one- or one-and-one-half-story frame structure developed in the 1840s. The Chicago bungalow's basic design was strongly influenced by both the Prairie School of architecture, from which it derived its low roof and overhanging eaves, and the English-based Arts and Crafts Movement, which gave it its characteristically simple lines.[1]

The popularity of the Chicago bungalow reached its peak in the 1920s, when some 100,000 of them were built throughout Cook County, most of them within Chicago proper, creating so-called bungalow belts in many neighborhoods, notably on the Southwest and Northwest Sides. Bungalows were heavily advertised in newspapers, real estate agents couldn't sell enough of them, and they even came in kit form, supplied by Sears, Roebuck and Company and other firms. Getting into the act, Tin Pan Alley turned out sentimental songs about the bungalow, and magazines such as *Good Housekeeping* published humorous verses about it.

Building a bungalow was a fairly easy task. One way was for prospective homeowners to build the structure themselves, following blueprints and specifications that could be ordered for about ten dollars.

Several factors fueled the bungalow building boom. The years after World War I saw a widespread desire for domestic stability, and satisfying this desire was made possible by the availability of funds from private wartime savings and loan associations. The average price of a typical bungalow in 1926 was, to many, an affordable fifty-five hundred dollars, and land was plentiful and cheap.

Expanding transportation services also helped the building boom by inducing many to move from congested neighborhoods to more distant but less crowded areas. Linking the new desire for home ownership, newspaper advertisements often noted the inclusion of garages with the houses being featured.

Through the years the bungalow underwent modifications as homeowners sought to personalize its basic design. The living room was sometimes made larger than the dining room, or both were combined to form one large living/dining area. Basements were converted into recreation rooms, attic space into extra bedrooms, and gables of varying designs raised in part the low-pitched roofs.

Today rows and rows of these bungalows still stand in many neighborhoods throughout the city, giving it one of its characteristic

Chicago bungalows (photo by June Skinner Sawyers). Throughout the city scores of modest brick or stucco bungalows were erected during the great building boom of the 1920s. This block on the Northwest Side is representative of many Chicago streets.

looks and continuing to provide countless Chicagoans with a solid, comfortable, and affordable means of realizing and enjoying their little piece of the Great American Dream.

Notes

1. Although bungalows are scattered throughout the city, one of the largest concentrations is the Villa District, a historic neighborhood on the Northwest Side bounded by Addison Street, Hamlin Avenue, Avondale Avenue, and Pulaski Road. Both the "Chicago" and "California" bungalows are represented here.

THE COMING OF THE AUTOMOBILE
AND THE "SUNDAY DRIVER"

Ever since Henry Ford popularized the new horseless carriage with the introduction of the Model T in 1908, Chicagoans, along with the rest of the nation, have been in love with the automobile.

Automobiles came into their own during the "Roaring Twenties," when lower prices and generous credit terms enticed many to buy their first cars. According to Harold M. Mayer and Richard C. Wade, authors of *Chicago: Growth of a Metropolis,* there were as few as 12,000 autos in Chicago in 1910, but less than two decades later this figure had soared to a massive 341,000. By 1963, there was one car for every three residents in the metropolitan area, say Mayer and Wade. All these vehicles transporting people around the city and from city to suburb and beyond led to the construction of an expansive—and expensive—network of multilane roads and expressways.

The easy mobility made possible by the automobile changed the pattern of the average Chicagoan's life—even introducing a new phrase, "Sunday driver." Entire families could now spend Sundays visiting relatives or enjoying leisurely sightseeing drives in the country. The pleasures of the rides, however, had a dark side in the form of early and equally exasperating versions of today's traffic jams and urban gridlock.

As owning an automobile—or two or more—quickly became an essential part of the typical Chicagoan's increasingly mobile lifestyle, the consequences of motoring were not always positive or pleasurable. To serve the rising numbers of motorists, for example, an automobile-related industry of tourist homes, roadside diners, and motels grew in and around the city to the delight of its operators. The new industry, however, cut deeply into the profits of the railroad industry—a heartfelt irony in a city once known as the railroad capital of the country. By 1933 car owners had, among other problems, to contend with auto thefts, which, according to contemporary newspaper accounts, had grown to a $10 million Chicago "industry."

Some leading citizens said the automobile weakened family life, reduced church attendance, encouraged crime, loosened morals, and caused senseless deaths on the nation's highways. Young drivers were especially subject to criticism. "The automobile moron is Chicago's deadliest criminal," said Morgan A. Collins, the city's chief of police, in 1926. Evangelist Billy Sunday blamed the "looseness" of youth on the easy availability of the automobile. "We've put the red-light district on wheels," he warned. A visitor to Chicago, spiritualist Jiddu Krishnamurti, commenting on what he considered the insatiable materialism of young men and women, lamented, "Girls and boys are . . . merely contented with jazz . . . clothes . . . money . . . and an automobile."

World War II changed Chicagoans' driving habits. Civilian auto production was halted in 1942 as Detroit became a center of war-production efforts. Gas rationing was introduced, first on the East Coast in May 1942, and then the rest of the nation by December of that year. Two or three gallons a week were allowed per family, gas ration stamps were issued, and a national speed limit of 35 miles per hour became mandatory. In 1943 Washington banned pleasure driving altogether; only essential trips such as driving to church or picking up groceries were allowed. Bus schedules were cut, and pleas were made for the public to "Please Stay Home."

Not everyone abided by the wartime rules, and many Chicagoans were among the transgressors. Government officials responded by encouraging the city's residents to carpool more and emulate their fellow citizens in Richmond, Virginia, who had taken to placing signs in car windows that indicated their destinations and thus made carpooling more efficient. Philip Harrington of the Office of Defense

Traffic jam on Dearborn Street near Randolph, 1909 (Chicago Historical Society, ICHi–04191).

Transportation went so far as to scold Chicagoans specifically for "wasting" the extra seats in their automobiles.

Having survived wartime gasoline rationing and the harsh constraints of the OPEC-induced oil crisis of the mid-1970s, Chicagoans still live in a world dominated by the automobile. On any given day they will be found streaming into drive-through fast food stands and bank stations; crowding by the thousands into vast parking lots of suburban shopping malls; heading out, bumper to bumper, to destinations near and far on ever-expanding but usually congested expressways—all clear signs that the American love affair with the automobile is as passionate and enduring as ever.

LAW AND DISORDER

The Everleigh Club, 2131–33 South Dearborn Street, shortly before demolition in 1933 (Chicago Historical Society, ICHi–00367). The Everleigh Club, located in the heart of the red-light district, opened its doors on February 1, 1900. Chicago's most famous brothel, it contained fifty rooms, fourteen of which were reportedly sound-proof. Mayor Carter Harrison II ordered the club shut down in October 1911.

Engraving, "Wright's Grove," Clark Street between Wrightwood and Diversey circa 1868 (Chicago Historical Society, ICHi–16083). Spacious picnic grounds in a German settlement on the North Side in what is now congested Lincoln Park.

THE GERMAN BEER RIOTS OF 1855
(OR "REAL" AMERICANS DRINK WHISKEY)

In campaigning for mayor in 1855, Dr. Levi D. Boone pledged to fire all aliens from city jobs and to enforce an obscure, virtually forgotten Sunday-closing law for saloons and beer gardens. He was, after all, the candidate of the Know-Nothing, or Native American—that is, native born—Party, which looked upon the growing number of immigrants and Catholics as a threat to its vision of a "pure" Anglo-Saxon and Protestant America. And candidate Boone, an ultraconservative physician and a relative of the famous Daniel, was a confirmed teetotaler who particularly disliked beer, regarding it as un-American. "Real" Americans, then, if they did indulge, drank whiskey, not the beer that the "foreigners" liked to guzzle.

Although roughly half of Chicago was foreign-born and of those immigrants half were of German stock with a professed fondness for beer, Boone won the election. Once in office, the new mayor quickly carried out his pledge to enforce the Sunday-closing law. Furthermore, he raised the liquor-licensing fee fifty dollars (or thirty dollars, according to one source) to three hundred dollars a year, recommending further that no new licenses be issued for three months. All this, however, applied only to saloons and taverns that sold beer, not to those that served whiskey.

The result was an uproar on the North Side (which was so heavily German that it earned the nickname of the *Nord Seite*). Though many saloonkeepers complied grudgingly, many others openly defied the Sunday-closing law, denouncing it as the most tyrannical measure since the Stamp Act, and stopped paying the new license fee. An association of saloonkeepers was formed to aid members prosecuted for violations of the law. Soon more than two hundred tavern owners were arrested, and of these, some were scheduled to appear before Judge Henry Rucker on April 21, 1855.

Early that morning about one hundred German workers came pouring out of several North Side saloons and, accompanied by a fife-and-drum band, marched down Milwaukee Avenue toward the courthouse downtown to protest the arrests. There they were met by some fifty special agents and more than 250 men hurriedly deputized by Mayor Boone to assist the policemen. As the angry crowd became unruly, the lawmen began using their heavy nightsticks and, after arresting many of the protesters, finally managed to disperse the crowd.

That afternoon a larger crowd of protesters gathered in Ogden Park on the North Side. Now some four thousand strong and including a group of like-minded Irishmen and some Swedes, the demonstrators ignored pleas from city officials that they return home. Instead, armed with shotguns, rifles, pistols, clubs, knives, and shillelaghs, they made their way downtown. As they approached the Clark Street Bridge from the north, more than two hundred men from units mustered from the National Guard, the Light Guard, Swift's Artillery, and special police waited on the other side, rifles lowered and nightsticks ready. The two groups then clashed, and gunfire broke out from both sides. When the fighting ended, there were scores of injuries and many arrests, but, oddly enough, only one fatality. He was Peter Martens, a twenty-six-year-old German shoemaker[1] who allegedly shot police officer George Hunt, wounding him in the arm, and then, according to newspaper reports, was pursued and killed by Sheriff James Andrews.

To prevent any further disturbances, martial law was declared and remained in effect for three days. Eventually all charges against those arrested were dropped. Two months after the disturbances, which came to be known as the "Lager Beer Riots," Chicagoans voted overwhelmingly against a prohibition measure proposed by Mayor Boone. By then it was clear that because of the riots, Boone and the Know-Nothings had lost both face and the goodwill of the citizenry, and the beer-loving immigrants, triumphant at last and spirits undoubtedly foaming high, staged a jubilant victory parade.

Notes

1. Other sources say he was twenty-year-old Peter Martin. See Richard Wilson Renner, "In A Perfect Ferment: Chicago, the Know-Nothings, and the Riot for Lager Beer," *Chicago History* 5, no. 3 (fall 1976), 168.

THE EYE THAT NEVER SLEEPS

Their motto was, "The eye that never sleeps." They chased bank robbers, rogues, and thieves. The legendary Jesse James, the train robbery Reno Brothers Gang of Indiana, and Butch Cassidy and the Sundance Kid were among their prey. They were the Pinkertons, at one time the best-known detectives in the United States.

Allan Pinkerton founded Pinkerton's National Detective Agency in Chicago in 1850, at a time when public distrust of police intrusion in private affairs was prevalent and the citizenry had little confidence in the poorly trained part-time constables and night watchmen who then comprised the "official police." Even after the Chicago Police Department was formed in 1855, wealthy residents continued to pay gladly for private police-related services. In addition, the growth of industry made adequate surveillance and protection a necessity for the expanding businesses. In such a climate, Pinkerton spawned the detective as entrepreneur, and other private agencies, following his lead, flourished during the 1850s and 1860s.

Pinkerton was already a successful businessman before becoming a master sleuth. An avowed social reformer in his native Scotland who aggressively advocated the rights of the working class, Pinkerton fled to America to avoid government persecution and eventually found employment as a cooper (barrel maker) in the little Scottish-American community of Dundee, Illinois. There he became active in local politics, making a name for himself in abolitionist circles (he was among those who helped John Brown escape to Canada).

Walking home one night in the late 1840s, Pinkerton accidentally discovered a counterfeiter's hideout and, returning with the county sheriff, helped make an arrest. The Scotsman's reputation quickly spread, and soon he became a Kane County deputy sheriff; then a special agent for the treasury department and the post office; and finally the head of the United States Secret Service and a personal bodyguard to President Abraham Lincoln.

In filling a need that government police agencies weren't meeting adequately, Pinkerton made private police work a million-dollar business. His detectives diligently kept watch over railroad conductors to ensure their honesty, infiltrated labor unions to discover their secrets, monitored employees to discourage company thefts, and used informers to trail the pickpockets who followed the traveling circuses and Wild West shows.

The railroad companies were especially lucrative customers. Because state police did not yet exist and the federal government refused to take responsibility for the protection of railroad property, the rail companies, then expanding rapidly across the desolate prairies, turned to Pinkertons for protection against vandalism and theft.

Trailing criminals became the domain of some of the most colorful, and sometimes notorious, detectives on record. James McParland infiltrated the Molly Maguires, an underground Irish terrorist group that operated in the 1860s in Pennsylvania. Tom Horn, a former Army scout and Indian fighter, was the scourge of train robbers and cattle rustlers. Charles Siringo and Frank Dimaio spent four years out West in search of Butch Cassidy and the Hole in the Wall Gang. Master detective story writer Dashiell Hammett was a Pinkerton man between 1913 and 1918 and later worked on the sensational rape-murder case of movie starlet Virginia Rappe, in which actor Fatty Arbuckle eventually was acquitted of rape and manslaughter charges.

When Allan Pinkerton died in 1884 and sons William and Robert took over, the agency had grown from a one-man operation to a force of more than two thousand competing with fourteen other private detective firms in the city. Robert was noted for his strong

administrative skills, but it was William, the more flamboyant of the two, who captured the limelight and became the darling of the press. He was always in the news. Known affectionately as "Billy," the mustachioed, two-hundred-pound gumshoe who frequented saloon hangouts and racetracks was an expert on the criminal activities of the underworld.

By the 1930s, city police departments had become competent enough to weaken the demand for the private agencies. So had the FBI, created in 1908 as a nationwide governmental police force, especially after it began using lie detectors, crime labs, and other sophisticated crime-fighting equipment.

On January 1, 1965, Pinkerton's National Detective Agency changed its name to Pinkerton's Inc., reflecting the change in its business to a mostly noninvestigative nature. Instead of chasing bank robbers and stagecoach bandits, today's Pinkertons, head-quartered in Van Nuys, California, but with branch offices in Chicago, Westchester, and Des Plaines, and more than 130 offices worldwide, manufactures electronic alarm and safety devices and tracks down fraudulent insurance claims.

Pulp literature, dime-store novels, and, lately, television and movies have kept the Pinkerton mystique alive, elevating the private detective to legendary status. Philip Marlowe, Mike Hammer, Lew Harper—in fact, all private eyes, both real and fictional—are beholden to Allan Pinkerton, the Caledonian sleuth.

Select historical sites

- *Allan Pinkerton burial plot.* Graceland Cemetery, 4001 North Clark Street, Chicago; 312-525-1105. The detective is buried here along with his family as well as several Pinkerton employees, including the grave of Kate Warn, Pinkerton's first woman detective.
- *Pinkerton historical marker.* Third Street, West Dundee, Illinois. A marker commemorates the spot where Pinkerton lived from 1844 to 1850.

Allan Pinkerton burial site, Graceland Cemetery, Clark Street and Irving Park Road (photo by June Skinner Sawyers). Final resting place for the Caledonian sleuth.

NIGHTMARE ON SIXTY-THIRD STREET

In the 1890s in a sprawling brick mansion that stood at Sixty-third and South Wallace Streets lived a man who was known to his neighbors as Dr. H. H. Holmes, a respectable and hard-working young fellow with a keen business sense. In fact, he was Herman Webster Mudgett, a master of deceit and a nineteenth-century Bluebeard who committed unspeakable acts of perversion and murder within the dark corridors of his three-story "castle."

Soon after coming to Chicago from his native New Hampshire, Holmes, a former medical student, secured a position as a prescription clerk at an Englewood drugstore. An impeccable dresser and a glib conversationalist, he attracted so many new customers that he was able to buy the establishment from its owner, a Mrs. Holden, who mysteriously vanished soon afterwards. Holmes said she went to California.

Holmes had already hired an attractive young woman, Julia Connor, and her husband to work in the store (the husband also later disappeared) when he began constructing his enormous mansion across the street. To finance this tremendous undertaking, Holmes concocted numerous schemes, some of which actually paid off. He marketed a "sure-fire" cure for alcoholism that he bottled and sold for fifty dollars a throw. He sold ordinary tap water as an all-purpose miracle drug for five cents a glass. And in one of his boldest moves, he "invented" a process that converted ordinary water into gas (the gas company inspector actually offered him twenty-five thousand dollars for rights to the process).

When completed, his mansion stood three stories high and contained some one hundred rooms of various sizes, staircases that led nowhere, false partitions, long dark corridors, trapdoors, and secret passageways. Young girls flocked to it to work for his various fly-by-night operations. Most were wealthy, single, or orphaned. According to a contemporary newspaper account, Holmes liked "a nice, green young girl fresh from a business college."

Holmes traveled extensively to finance his bogus operations, swindling people left and right. On one particular journey he renewed a friendship with a Southern girl, Minnie Williams, and proposed to her. She returned to Chicago with him, unaware that not only was he living with Julia Connor, but he was also still married to two other women, his first wife in New England and a second from Wilmette, Illinois. Connor then conveniently "disappeared." Another time, in Denver, Holmes married another woman, Georgie Anne Yoke, with Minnie Williams, in a bizarre twist, serving as witness. Soon Minnie, too, vanished.

Broke, Holmes concocted perhaps his most elaborate scheme. He and his sometime partner in crime, a small-time thief named Benjamin Pitezel (or Pitzel, according to some records), plotted to defraud an insurance company by faking a fatal accident, planting a stolen cadaver, identifying it as Pitezel, and collecting from the insurance company. Stuck in a St. Louis jail one night on a charge of petty fraud, Holmes took a fellow inmate, a train robber named Marion Hedgepath, into his insurance scam, promising Hedgepath five hundred dollars from the loot if Hedgepath would find a willing lawyer to handle the fraudulent claim. An industrial accident was then staged in Philadelphia, but with Pitezel actually dying as an unwilling victim, and all involved shared in the money—except Hedgepath.

An angry Hedgepath then notified the authorities, and Holmes was eventually arrested in Boston and brought back to Philadelphia to face murder charges. Meanwhile, the Chicago police had entered the Holmes mansion on the South Side and found such horrors as rooms with gas pipes but with no gaslight fixtures and windowless chambers lined with asbestos. In the dank cellar were a crematory, lime pits, vats of acid, and bloodstained clothing.

Found guilty of the Pitezel murder, Holmes confessed to a total of twenty-seven murders. But he later disavowed that confession, amid estimates his victims numbered as many as 150, most of them young women.[1]

Holmes was sentenced to death by hanging and met his executioner on May 7, 1896. "Ready, Holmes?" asked the hangman. "Yes, don't bungle," answered the murderer.

The mysterious Dr. Holmes then went to the grave carrying with him many of his dark secrets.[2]

Notes

1. For a modern look at Holmes see Todd Savage, "Horror Hound: Tracking Down a 19th-Century Serial Killer," *Chicago Reader,* January 6, 1995, 37–38.

2. Chicago has seen its share of sensational murderers from Richard Speck to John Wayne Gacy. Perhaps the most notorious is the case of Leopold and Loeb. In 1924 eighteen-year-old Nathan Leopold and seventeen-year-old Richard Loeb, two precocious graduates of the University of Chicago, kidnapped and murdered fourteen-year-old Bobby Franks. Their brilliant attorney, Clarence Darrow, convinced the judge to spare their lives and grant them a life sentence. Loeb was killed in prison in 1936; Leopold served thirty-three years and was paroled. He died in 1971.

STREETS ON FIRE:
THE CHICAGO RACE RIOTS OF 1919

O n Sunday, July 27, 1919, the temperature soared into the nineties. Five African-American teenagers decided to go to the lake to find relief from the scorching heat. It would be a day they would soon wish to forget.

It was early afternoon when the teenagers hitched a ride on the back of a produce truck. The boys jumped off at Twenty-sixth Street and Wabash Avenue, near the railroad tracks, and began walking briskly, sprinting almost—they were in the heart of Irish street gang territory—the rest of the way to the lake. At that time, Chicago beaches were highly segregated. Blacks frequented the Twenty-fifth Street beach; the Twenty-ninth Street beach, farther south, was, by custom, exclusively for whites. But the boys had other ideas. They were heading toward a private spot that they had discovered in between the two beaches. They had even built a raft of logs and chains.

At two o'clock the boys were enjoying the pleasures of the raft. Meanwhile, unbeknownst to the teenagers, there was friction at the Twenty-ninth Street beach. Several black men and women had apparently entered the whites-only beach. They were greeted with profanity and hurling of rocks, which made them leave. Minutes later, though, they returned with a group of friends and companions, who returned the volley. This time the white bathers fled. When the whites returned, the battle had begun in earnest. The race riot of 1919 was on.

The boys were still unaware of the fracas. As they drifted toward the breakwater near Twenty-sixth Street, a white man hurled rocks in their direction, fatally striking young Eugene Williams. When Eugene's companions later identified the white man to a white police officer, Daniel Callahan, Callahan refused to arrest the suspect. He did, however, at the insistence of a persistent white man, arrest at the scene a black man who reportedly was uncooperative.

In the meantime, rumors spread like prairie wildfire that Officer Callahan had "prevented" swimmers from rescuing Williams and that he encouraged whites to throw rocks at the black swimmers. Hundreds of angry onlookers from both races gathered at the beach as the police took the black man into custody. In the subsequent turmoil, another black man, James Crawford, reportedly pulled out a gun and shot at the officers. One of them was wounded. A black officer fired back, killing Crawford.

The death of James Crawford set the rest of the tragic consequences in motion. The riot raged for five days: White preyed on black, black on white. According to William Tuttle, the violence was random and indiscriminate. At one point, white gunmen in automobiles sped through the Black Belt shooting wildly while black snipers returned the gunfire.

The Chicago race riot of 1919 was hardly unique in the annals of American history. The twentieth century had already seen its share of rioting before the Chicago riot: New York City in 1900, Atlanta in 1906, and, closer to home, Springfield, Illinois, in 1908 and East St. Louis, Illinois, in 1917.

The reasons for the violence were complex, ranging from xenophobia, unemployment, and a pervasive sense of disillusionment following the end of World War I. The "Red Scare" of the postwar years also made an impact. Thus anyone who was somewhat different or gave even the slightest hint of nonconformity was met with suspicion and his or her patriotism questioned. Tuttle believes that African-American men and women became the scapegoats, easy objects of ridicule and fear who threatened the status quo by competing with whites for jobs and housing. Thus, the major cause of the riot, he suggests, was the influx of Southern blacks into the city. Racial tensions had existed before, but now they reached frightening proportions.

For many whites the mass migration of blacks from the rural South was alarming. During World War I, for example, more than 450,000 Southern blacks moved to the great Northern cities. By 1919 the population in the Black Belt totaled at least 125,000. Most came from the Deep South—Mississippi, Arkansas, Alabama, Louisiana, and Texas. Few institutions were as fundamental in stimulating the migration north than the *Chicago Defender*, the leading African-American newspaper in the city. On January 6, 1917, the *Defender* published a prophetic headline: MILLIONS TO LEAVE SOUTH.

The *Defender* even attached a specific date to the so-called Great Migration—May 15, 1917— even though, as the paper later admitted, the date was arbitrarily set. But the die had already been cast. Thousands upon thousands of poor Southern blacks left their hometowns in search of the Promised Land of the North. They were looking for the same elusive dreams as countless immigrants before them: a good job, proper housing, and a better education for their children. The new arrivals were helped by various organizations, including the Urban League, the Wabash Avenue YMCA, and other social service agencies.

What's more, blacks had returned home after serving during World War I expecting to be accorded dignity and respect or, at least, some measure of tolerance. Instead, residential segregation created two worlds—one black, one white—fostering a volatile atmosphere based on ignorance and misunderstanding.

On that hot summer day in July, when racial tensions came to a head, the police force was largely ineffective. Although encouraged to call in the National Guard, Mayor William Hale Thompson dragged his heels, preferring instead to rely on the local police to keep the violence under control. Finally, the state militia was called in to quell the disturbance. When the heavens opened up and a soothing rain fell from the sky, the violence subsided. Even so, sporadic incidents occurred for the better part of a week.

After order was finally restored, the city was left with disturbing statistics: 38 dead, including 23 black men and boys; at least 537 injured, of whom 342 were black.[1]

Notes

1. See William S. Tuttle, *Race Riot: Chicago in the Red Summer of 1919* (New York: Atheneum, 1970), 64. Carl Sandburg in his classic study, *The Chicago Race Riots, July 1919* (New York: Harcourt, Brace, 1919), reported that twenty blacks and fourteen whites were killed.

 SHUTTING DOWN THE LEVEE

It was a relatively small book of four hundred pages, but when it came out in the spring of 1894, it startled, shocked, and angered thousands of Chicagoans. Titled *If Christ Came to Chicago* and written by William T. Stead, an English journalist and social reformer, it was packed with accounts of debauchery and depravity more sordid than those that could be found in the most debased fictional works of the day—and it was all happening, the author told his readers, right in their midst.

Drawn to what he had called "one of the wonders of the 19th Century," Stead came determined to get as full a picture as he could of the entire city. He got himself invited to dinner in Prairie Avenue mansions, spent time with businessmen and politicians, and even gave public lectures touching on public morality, civic duties, and political corruption.

Above all, he frequented the saloons, brothels, and dives of what had come to be known as the Levee, the red-light district that stretched roughly from South Wabash Avenue west to the Chicago River between Van Buren and Twenty-second Streets. The heart of the district, however, centered around Nineteenth Street to Cermak Road (Twenty-second Street) and from State to Clark Streets. Wandering through the district day and night, he talked with bums, madams, and prostitutes and witnessed firsthand the daily goings-on there. The city's most famous brothel, the notorious Everleigh Club at 2131–33 South Dearborn, was located here in a three-story brownstone. Other popular attractions included the House of All Nations, the Bucket of Blood, and Freiberg's Dance Hall.

When his book came out, critics called him a crank and accused him of being part of a Republican conspiracy to destroy the city's Democratic Party. The *Chicago Tribune* assailed the book as "a directory of sin" and demanded that it be suppressed. Mothers warned their children not to read it. Denounced in some quarters as the ravings of a maniac, it was, however, also praised by others as the voice of a prophet.

Within its covers, Stead listed addresses of brothels, pawn shops, lodging houses, and saloons; gave detailed maps of the Levee; and named gamblers and saloonkeepers. With indignation he castigated city council members as opportunists and rogues, accused politicians of buying elections with glasses of whiskey, and called aldermen "the swine of our civilization."

Amid the shock and the controversy, Chicagoans scooped up vast quantities of the book. Within a week, the first printing, one hundred thousand copies in all, was sold out.

But reform, Stead's apparent goal, was a long time coming.

Fifteen years later, the Levee was still flourishing—well enough to become once again the target of another reformer from England. On a balmy night in October 1909, evangelist Rodney "Gipsy" Smith and a host of followers, led by a Salvation Army band, marched in protest into the district. Block after block they went, sometimes filling the streets from curb to curb as their numbers grew to as many as twenty thousand. At the height of their demonstration, Smith and his marchers sank to their knees, shouted prayers, sang hymns, and invoked the judgment of God upon the Levee and its denizens. After a soft rendition by the band of "Where He Leads Me I Will Follow," the protesters quietly dispersed.

Forewarned about the march, the Levee residents had closed down everything and discreetly stayed behind shuttered doors and darkened windows. But as soon as the marchers left, the district came back to life. Lights were turned back on, doors were reopened, piano music again filled the night air, and customers began to crowd on the streets and stream into the saloons and brothels. Before the night was over, the Levee, ironically, would enjoy the best business in its history.

Oriental Music Room, Everleigh Club, 1902 (Chicago Historical Society, ICHi–00379). A typically plush interior.

The Everleigh Sisters. Ada (1866–1960) and Minna Everleigh (1878–1948), Chicago's notorious brothel queens.

But Smith's march and Stead's book, though seemingly ineffective, did take their toll on the district. Along with a number of ugly incidents that time and again grabbed the city's shocked attention, they finally forced Chicagoans to take a hard look at the squalor that was in their midst. One such incident was the suicide of a teenage waif known only as Red Top.

Typical of the many homeless boys who roamed the mean streets of the Levee, Red Top was forced to sleep under stairwells and survive on handouts and odd jobs. Finally, it became too much for him, and one day, according to historian Finis Farr, Red Top hanged himself in a woodshed, leaving behind a pathetic note: "They ain't no fun living this way and I'd sooner be dead. I never had no mother or no father or no home. I don't owe nobody nothing and I don't want nobody to cry over me. So Goodbye."[1]

Slowly but surely, Chicagoans lost their tolerance for the Levee and the corruption it spawned in the city's political and social life. After countless police raids, grand jury investigations, vice commission reports, and denunciations by reformers, the old South Side red-light district was gone, and thus came to an end an inglorious though colorful chapter of the city's history.

Notes

1. The Levee had a strange pull on many well-known people, too. In 1905 Marshall Field, Jr., died in his Prairie Avenue mansion of a gunshot wound to the head. The mainstream press called it an unfortunate accident. According to the rumor mill, though, he had allegedly spent the previous night at the Everleigh Club. Five years later the heir to the Rock Island Railroad was found dead at a Levee brothel on South Dearborn Street. See Richard Lindberg, *Chicago Ragtime: Another Look at Chicago, 1880–1920* (South Bend, Ind.: Icarus Press, 1985), 137.

# THE GANGSTER AND THE SONGBIRD

An underworld vice lord from Chicago and a sweet-voiced choir singer from Grand Rapids, Michigan, may seem to have little in common, but for a few brief weeks in the spring of 1920 Jim Colosimo and Dale Winter became a couple whose romance caught the city's fancy.

An Italian immigrant with no formal schooling, Colosimo acquired culture while making money from gambling and prostitution. In the late 1890s, he was a street cleaner with hardly more than a broom, shovel, and cart to his name. But he began to acquire both wealth and power when, in distributing grapes to Sicilian families on the Near West Side and then selling the wine they made, he made contacts with various underworld figures. Then he organized the city's street sweepers into an influential political organization. Soon he was reputedly pulling in fifty thousand dollars a month from various legal and illegal operations.

Along with a weakness for diamonds and fancy suits, Colosimo also had an insatiable urge to better himself. Each night his wife, Victoria Moresco, read the classics to him while recordings of Italian opera selections played in the background. Together they opened their first nightclub, a bawdy parlor house called the Victoria, at Armour and Twenty-first Streets, where a "professor" named "Izzy the Rat" pounded on a tinny piano.

In 1910 Colosimo opened his famous cafe at 2126 South Wabash Avenue, a splendid nightclub that featured good music, excellent food, and fine wine. Soon it became the rendezvous for those who sought an illicit but oh-so-sophisticated atmosphere. It was *the* place to go after the rest of the city went to bed.

Despite the club's wicked reputation, the underworld's presence there was unobtrusive. Certain characters were allowed entry only if properly dressed and, once inside, were strictly bound to behave in a civil manner. Hence, thieves and gamblers, million-aires and merchants, bankers and schoolteachers, and even the chief of police patronized the cafe. The establishment became so popular that Colosimo had to build an annex next door. One section would stay open until one in the morning, in observance of the city's tavern-closing law, but patrons then moved into the "north room" to continue their carousing.

Into this glitzy setting walked pert Dale Winter. Colosimo had met her earlier in Grand Rapids through an orchestra leader. Seeing her now at the club for an audition arranged by *Chicago Tribune* writer Jack Lait, Big Jim quickly fell in love with her. Winter, who still lived with her mother in a South Side hotel and for some months sang in the choir of the South Park Methodist Church, was soon given star billing along with singing lessons from Giacomo Spadoni of the Chicago Opera and a course in etiquette. In turn, she exerted a subtle influence over the smitten Colosimo, persuading him to wear quieter clothes and urging him to speak more softly.

Colosimo secured an uncontested divorce from his wife in March 1920. The next month he and Winter eloped to West Baden Springs, Indiana, and enjoyed a two-week honeymoon. Upon their return, he bought a handsome home on the South Side for his new bride.

But their romance was short-lived. At 4:30 P.M. on May 11, 1920, Colosimo arrived at the almost deserted cafe and walked to the rear office, where his secretary, Frank Camilla, sat. "Hello, Frank. What's doing?" the kingpin said cheerfully. "Nothing," came the noncommittal reply. After a few moments, he went alone to the front. When he reached the lobby, a dark figure emerged from the shadows. Two shots rang out. One splintered a glass pane, the other struck Colosimo in the head. He fell facedown on the porcelain floor, dead at age forty-nine.

Colosimo's night club and restaurant, 2126–30 South Wabash Avenue, 1953 (photo by J. Sherwin Murphy. Chicago Historical Society, ICHi–01432). "Big" Jim Colosimo was gunned down in the lobby of his popular cafe on May 11, 1920.

Many theories exist about Colosimo's death. Some think his ex-wife, unhappy with the financial arrangements of the divorce, arranged the murder. Some say Al Capone did it; others, New York gunman Frankie Yale. Three years after the slaying, a Chicago salesman, James Mulcrone, told St. Louis police that he shot Colosimo in a drunken rage because he had been ejected from the cafe. The confession was later dismissed because, according to Sergeant Felix Kosinski, Mulcrone was suffering from "hallucinations produced by drugs."

The most popular theory is that Big Jim's nephew, Johnny Torrio, thinking his liaison with Winter had made his uncle "go soft" and that a "reformed" Colosimo would be unable to hold the city's crime syndicate together, ordered the assassination.

A widow after being a bride for only a few weeks, Winter returned to the stage, married an actor in 1924, and settled in Los Angeles. Colosimo's famous cafe eventually went out of business in 1945, and the site later became a parking lot.

Law and Disorder

 "SCARFACE" TAKES OVER CICERO

If you smell gunpowder, you must be in Cicero. That, or words to that effect, was a popular saying around town during the 1920s. Until early in that decade, Cicero was a pleasant lower- middle-class suburb populated largely by people who worked in the steel mills and the stockyards and took quiet pride in their modest homes and neat little yards. To them, it was an ideal place to raise a family.

Enter the Johnny Torrio gang. The town quickly became an underworld haven seething with gangster types and spawning dance halls, gambling parlors, bookie joints, and all-night saloons. The "fall" of Cicero came during the particularly violent village election year of 1924, during which the body count of dead victims almost seemed to surpass the total number of votes cast.

Torrio's domain already encompassed the Loop, most of the South Side, and scattered pockets north of Madison Street, and reached out into such suburban areas as Chicago Heights, Blue Island, Burr Oaks, Stickney, and Forest View. But the well-dressed mobster with the benign face wanted more. So he summoned a new protegé, a hot-headed punk fresh from the mean streets of New York by the name of Al Capone, and he gave him an order: Take Cicero.

For years Cicero's mayor, Joseph Z. Klenha, a Republican, and his largely corrupt administration ran the suburb with little or no political opposition. That all changed in 1924, when the Democrats decided for the first time to put up a real challenge to the incumbent. But more than simple politics was involved. The Torrio gang had already controlled the beer-running operation that supplied Cicero's saloons. Rival factions, wishing to get a piece of the action, aligned themselves with the Democrats, and Klenha, fearing for his political career, asked Capone for help. "Big Al" was only too happy to oblige.

Capone, in fact, had by this time already moved in by ousting Eddie Vogel, a local politician who owned a chain of slot machines and actually ran the suburb, with Mayor Klenha serving as titular head. Come election time, Capone ruthlessly set about demolishing the opposition and establishing full control.

The methods Capone's hoods used to control the election were so ruthless that the *Chicago Tribune* felt compelled to call the violence "unsurpassed in any previous Cook County political contest." On election day itself voters were accosted by armed goons who gruffly asked them how they were going to vote. If the answer was unsuitable, the voter was bluntly told to change his or her mind. Those who refused or dared to argue were pummeled until comonsense or the desire to stay alive prevailed.

Automobiles filled with gunmen sped up and down the streets. A Cicero police officer was disarmed and badly beaten. Polling places were raided by thugs and ballots torn forcibly from the hands of voters. One Democratic worker was kidnapped, blindfolded, and carried to a Chicago basement, where he was kept captive until the polls closed; then he was tossed out of a moving car. Another was kidnapped and shot through both legs.

At one point police in a squad car came across three known gang figures—Frank Capone, Al's brother; Dave Hedlin; and Charles Fischetti—standing at a street corner with a "short stocky man with two guns." As two police sergeants, William Cusack and William Riley, jumped out of the car with their guns drawn, Frank Capone began firing. In the ensuing gunfight, joined in by two other police sergeants, Frank Capone was shot dead through the heart, Hedlin was wounded, and Fischetti, after fleeing to a nearby field, surrendered. The mystery man, later identified as Al Capone, escaped into the darkness.

Investigations of this gunfight followed, but no one was prosecuted. Fischetti later denied he even knew an election was taking place. "Frank and I were thinking of opening a restaurant in Cicero," he explained, lamely.

Despite police efforts, Cicero almost overnight became "Caponeville," and everyone, from the police department to local businesspeople to the mayor's office, took instructions from the Capone headquarters.

It was an underworld empire built on blood, and from 1924, when Al Capone became its undisputed boss, until 1931, when he was sent to prison on tax evasion charges, Cicero was its capital.

Museums

- *Capone's Chicago.* 605 North Clark Street, Chicago 60610; 312-654-1919. Hours: Daily from 10 A.M.–10 P.M. Admission: Adults, $4.75; children under 12 and senior citizens, $3.75. Recreation of the Prohibition era and the city's notorious gangster history.

Select historical sites

- *Lexington Hotel.* 2135 South Michigan Avenue, Chicago. Built in 1892, this building once served as Capone headquarters.
- *Capone family house.* 7244 South Prairie Avenue, Chicago. Capone bought the two-story house in 1923. He lived here with his mother and brothers until 1931, when he was convicted of income tax evasion.

"TEXAS" GUINAN:
THE MAGIC TOUCH OF A SASSY PROHIBITION BABY

The name "Texas" Guinan was as unique as the woman. Queen of the Nightclubs, they called her, and by all accounts the vivacious performer who mixed satirical jabs with illegal brew deserved her title. She was a dancer, a hostess, a nightclub owner, and quite a con artist who could make her customers come back to be fleeced yet again . . . and again.

Guinan, christened Mary Louise Cecilia, was a Prohibition baby, and as a true child of that freewheeling era, she did what she wanted, when she wanted, and usually got away with it. Born in Waco, Texas (hence the nickname), Guinan came to Chicago as a girl with a scholarship to the Chicago Conservatory of Music. But she soon moved to New York, where she gained favorable notices as a dancer in all-women revues. "Keep your eyes on that girl," wrote one admiring reviewer. "She'll be big some day. She has zip and fizz, and that's what the public wants."

It wasn't long before Guinan became a nightclub owner herself and began staging elaborate floor shows in New York (Ruby Keeler and Barbara Stanwyck supposedly got their breaks working for Guinan), during which she coaxed the audience to "give this little girl a great big hand." In 1928 federal authorities shut down her Salon Royale, charging Guinan with "maintaining a nuisance." Acquitted of that charge, Guinan returned to Chicago and ran the show at clubs such as the Planet Mars, the Club Royale, and during the spring and winter of 1930, the Green Mill. She had, wrote Charles Collins of the *Chicago Tribune,* "form, rapid tempo and the carnival spirit."

Guinan openly greeted customers with a sassy "Hello, sucker," which, from her, sounded as smooth and inviting as a velvety quaff of illicit hooch. Guinan herself neither drank nor smoked, allowing her to boast that she had no "minor vices." But she knew what the public wanted, and she gave it to them. Tabs for a few glasses of illegal liquor and a show could run as high as one hundred dollars, but she would massage the ego of a customer until he felt that the extortionate prices he was being charged were not only reasonable but well-deserved. Guinan would tease, flirt, and cajole until her happy victim, like a good sport, gladly surrendered his money.

"A sucker," she once said, "is a guy who was born all softened up and ready for the touch."

She had the touch. Even women were curious about what she had to say. In 1929 Guinan gave a lecture entitled "Why Husbands Stay Out Nights" to a group of ladies who gathered in the ballroom of the Illinois Women's Athletic Club to hear her. "Men are like children," said the thrice-divorced entertainer, "and they must be treated like children. If they wanta play boss, let 'em play boss. What do you care? You know you have the edge on 'em."

With the pouring of forbidden alcohol came more police raids. Guinan, however, was always cooperative. "Oh, a raid," she said one time, good-naturedly pulling a reluctant officer by the arm toward a piano. "Listen, folks, listen," she told the crowd, "these men are Prohibition agents. They won't harm you. Let's give three cheers for Uncle Sam." During a New Year's Eve raid at the Planet Mars, Guinan placed her arm around one agent and whispered, "Welcome." When asked if she owned or had part interest in the club, Guinan, who in fact was the owner, meekly said: "Why, I'm only a little girl from New York in Chicago. I just work here."

Police raids, however, were not the only problems Guinan had to face. At 4 A.M. one Sunday in March 1930, three shots rang out in the Green Mill, where Guinan and her girls were performing, and a man named Leonard Sweitzer fell wounded. His assailants, police later said, were Harry O. Voiler, the club's manager; and his bodyguard, Arthur Reed, though both denied firing any shots.

Apparently Sweitzer, who co-owned the Green Mill, had sublet it to Guinan, who got Voiler to run it for her, and the shooting resulted from Voiler's refusal to pay rent as agreed upon. The police temporarily shut down the club.

After a raid that closed down the Planet Mars in 1932, Guinan moved back to New York and later to Hollywood, producing and touring with theatrical revues but never regaining the limelight she once had as the "high priestess of whoopee." Her last visit to Chicago was at the 1933 world's fair. Later that year the final curtain came down for the former toast of Chicago's nightlife when she died, from an intestinal infection, while performing in Vancouver, British Columbia. She was not quite fifty.

WHISPERING IN THE DARK:
THE SECRET WORLD OF SPEAKEASIES

The Prohibition era was a colorful time of pinstriped gangsters and honky-tonk piano players, of Babe Ruth and F. Scott Fitzgerald, of Eliot Ness and Al Capone. Its roots went back to the temperance societies of the eighteenth century, the first demands in the 1830s for outright prohibition, the "dry bills" of the 1850s that did become law in a number of states, and the post–World War I crusade led by the Anti-Saloon League and the Women's Christian Temperance Union (WCTU). All this finally led to the Eighteenth Amendment, ratified on January 16, 1919, and effective exactly a year later. New phrases entered the language—"rum runner," "real McCoy" (a drink not watered down), "bathtub gin," "G-man"—and a new establishment was born: the speakeasy.

Countless speakeasies sprouted in Chicago. Settings varied from dank basements and seedy back rooms to elegant homes and clubby cellars. Places like the Moulin Rouge, Colosimo's, the Midnight Frolic, and the Rendezvous attracted a steady stream of thirsty customers. Many speakeasies catered to members of the upper class; for the common folk, there were the less pretentious speakeasies known also as "beer flats." A secret password spoken softly (hence the term *speakeasy*) through a tiny peephole was all that a customer needed to get by the guard at the door. The speakeasies were illegal, of course, and were targets of continuing raids by the authorities. But when one closed, another opened.

Many of today's well-known bars in Chicago were once speakeasies: Butch McGuire's, a favorite of singles; Durkin's, once known as Prohibition Willy's Speakeasy; Marge's, where gin was made in the bathtub on the second floor; Riccardo's; Twin Anchors; the Green Mill, where entertainer Joe E. Lewis's throat was slashed when he decided to leave for a gig at a competing club;[1] and Schulien's, owned by Matt Schulien, a hefty, amiable, cigar-chomping ace of a card dealer who as host of an illegal establishment spent many nights in jail but kept his customers happy with pinochle and nickel-dime poker games that lasted into the wee hours of the morning.

Despite their reputation as haunts of shady characters and corrupt officials, speakeasies were far from the devil's dens many made them out to be. Most were respectable establishments where the values were middle class, the manners genteel, and the food tasty and inexpensive. In the classier places, gentlemen even wore jackets and ladies white gloves. Many of them, like Durkin's, started life as restaurants, and the transition from restaurant to speakeasy and back again to restaurant after Prohibition was an easy one. But even after the end of Prohibition, no establishment could legally call itself a "saloon." Not until 1974 was this ban lifted, allowing Schulien's, among others, happily to reclaim "saloon" as part of its name.

It was the mounting criminal activity surrounding illegal liquor that aroused civic concern and gave the speakeasy its bad reputation even though hoodlums often maintained a low profile and mostly kept to themselves. But there was money to be made. Major mobs controlled well-defined territories, their take reportedly running well into the millions. Lost tax revenues have been estimated at as much as $1 billion a year and the total bill to the taxpayers for bootlegged liquor throughout the era at close to $36 billion.

The Great Depression changed everything—and with it came empty pockets, short tempers, and a bad taste in the mouths of many who came to see the "noble experiment" as an utter failure that bred nothing but violence, corruption, and a general disdain for the law. More than five hundred people were killed in Chicago alone, victims of the gang wars over control of the city's illicit liquor traffic.

So when Franklin D. Roosevelt, campaigning for the presidency, endorsed repeal of the Eighteenth Amendment in 1932, a great collective cheer erupted on many American streets and behind the doors of many a speakeasy. Repeal finally arrived on December 5, 1933, with the ratification of the Twenty-first Amendment. Inside the Palmer House an all-male crowd watched intently while noted meatpacker Oscar Mayer became the first Chicagoan to drink legal liquor again after thirteen years, ten months, and nineteen days.

The long alcohol drought was over and with it the colorful era of the speakeasies.

Notes

1. Few clubs anywhere have as rich a history as the Green Mill. Many people have walked through its door. Actors Charlie Chaplin, Wallace Beery, and Bronco Billy Anderson, who worked nearby at the old Essanay Studios, dropped in. Vaudevillians Al Jolson and Eddie Cantor sang here as did, in a later era, Billie Holiday. Benny Goodman was known to stop by for a late-night jam session. Al Capone had his favorite booth. For a description of the Green Mill during its earlier heyday, see Chet Jakus and Jacki Lyden, *Landmarks and Legends of Uptown* (Chicago: Privately published, n.d.), 29–31. Howard Reich offers an entertaining look at the club—past and present—in "A Joint for the Ages," *Chicago Tribune,* March 5, 1995, 15–16.

THE TRUE STORY BEHIND *NORTHSIDE 777*

The ad that appeared in the classified section of the October 10, 1944, issue of the *Times* in Chicago read:

$5,000 Reward for killers of Officer Lundy on Dec. 9, 1932. Call GRO. 1758, 12–7 p.m.

By then two young Chicagoans, Joe Majczek and Ted Marcinkiewicz, had been arrested, brought to trial, and convicted of murder—the killing of Officer William Lundy during a holdup of a delicatessen in the city's Stockyards district—and had each already served eleven years of their ninety-nine-year sentences.

Their conviction was based mostly on the testimony of the state's key witness—Vera Walush, owner of the delicatessen at 4312 South Ashland Avenue—who during the trial positively identified both Majczek and Marcinkiewicz as the killers of the officer. "Those two guys . . . they were right in my face," she said in court, countering the testimony of Majczek's brother, Stephen, who said under oath that he and Joe were both at home at the time of the robbery.

But Tillie Majczek, a Polish cleaning woman, never believed her son was guilty of the crime. So she scrubbed floors at a downtown office building and saved her money until she had five thousand dollars to offer as a reward to anyone who could help her prove her son's innocence.

The ad caught the eye of two veteran reporters of the *Times*—Jack McPhaul and James McGuire—who, as McPhaul recounts in *Deadlines & Monkeyshines: The Fabled World of Chicago Journalism*, started digging into the case and discovered a few interesting details, which included the following: the delicatessen was also a speakeasy where Walush purveyed illicit brew; the jury wasn't

informed that Walush had originally told the police she could not identify the holdup men and had no suspects in mind; and Majczek, who was on probation at the time for a neighborhood robbery that netted him two dollars, had been put twice on a police lineup—and twice Walush had failed to pick him out as a suspect.

It was also discovered that Walush later gave the police another statement that she had recognized one of the robbers as a neighborhood acquaintance named Ted; that when word went out on the streets indicating Ted Marcinkiewicz was wanted as a murder suspect, he panicked and hid out in the home of Majczek, who happened to be a boyhood friend; that when police came looking for Marcinkiewicz at Majczek's house, he reportedly said: "Let them in. I have nothing to hide"; and that it was only after the police had threatened to arrest Walush for bootlegging did she positively identify Majczek and his friend as the robbers who killed Officer Lundy.

Meanwhile, a detective informed Judge Charles P. Molthrop, who had presided over the case, that Majczek had been framed. Convinced now that justice had been miscarried, Molthrop accused Walush of perjury and vowed to push for a new trial "even if," he said, "I have to pay for it out of my own pocket." Molthrop, however, did nothing further, allegedly because a prosecutor in the state's attorney's office told the judge that if he persisted in pursuing the case, his career would very quickly come to an end.

But the truth finally came out, and Majczek became a media sensation. His story was splashed across the front pages of daily newspapers. After all the evidence was presented to the Illinois Department of Corrections, Governor Dwight H. Green granted a full pardon to Majczek. On August 14, 1945, Majczek walked out of prison and, as compensation for the twelve years he was unjustly kept behind bars, received twenty-four thousand dollars and a new suit.

Somehow all the attention was focused only on Majczek, but five years later Marcinkiewicz was also freed after the courts formally determined he, too, had been denied a fair trial and that his constitutional rights had been violated.

Why the convictions of two apparently innocent men? McPhaul notes that six murders had been committed in the city during the week Lundy was killed, and that with the Century of Progress exhibition scheduled for the following spring, business leaders became fearful of what the violence might do to the city's image. Pressured to "do something," Mayor Anton Cermak in turn ordered the police to "do something." If one accepts this theory, Majczek and Marcinkiewicz then became unfortunate victims of the resulting "war on crime."

Finding the story irresistible, Hollywood brought Majczek's tragedy to the movie screen in 1948, with James Stewart playing the role of an unrelenting reporter in *Call Northside 777*. Majczek reportedly received one thousand dollars for film rights from the studio.

But there was to be no happy ending. After his release from Stateville Penitentiary in Joliet, Majczek remarried the wife he had divorced when he was sent to prison, moved to Oak Lawn, and worked as an insurance broker. In 1979 he suffered severe head injuries from a car accident and had to be confined in a sanitarium, where he died in the early 1980s. Marcinkiewicz changed his name to Ted Marcin and moved to California. With his eyesight failing and fearing that he would be placed in a convalescent home, he committed suicide in 1982. Tillie Majczek, the woman who believed so strongly in her son's innocence, died in 1964.

The killer was never found.[1]

Notes

1. For a recent update of the Majczek case, see Gary Houston, "A Real-Life Chicago Murder Mystery," *Chicago Tribune*, January 9, 1995, 1–2.

THE SPIRITUAL LIFE

Fourth Presbyterian Church, taken shortly after dedication ceremonies in 1914 (courtesy Fourth Presbyterian Church). Gothic revivalist Ralph Adams Cram (1863–1942) designed the English Gothic church; the cloister, manse, parish house, and the Blair Chapel building—all done up in an English Romantic style—is the work of Howard Van Doren Shaw (1869–1926).

THE PERILOUS JOURNEY OF JACQUES MARQUETTE

On May 17, 1673, the French Jesuit missionary Father Jacques Marquette left the relative security of his mission chapel in Saint Ignace in what is now Michigan's Upper Peninsula and went out into the uncharted wilderness to seek new converts among the natives of the New World. The long and arduous journey, which eventually cost him his life, took him along great rivers, through dense forests and the wild Illinois prairie and, for one historic winter, to a desolate spot by a huge lake that local Indians called *Checagou*.

Actually, Marquette's spiritual mission was but part of an expedition of five French-Canadian woodsmen, several Indian guides, and a twenty-eight-year-old cartographer from Quebec named Louis Jolliet. Commissioned by Comte de Frontenac, the governor of New France (Canada), its purpose was more down-to-earth than that of the missionary's—to make further explorations of the Mississippi River with an eye to establishing future fur trading posts and to see if the "Big Muddy" might at some point lead to the China Sea and to the presumably vast sums of the Orient.

Marquette first and briefly set foot on what is now Chicago late in 1673 after he and Jolliet had gone down the Green Bay, the Fox and Wisconsin Rivers and into the Mississippi, and had determined that the mighty river flowed into the Gulf of Mexico. Seeking a shorter route back to Lake Michigan, they traveled up the Illinois and the Des Plaines Rivers and then along an ancient route of mud and shallow water—the Chicago Portage[1]—that led them to the Chicago River and Lake Michigan. The group then paddled on to Green Bay, where a sick and tired Marquette sought to regain his health while Jolliet proceeded to Quebec to report to the governor.

By the fall of 1674, Marquette, still not quite fully recovered, was on his way back to Chicago, though his real destination lay beyond—to the Kaskaskia Indians living near what is now Utica,

Illinois. Warmly received by the natives when he first encountered them the previous year, the missionary had promised to return and bring Christianity to them as soon as he could.

On December 4, Marquette and two other Frenchmen, Jacques Largillier and Pierre Porteret, reached the mouth—then located at Madison Street—of the frozen and snow-covered Chicago River. Suffering from severe dysentery and chronic fever, the Jesuit decided he was too sick to move on and established winter quarters in a log cabin at what is now Damen Avenue and the south branch of the Chicago River, becoming thereby, with his two companions, the first white settlers on record to live in Chicago.

It was a severe winter that year. The wind blew hard across the open prairie. The cabin was continually flooded by waters from the river, at times forcing Marquette and his companions to scamper up the nearest tree to avoid drowning.

Help came in the form of beaver skins and such food as bread, corn, dried meat, and blueberries brought, according to historian A. T. Andreas, once by two visiting Frenchmen—a voyageur named Pierre Moreau and a doctor who Marquette referred to as "the surgeon"—and on several occasions by neighboring Indians. Moved by the Indians' generosity, trust, and respect and "to reward them for their trouble and for what they had brought me," Marquette in turn gave them a hatchet, knives, sets of gold beads, and two mirrors, according to another historian, Robert Shackleton.

As soon as the ice on the Chicago River began to melt, Marquette resumed his journey, reaching the Kaskaskians by Easter. He was received, he wrote, "like an angel from heaven." At the end of his work among the new converts, the black-robed Jesuit preached what was to be his last sermon on this earth before hundreds of chiefs, braves, women, and children during a mass he offered from the back of an overturned canoe. Aware of his rapidly failing health,

he expressed the wish to see his beloved mission in Saint Ignace once more before he died, and about one hundred braves set out to take him back home.

While still on Lake Michigan, Marquette, realizing that the end had come, asked his entourage to pull ashore near what is now Ludington, Michigan. There, under a hastily built hut, the missionary/explorer died on May 18, 1675, weeks short of his thirty-eighth birthday, and was buried under a wooden cross. A year later, a group of Ottawa Indians retrieved his remains and carried them home to his mission at Saint Ignace.

For his sojourn here in the winter of 1674–75, Chicagoans have been honoring Father Marquette as "the first visitor" to Chicago. In 1907, a fourteen-foot mahogany cross was erected at the site of his cabin, and today parks, buildings, and churches still bear his name, serving as modest reminders of the gentle priest who spent a cold winter in a bleak cabin on what one day would become a great city.

Notes

1. The Chicago Portage, gateway to the Illinois Valley, was a low divide between Lake Michigan and the Des Plaines River that linked the Great Lakes to the Gulf of Mexico. A popular artery of travel since prehistoric times, the Chicago Portage was used frequently by Indian tribes, early French pioneers and explorers, fur traders and trappers, and missionaries. Jolliet and Marquette were reportedly the first white men to use the portage.

Select historic sites

- *Father Marquette camp.* Site of Marquette's cabin; what is now the intersection of Damen Avenue, Twenty-sixth Street, and the south branch of the Chicago River. Dedicated in October 1930, it consists of

---

Jacques Marquette (1637–75). Father Marquette was the first white man on record to live in Chicago. He spent the winter of 1674–75 near what is now the intersection of South Damen Avenue and Twenty-sixth Street. Bronze tablets commemorate his brief visit.

two bronze tablets on a granite slab. At the same site is a twenty-foot cedar cross dedicated on September 1, 1973.

- *Chicago Portage National Historic Site.* Forest Preserve District of Cook County, Cummings Square, 536 North Harlem Avenue, River Forest, Illinois, 60305; 708-771-1330. Marquette and other early explorers would carry or "portage" their canoes across the open prairie to the Chicago River. The portage stretched from the Des Plaines River to the south branch of the Chicago River. The Forest Preserve District of Cook County with the cooperation of the Illinois and Michigan Canal Civic Center Authority are developing a major interpretative facility that will eventually include a museum, an archeological center, a replica of an early trading post, a library, and other historical resources.

MINISTRY FOR ALL:
THE FOURTH PRESBYTERIAN CHURCH

Fourth Presbyterian Church stands at the corner of Michigan Avenue and Chestnut Street, a stately presence on the Magnificent Mile and a spiritual alternative to the symbols of Mammon that surround it. Throughout its long and illustrative history, the Fourth Presbyterian Church has taken great pride in its effort to minister to a cross section of the diverse population. The leadership has adapted to the times, applying, whenever necessary, new solutions to age-old problems.

The history of the Presbyterian church in Chicago is a volatile one, full of strong personalities and oftentimes intractable conflicts. The early days of the church, for example, consisted of two fundamentally opposing factions: the conservatives of the Presbyterian or Old School sect versus the liberals of the Congregational or New School sect.

With the passage of the Plan of Union in 1801, the Presbyterian General Assembly, the church's governing body, allowed Presbyterian and Congregational ministers to address the spiritual needs of either group. This ostensibly generous act had its share of pitfalls. Conflict between the two denominations soon arose. Presbyterians felt that churches on the rapidly expanding frontier were becoming too Congregational; that is, too lax in their interpretation of church doctrine. Conservatives began to pull away and began urging the establishment of their own strictly Presbyterian church. At the heart of the division was each denomination's attitude toward slavery. The Old School tended to favor the status quo—change was acceptable but only if it was implemented gradually. The New School, on the other hand, leaned toward complete abolition.

In June 1833, Jeremiah Porter organized, with twenty-five members, the First Presbyterian Church of Chicago, which fell in the New School camp. The Second Presbyterian Church was founded in 1842 and the Third Presbyterian Church in 1847.

A number of prominent Chicagoans, including the reaper king Cyrus McCormick, used their influence to establish yet another Presbyterian church in the city. Consequently, in August 1848, a fourth Presbyterian church was formed—the North Presbyterian Church. The new congregation's first building was constructed at the corner of Clark Street and what is now Hubbard Street. The congregation grew rapidly and within two years moved to a new and larger structure at State and Illinois Streets and moved again in 1861 to the corner of Cass and Indiana Streets (Wabash and Grand Avenues).

At the same time, members of the New School faction began constructing their own church, giving it the name of Westminster Presbyterian Church. Initially they met in the lecture hall of Rush Medical College until they were able to erect their own building at Dearborn and Ontario Streets. In 1866 David Swing, a classics professor at Miami University in Oxford, Ohio, accepted the pastorate at Westminster. Noted for his fiery eloquence and his passionate stands on the issues of the day, Swing not only became one of the most famous preachers of his time but also eventually became embroiled in the Presbyterian struggles between conservatism and liberalism, between Old School and New School.

In 1871 the two branches of the Presbyterian church came together when Westminster and North merged to form the Fourth Presbyterian Church of Chicago with Swing as their pastor. Swing was a popular minister, drawing crowds whenever he spoke. Indeed, he was so popular that newspapers printed his sermons.

Swing reacted to the new religious skepticism—a brand of liberalism and modernism—that was sweeping across post–Civil War America with a controversial interpretation of Presbyterian tenets. Salvation, he told his congregation, was available to everyone through Christ and the exercise of free will. Old School Presbyterians rejected such claims, finding it threatening to the sovereignty of God and the doctrine of predestination. In particular, they charged that Swing "failed to preach the central doctrines of Evangelical Christianity." The conflict heightened, culminating with heresy charges brought against Swing in 1874. The trial lasted fourteen days. Although ultimately acquitted, Swing had had enough of mainstream Presbyterianism. Weary of litigation, he resigned from the Fourth Presbyterian Church and, in late 1875, organized an independent church, the Central Church.

Succeeding pastors at Fourth Presbyterian, each in their own way, have proved to be as passionate and outspoken as Swing.[1] John Timothy Stone became pastor in the early years of the twentieth century. During his tenure, the church saw many changes, including the construction of a new building on Michigan Avenue. The cornerstone was laid in 1912 and the handsome English Gothic structure opened in 1914. At that time, one must remember, Michigan Avenue was a narrow and muddy street—a far cry from the tony boulevard of later years. The church's community served two worlds: wealthy Gold Coast residents and a "rooming house" district of mostly single young men and women. Then as now, the church sought to minister to both worlds through worship services, Sunday school, and missionary programs. Later generations brought expanded services in the form of outreach programs, student and adult ministry, and pastoral counseling.

During the turbulent 1960s and 1970s, the Welsh-born pastor Elam Davies played an active role in the community. Like Swing, he was not one to fear or avoid controversy. During the early 1970s he granted protection to a group of Native Americans who had been involved in a violent confrontation with police over poor living conditions and had sought refuge in the church. Davies not only granted them asylum but also defused the situation entirely by arranging for them to discuss their demands with the appropriate authorities.

From David Swing to the current pastor, John Buchanan, the goal of Fourth Presbyterian has always been to reach out to all elements of society. Throughout its history, the church's commitment to Christian education, fellowship, and service have remained absolute and unswerving.

Notes

1. Fourth Presbyterian has been known for its stable leadership. During an eighty-five-year period, the church has had only four pastors: John Timothy Stone (1908–30), Harry Ray Anderson (1928–61), Elam Davies (1961–84), and John Buchanan (1985–present).

DWIGHT MOODY AND THE BUSINESS OF SAVING SOULS

It was an age of enterprise, those last decades of the nineteenth century, when self-made men made huge fortunes, and the spirit of the frontier surged unbridled in many a strong heart. It was also the era that in Chicago produced the first "religious tycoon," Dwight L. Moody.

Moody, an outspoken Yankee from Massachusetts, had no formal education and never was an ordained minister. But he became reputedly the greatest evangelist of the nineteenth century, who, it was said, traveled nearly a million miles, spoke to more than one hundred million people, and reduced the population of hell by one million souls.

Moody was a doggedly persuasive salesman at heart, whether pushing shoes or preaching the gospel. As a representative for Wiswall's Bootshop on Lake Street near Clark Street, a job he snared two days after his arrival in Chicago, he would hawk his wares outside the store, not content to wait for customers to come inside. Sometimes he followed them to train depots and hotel lobbies. He often said his ambition was to amass a fortune of one hundred thousand dollars, and he was well on his way to that goal when, at the age of twenty-three, he decided to take up missionary work.

There were many obstacles to overcome. Chicago was a rough town where churchgoing took a back seat to dancing, card playing, and hard drinking, and few took kindly to the solemn-faced man admonishing them to find God. Though some affectionately referred to him as "Brother Moody," others called him "Crazy Moody," and he was sometimes threatened with bodily harm if he did not move on.

Undaunted, he rented space—one pew—in a church and canvassed the neighborhood for clients. Visiting saloons and dives, he persuaded hoodlums, beggars, thieves, and street urchins with such nicknames as Red Eye, Billy Bucktooth, and Madden the Butcher that there was a place for them in God's kingdom. In this manner, he built up his ragamuffin Sunday school group. Considering it a great sin to preach to empty seats, Moody advertised in newspapers and once bought a pony to promote attendance by, reportedly, parading it up and down the street with several motley youngsters clinging happily to its back.

In due time Moody became one of the best-known evangelists in the country and on the revivalist circuit. A forerunner of the tradition that would later produce Billy Graham, Oral Roberts, and Pat Robertson, Moody supplied the sermons, relying for the hymn-singing on his partner, Ira D. Sankey, a tax collector from Pennsylvania whose rich baritone voice virtually guaranteed large audiences. At his meetings Moody sought controlled emotionalism, not frenzied passion. Whenever the crowd grew too excited, he would stop and announce, "We will now have some hymns." Then Sankey would sing.

In the summer of 1873, Moody and Sankey took their revivalist program to the United Kingdom, where they met with rousing success. Over two and a half million people filled the old halls in Edinburgh, Glasgow, Dundee, Belfast, Londonderry, York, Sheffield, Birmingham, Newcastle, and London. So successful was the tour—and the team's popular hymnbooks (sold at sixpence a copy)—that Moody had enough money to complete the church he had begun in Chicago at Chicago Avenue and LaSalle Street.

The pair returned home famous and with ambitious plans for a similar campaign in America, which was then praised as "a vast business enterprise, organized and conducted by businessmen who put their money into it on business principles for the purpose of saving souls."

Above all, Moody wished to reach the mass of people who never went to church. Seeing a need for a new kind of Christian

worker, a "gap man" able to bridge the gulf between the regular clergy and the lower classes of society, he founded the Moody Bible Institute in 1896 as a missionary training school, then continued his cross-country evangelical tours until he died of a heart attack in 1899. At his death, a *Chicago Tribune* editor commented, "It was Chicago which found him and then in due time gave him to the rest of the world."

Today the institute, on North LaSalle Street, has an enrollment of fourteen hundred and is one of the largest Bible-training schools on the globe. Through its curriculum and various operations—outreach programs, a radio station, the *Moody Monthly,* and the Moody Press—it is a living extension of Dwight Moody seeking to bring the Word to the world.

Dwight L. Moody (1837–99). From its humble beginnings as a Sunday school to its contemporary status as a world-class religious institution, the Moody Bible Institute stands as a monument to the vision of Dwight Moody.

THE BUILDING OF A GREAT TEMPLE
ALONG THE NORTH SHORE

The Bahá'í House of Worship is a familiar Chicago-area landmark, an imposing domed structure just off Lake Michigan in Wilmette that attracts some two hundred thousand visitors a year, but its history is not so well known.

Completed and dedicated in 1953, the building is an expression of the Bahá'í faith, which originated in Iran in 1844 when Mírzá 'Ali-Muhammad, said to be a direct descendant of the prophet Muhammad, proclaimed himself a new messiah. As the Bahá'u'lláh, the Glory of God, he preached universal peace, equality of the sexes, compulsory education, and a common international language. His writings, more than one hundred books of poetry and prayers, now form the scriptures of the faith. Branded a traitor by traditional Moslems, Bahá'u'lláh died in a prison in Palestine in 1892, but his son, 'Abdu'l-Bahá, carried his teachings to the Mideast, Europe, and eventually the United States.

The Bahá'í religion was introduced to Chicago by a missionary who came to the Columbian Exposition in 1893. One of his converts was Thornton Chase, a local insurance salesman and Civil War veteran, who then sought other converts. Small Bahá'í groups soon formed in Chicago and Kenosha, Wisconsin.

Answering the Bahá'u'lláh's desire to erect worthy Bahá'í houses of worship on every continent, local adherents pooled their resources and bought the Wilmette site in 1906, and a symbolic groundbreaking ceremony was conducted in 1912 by 'Abdu'l-Bahá himself.

Designs for the building were presented by leading architects during a national Bahá'í convention in New York. The winning design was that of the French-Canadian Louis Bourgeois, and construction began in September 1920.[1] Work progressed slowly as funds became available from Bahá'í followers around the world and specially developed materials, such as the panels made of quartz and white cement at the John J. Earley studios in Washington, D.C., were shipped in.

Completed in 1953, the "Temple of Light" envisioned by Bourgeois is an intricately decorated domed building of concrete, glass, and steel. The number nine, the Bahá'í symbol of unity, is the dominant architectural motif. The structure is nine-sided, each pylon is 45 feet tall, and the dome rises to a height of 135 feet. Eighteen steps lead to the main floor, and there are nine entrances to the main hall. By night, twenty-seven floodlamps mounted on nine poles bathe the entire building with light. On the pylons are emblems of the world's major religions: the Jewish Star of David, the Christian cross, the star and crescent of Islam, and, surprisingly, the swastika, which, of course, has come to be indelibly associated with Hitler and the Nazis but is also the ancient symbol of the Hindus, Buddhists, and American Indians. Nine inscriptions are carved above entrances to the temple,[2] nine inscriptions appear in alcoves within the temple.[3] In May 1978, the temple was placed on the National Register of Historic Places.

"It is the first new idea in architecture since the thirteenth century," said H. Van Buren Magonigle, onetime president of the New York chapter of the American Institute of Architects. In keeping with Bahá'í's goal of world harmony, the structure incorporates contrasting styles from many lands into its architectural scheme: Arabic and Egyptian as well as Gothic, Greek, and Romanesque.

A Bahá'í service, incorporating devotions from the world's major religions, is held every Sunday afternoon. Other Bahá'í services, including a simple fifteen-minute wedding ceremony popular even among non-Bahá'í's, are held either in the surrounding gardens or in a room under the main hall. Through the years interfaith conferences, concerts, and "Family of Man" programs seeking religious harmony while respecting sectarian differences have been held here.

The Bahá'í faith—which has no clergy or hierarchy but instead is headed in each country by an elected nine-member National Spiritual Assembly and overall by a nine-member Universal House of Justice based in Haifa, Israel—has spread to 166 independent countries and 48 dependent territories.[4] Of its more than 5 million adherents, 110,000 reside in the United States. Some 1,300 of them are in the Chicago area and include former Protestants, Catholics, Jews, agnostics, and atheists.

To them and to their fellow Bahá'í's throughout the world, the domed house of worship dominating the lakeshore at Wilmette Harbor stands as an enduring symbol of peace, hope, and the unity of humankind.

Notes

1. Bourgeois actually started working on his plan as early as 1909. Finally, in 1917, he created the image of a bell-shaped temple. After many years of frustration and hard work, his plan was unanimously accepted by delegates from Bahá'í communities throughout North America.
2. "[The] earth is but one country, and mankind its citizens"; "the best beloved of all things in My sight is Justice; turn not away therefrom if thou desires Me"; "My love is My stronghold; he that entereth therein is safe and secure"; "Breathe not the sins of others so long as thou art thyself a sinner"; "Thy heart is My home; sanctify it for My descent"; "I have made death a messenger of joy to thee. Wherefore dost thou grieve?"; "Make mention of Me on My earth, that in My heaven I may remember thee"; "O rich ones on earth! The poor in your midst are My trust; guard ye My trust"; "The source of all learning is the knowledge of God, exalted be His Glory."
3. "All the Prophets of God proclaim the same faith"; "Religion is a radiant light and an impregnable stronghold"; "Ye are the fruits of one tree, and the leaves of one branch"; "So powerful is unity's light that it can illumine the whole earth"; "Consort with the followers of all religions with friendliness"; "O Son of Being! Thou art My lamp and My light is

Bahá'í Temple, Wilmette (photo by June Skinner Sawyers). Louis Bourgeois' Temple of Light remains an enduring Chicago-area landmark.

in thee"; "O Son of Being! Walk in My statues for love of Me"; "Thy Paradise is My love; thy heavenly home is reunion with Me"; "The light of a good character surpasseth the light of the sun."

4. The Bahá'í faith encourages the following rules: fostering of good character, eradication of prejudice, achieving balance between the spiritual and the practical, development of the unique talents of each individual, equality of men and women, and universal education.

Select historic sites

- *Bahá'í Temple*. Linden Avenue, Wilmette, Illinois 60091; 708-256-4400. Open daily throughout the year between October 1 to April 30 from 10 A.M. to 5 P.M.; from May 1 through September 30 from 10 A.M. to 10 P.M. Group tours may be arranged by contacting the House of Worship Activities Office at 708-853-2300.

A RED HAT FOR CARDINAL MUNDELEIN

Because he was the first cardinal in America west of the Alleghenies, Archbishop George William Mundelein, returning to Chicago from Rome on May 11, 1924, after being elevated to that rank by Pope Pius XI, was greeted by a princely welcome the moment he stepped off the platform at the Baltimore and Ohio station at West Fifty-fifth and South Leavitt Streets.

As his special train arrived, a cheering crowd quickly surrounded it. Waving to the throng in appreciation, the prelate was escorted by detectives in long coats, striped trousers, and top hats into a car bearing his new cardinal's coat of arms. Led by Mayor William E. Dever, a colorful and festive motorcade and parade—with marching bands and representatives from various civic and church groups—then took him to Holy Name Cathedral at State and Superior Streets.

Lining the streets from the train station to the cathedral were crowds of smiling faces representing all creeds, nationalities, and religious persuasions. One particularly emotional young man, perched on a tall sign on West Fifty-fifth Street, swung his arms about and yelled so forcefully that he fell backward to the ground, then arose as if nothing had happened and began cheering again. Police officer Patrick Kelly, on duty on the parade route, was so moved that he left his post and jumped on the running board of the cardinal's car to shake the prelate's hand.

At the cathedral main altar Cardinal Mundelein's first act was to give his blessing to the various groups who had gathered for the occasion, among them young men—the future of the Catholic clergy—from Saint Patrick's, Saint Mel's, De La Salle, Saint Ignatius, and other Catholic high schools; frock-coated gentlemen and gowned ladies of an older generation; and ranks of priests, brothers, and nuns.

In his address during the benediction service, Mundelein said: "It was forty years ago that I went to see the first cardinal of the American church, but his lips were still and his great red hat lay at his feet. For he was dead." Then, obviously referring to his relatively youthful age of fifty-two, he said, "But the first cardinal of the western portion of this country comes to you in the flower of his youth, with strength and energy."

At the public reception attended by five thousand that night at the Auditorium Theatre, the cardinal delivered the pope's message to Chicago—"You have done great things, and we are grateful"—and encouraged the United States to take its place as a leader of nations in "gentlemanly conduct and brotherly love."

Even before he became a cardinal, Mundelein had earned the city's esteem during the nine years that he exercised the spiritual, charitable, civic, and educational aspects of his office as head of the Chicago Roman Catholic archdiocese. When he became archbishop in 1915, he was given one of the largest church territories to govern (its physical properties alone were estimated then to be worth in excess of $100 million). But Mundelein, then at forty-three the youngest in the nation to hold the office of archbishop, proved equal to the task. "The church certainly gained one of the clearest-headed businessmen in the country, and the business world lost one when George Mundelein became a priest," noted one banker.

As a moral leader, Mundelein did not hesitate to speak out on public issues. On the eve of World War II, he publicly took Adolf Hitler to task, triggering formal protests by the Nazi government to the Vatican, and earning him praise from the pope instead of the censure demanded by the Nazis.

As an educator, Mundelein sought to establish a Catholic center of higher learning for Chicago and the Midwest composed of Saint Mary of the Lake Seminary and a cluster of Catholic colleges. To that end he had the seminary built in Area, northwest of Chicago, and though his dream of a great Catholic university in the Midwest never fully materialized, the predominantly Protestant residents of Area did vote to rename their town Mundelein.

The archbishop died quietly in his sleep in October 1939, at Saint Mary of the Lake. As at the triumphal welcome the city gave him when he became a cardinal, Chicago again turned out to honor Mundelein, this time with a vast funeral procession through downtown streets, with all of the city's 3.5 million residents named honorary pallbearers. A private party then brought him to his final resting place on his beloved seminary campus.

POLITICAL BEDFELLOWS

William Hale Thompson (1867–1944).
The flamboyant Thompson captured in
an unusually dignified mood.

THE DAY THE MAYOR FIRED THE POLICE DEPARTMENT

On the morning of March 22, 1861, Chicagoans woke up to find they were without a police force. Hours before, as the city, then the ninth largest in the nation, slept, Mayor John Wentworth had dismissed the entire department in a moment of typically impetuous anger.

Chicago by then had earned an unenviable reputation as a center of crime, filth, and corruption. One Chicagoan out of ten, wrote historian Finis Farr, was engaged in thievery or some other kind of criminal activity. Many of the city's unsavory goings-on were centered in a shabby area north of the Chicago River known as the Sands. Here, in tottering shanties and hovels, jerry-built gambling dens, saloons, and brothels, a horde of pickpockets, gamblers, and prostitutes thrived. Robberies were commonplace, murders a fact of life. The crime that was so rampant here spilled out into the rest of the city, prompting many citizens to arm themselves. "The city is at the mercy of the criminal classes," the *Chicago Tribune* said.

Within weeks of his first term as mayor, in 1857–58, Wentworth issued an ultimatum to the denizens of the Sands: Clean up your act or pack up and leave. Accustomed to getting their own way and unimpressed by the impertinence of the man from New Hampshire, they laughingly dismissed the warning as the fanciful rambling of a naive political outsider.

But the mayor had a trick up his sleeve. After scheduling a dogfight on the outskirts of town to lure the area's adult males away, he marched into the Sands leading a column of thirty police officers and a bailiff bearing writs of removal. "Move your furniture into the street," he bellowed at the disbelieving residents. "You have a half hour!" Shanties were then pulled down or set on fire.

Wentworth's unconventional ways, however, proved to be his own undoing when he turned them against his own police force during his second term, in 1860–61. The police in those days,

according to Virgil W. Peterson in *Barbarians in Our Midst*, were a poorly organized and poorly trained ragtag group equipped only with canes in the daytime and batons at night. When an officer made an arrest, his only means of transporting the supposed lawbreaker to the police station was a wheelbarrow, and usually a borrowed one at that. One thing the officers felt proud of, though, was their uniforms—short blue coats, blue caps with gold braid and brass stars. Wentworth, however, considered the uniforms an extravagance, and he ordered the men to discard them and instead wear a simple leather badge on their caps.

To make matters worse, Wentworth, citing economic reasons, reduced the number of men on the already undermanned force. Eventually, according to Peterson, the department was reduced to a captain, six lieutenants, and fifty patrolmen. The cutback prompted citizens to clamor for more and better police protection. Wentworth's response was to impose a citywide curfew. Anyone found wandering the streets after midnight would be arrested, he warned. Unfortunately, according to the *Tribune*, the first victims of this dubious attempt at crime prevention were three private detectives who had been hired by concerned merchants to guard their shops. As the public uproar intensified, the state legislature intervened and established an independent board of police commissioners. Furious at what he saw as a personal affront, the mayor vowed revenge.

At 2:00 on the morning of March 22, 1861, Wentworth assembled the officers at City Hall, railed against the new system, and dismissed the entire force. For twenty-four hours the city was without police protection. Criminal elements, however, failed to take advantage of the situation—probably because it was over before most people knew it—and the new police commissioners hastily appointed new officers and got many of the dismissed policemen to sign up again.

Soon afterward came the next mayoral election, and Wentworth realistically chose not to seek reelection. Instead he later won a seat as a United States representative, which he had been before becoming mayor. After a total of six terms in Congress, he spent some time in farming and real estate and began work on a massive Wentworth genealogy project. He died on October 16, 1888, best remembered perhaps as the mayor who took on an entire police force—and lost.

Select historical site

- *"Long John" Wentworth memorial.* Rosehill Cemetery, 5800 North Ravenswood. Wentworth is one of twelve mayors buried at Rosehill. Befitting his name, "Long John's" seventy-two-foot obelisk is the cemetery's tallest monument.

THE FIRST WARD BALL

Around the turn of the century, Chicago's First Ward had the dubious honor of being the wealthiest and most sinful in the city. The ward—then extending roughly from the Chicago River south to Twenty-ninth Street and from the lake west to the river's south branch—encompassed the central business area and the red-light districts, variously known as the Levee, Hair-Trigger Block, Little Cheyenne, Gamblers' Alley, Bad Lands, Bedbug Row, and Hell's Half Acre. Here, amid its prosperous stores, fine office buildings, and handsome churches as well as brothels, gin mills, dime hotels, and free-lunch saloons, the city's elite rubbed elbows with pimps, prostitutes, thieves, and gamblers.

Reigning over it all for nearly half a century were the ward's two aldermen (each ward then had two aldermen), Michael "Hinky Dink" Kenna and John "Bathhouse" Coughlin.

Of the two "lords of the Levee," to borrow the title of the same name by historians Lloyd Wendt and Herman Kogan, Kenna was the tight-lipped and humorless one, a lifelong teetotaler who preferred to remain in the background, while Coughlin was the epitome of the back-slapping, loud-mouthed machine politician who loved the company of the prizefighters and the jockeys, the senators and the merchants who patronized the ward's establishments.

Despite almost limitless access to easy money—culled from outright fraud and the sale of protection from arrest to the madams—the two men were always looking for ways to raise additional funds. One autumn day in Hinky Dink's saloon, the Workingman's Exchange at Clark and Van Buren Streets, the aldermen were lamenting the demise of the annual benefit party for "Lame Jimmy," the handicapped pianist and violinist at Carrie Watson's, one of the city's most expensive brothels. Coughlin estimated that a lavish ball held in a large venue, say the Seventh Regiment Armory at 3401 South Wentworth Avenue, could produce thousands of dollars for the Democratic organization. Thus was the First Ward Ball born.

To say that the first ball, in 1897, was a success would be an understatement. As soon as invitations were issued, brewers, wine merchants, and distillers offered supplies of liquor at discount prices. Waiters, anticipating huge tips, eagerly paid five dollars each for the right to serve at the event. Police officers and politicians came and mingled with pickpockets and common criminals. Prostitutes, in scanty but expensive costume gowns, arrived with police escorts. At the stroke of midnight the corpulent Coughlin—attired in a green dress suit, mauve vest, pale pink gloves, yellow pumps, and silken top hat and flanked by Minna and Ada Everleigh, the brothel queens—led the ball's grand march. "All the business houses are here, all the big people," boasted Hinky Dink. "Chicago ain't no sissy town."

In later years the ball proved so popular it had to be held in the larger confines of the Coliseum on South Wabash Avenue, where thousands danced and drank into the night. In 1907 one reporter counted 2 bands, 200 waiters, and 100 policemen at the ball and estimated that 20,000 guests drank 10,000 quarts of champagne and 35,000 quarts of beer.

As the ball came to symbolize the "wickedness" of life in Chicago, reformers, and there were many, denounced the affair as "a Saturnalian orgy," "a bawdy Dionysian festival," "a carnival of evil," where liquor flowed, tempers flared, and violence often erupted. One year when the *Chicago Tribune* announced that it would print the names of those attending the ball, the revelers came anyway, many of them discreetly masked.

By 1909 the forces of reform were reaching their peak, and the political winds were blowing in their favor. As evangelists led thousands to march in antivice parades in the red-light district and to pray at brothel steps, demands from religious and civic leaders to ban the ball and clean up the First Ward grew louder and more insistent. In 1910, when the Roman Catholic archbishop threatened to denounce the ball from the pulpits of Catholic churches, Mayor Fred Busse finally issued a ban against it.

With the demise of the First Ward Ball came further reforms. On October 24, 1911, the new mayor, Carter Harrison II, closed down the Everleigh Club—the city's most famous brothel—and soon thereafter State's Attorney John E. Wayman ordered that all the brothels and gambling dens in the Levee be raided until they closed down for good. It was the end of a notorious era in the ward and the city.

THE SHOOTING OF THE MAYOR

Carter Henry Harrison I and the city he liked to call "my bride" were made for each other. Full of hope and vigor, he came here as a young man from his native Kentucky. And it was here that he rose to prominence by winning the city's highest office, not once but five separate times. It was also here, on an October night in 1893, that he died, at age sixty-eight, the victim of an assassin's bullet.

Harrison was very much a man of his time. As with his adopted city, he was genial, robust, and tolerant, a larger-than-life figure who embodied the best and the worst that the burgeoning metropolis had to offer. He was also the most contrary of men. Of aristocratic stock (President William Henry Harrison was a relative), he was born in a humble log cabin but later, as mayor, lived in an elegant mansion in the most elite part of town. An honest man, his laissez-faire attitude as mayor helped create, in the words of one critic, "the Gomorrah of the West." A popular politician, he was despised by reformers and the press alike. A worldly sophisticate, he also appealed to the common citizen.

Harrison was first elected mayor in 1879, then reelected in 1881, 1883, and 1885 (mayoral terms then were for two years). He ran again, as an independent Democrat, in 1891 but lost to Republican Hempstead Washburne. Washburne served only one term. As the city prepared for the 1893 World's Columbian Exposition, held in honor of the four hundredth anniversary of the discovery of America by Christopher Columbus, the citizens began looking for someone to symbolize their verve, celebrate their entrepreneurial success, and exude the spirit of the New World. The Republican candidate, Samuel W. Allerton, was perfectly respectable but lacked the necessary spunk. Aware of the nationwide attention the city was about to get, Chicagoans went to the polls and for the fifth time chose the dapper Harrison as their leader.

In late October 1893, Harrison addressed a gathering of big-city mayors who had come to the fair from around the country. Proclaiming a new future he claimed to see on the horizon, he ironically said, "I intend to live for more than a half-century, and at the end of that half-century London will be trembling lest Chicago shall surpass her."

He returned home that evening to his mansion at the southwest corner of Ashland Avenue and Jackson Boulevard to enjoy a leisurely dinner with his youngest son, William Preston. Another son, Carter Henry II, was still at the fair. After a brief nap, Harrison received a visitor who had gained entry simply by telling a servant that he wished to have a word with the mayor. This was not unusual: The mayor's door was always open to all citizens. The visitor was Patrick Eugene Prendergast, a twenty-five-year-old newspaper carrier who had illusions of becoming the city's corporation counsel even though he was not a lawyer and his only legal "training" consisted of reading a popular legal tome, *Every Man His Own Lawyer*. Approaching the mayor and without saying a word, Prendergast pulled a six-shooter from his overcoat pocket and fired three shots at the mayor.

Hearing the shots, the family coachman raced into the room and saw Prendergast fire a final round at the mayor. The coachman then ran out to get his own revolver, but by the time he returned, Prendergast had vanished. William came in next and found his father lying across the doorway of a pantry passageway, moaning and bleeding profusely. W. S. Chalmers, president of the Allis-Chalmers steel company, who had rushed over from across the street upon hearing the shots and the ensuing commotion, helped William carry the mayor to a sofa. "Chalmers," reportedly said the dying Harrison, "this is death. I am shot over the heart."

Meanwhile, the assassin ran for several blocks, caught a street-car, alighted, and walked to the Desplaines Street police station, where he calmly told the desk sergeant that he had killed the mayor. Later, in a formal statement, Prendergast justified his action by saying: "He deserved to be shot. He did not keep his promise to me."

The assassination cast a pall over the city. "Our Carter," the man who had been a leader to a generation of Chicagoans, was gone. Mourners lined up outside the Harrison mansion into the night, talking, crying, trying to make sense out of a senseless act. At the world's fair, the closing festivities were canceled, putting a mournful end to what had begun as a joyful celebration.

Prendergast was convicted of murder and sentenced to die by hanging. "I had no malice against anyone," he reportedly said as the noose was placed around his neck. The Harrison legacy, however, did not end with the mayor's death. Mirroring his father's political career, Carter Henry Harrison II also served five terms as Chicago's chief executive, establishing a family record unmatched in Chicago political history.

Carter Harrison I (1825–93). From 1879 to 1887, Harrison served four consecutive terms as mayor of Chicago. In 1893 he won an unprecedented fifth term only to be cut down by an assassin's bullet in his Ashland Avenue mansion on a late October evening.

"BIG BILL" AND THE KING

Chicago has had some strange mayoral campaigns, but none was stranger than the 1927 run for a third term by William "Big Bill" Thompson, who had won the office in 1915 and in 1919 but had stayed out of the race in 1923.

Proclaiming an "America First" platform, Thompson promised to rid the city's schools and public library of British propaganda, oust school superintendent William McAndrew for being a "stool pigeon of King George V," and, for good measure, "swat" the king on the "snoot."

McAndrew, a blunt, outspoken New Yorker whom many Chicagoans disliked as an "insolent" outsider, was charged with insubordination, apparently because of a disagreement with the school board concerning the classification of "extra teachers" with largely clerical functions as civil service employees. But he was also perceived as "unpatriotic," and public attention centered instead on his alleged pro-British activities. On August 29, 1927, the school board suspended the superintendent, and a month later he was brought to "trial" before the board.

To support the case against McAndrew, the school board president, J. Lewis Coath, had authorized John J. Gorman, a former United States congressman who was appointed special assistant corporation counsel by Thompson, to comb school textbooks for lies and distortions. After a six-month "study," Gorman, a rabid Anglophobe, concluded that the books in the Chicago public school system were "poisoned" with British dogma and that the British were conquering America "not by shot and shell but by a rain of propaganda."

Thompson also ordered the public library's books examined because Britain had once donated books to the city after the Great Chicago Fire of 1871. For this task, he chose Urbine J. "Sport" Hermann, a close friend and a library board member. Hermann gladly accepted the challenge, promising to burn every book that he considered pro-British. Asked if he was going to seek the aid of an unbiased historian, Hermann replied, "Hell, no! I'll be my own judge, and Mayor Thompson will help me." Although wiser heads prevailed and no books were ever thrown into a patriotic bonfire, Chicago soon gained dubious fame as the book-burning capital of the free world. "Is there no end to absurdity?" the *Chicago Tribune* asked. "Why, it's the craziest thing I ever heard of," cried noted lawyer Clarence Darrow. Head librarian Carl B. Roden then suggested that the so-called pro-British books be placed in a cage and be read under guard only by "mature" historians.

On the first day of his trial, McAndrew was in a rather frivolous mood. Leaning back in his swivel chair as he read a newspaper, particularly the comic pages, the sixty-four-year-old educator hardly listened to the sixteen charges being leveled against him.

As the trial dragged on, Chicagoans were not quite sure whether to take the proceedings seriously or, along with the rest of the world, laugh at a ridiculous spectacle. Sedition was being taught in public schools, Mayor Thompson charged. American schoolchildren were being taught that George Washington and other heroes of the Revolution were traitors and that members of the Continental Congress were "quarrelsome lawyers and mechanics," cried Thompson's allies. McAndrew, they also said, had conspired with Charles C. Merriam and others at the University of Chicago—that "stronghold of King George"—to "destroy love of America in the hearts of children." Other accusations were directed at the American Library Association, which at one time was headed by a Canadian, as being an agent of British propaganda.

Speaking at one of the trial sessions, Charles Edward Russell, a New York writer and lecturer, claimed that the most dangerous organization in the world was the English Speaking Union. "The world is threatened now with the greatest menace—the advance of the Anglo-Saxon," Russell said. Others expressed the fear that Cecil Rhodes, the founder of the Rhodes scholarship program, was seeking to unite all the English-speaking peoples under one flag—the Union Jack. And some even talked of an impending war between Britain and the United States.

After twenty-seven hearings, one hundred witnesses, and more than six thousand pages of testimony, the board of education voted on March 21, 1928, to remove McAndrew from his office, even though his term had already expired the previous month. The verdict was given in absentia because six weeks into the trial, McAndrew had refused to attend the sessions, calling them a "burlesque."

McAndrew appealed, and in December 1929, Judge Hugo Pam overturned the verdict and dropped all charges, citing insufficient grounds for the insubordination charge and calling the pro-British accusations "improper."

By then Thompson had won the mayoral election, staying in office until 1931, when he lost by an overwhelming margin to Anton Cermak. That defeat effectively put an end to the political career of Chicago's last Republican mayor. After running unsuccessfully for governor in 1936 and for mayor again in 1939, Thompson died at age seventy-four on March 19, 1944.

A MARTYR COMES HOME TO REST

The funeral train sped northward from Florida under ominous winter skies, bearing the body of Anton J. Cermak, the unschooled Czech immigrant boy who had become the mayor of Chicago.

For nineteen days Cermak had wavered between life and death. He had gone to Miami to discuss federal aid for Chicago with President-elect Franklin D. Roosevelt. There was talk, too, that the scrappy mayor would be offered a position in the Roosevelt cabinet. But on February 15, 1933, Giuseppe Zangara, a frustrated immigrant from southern Italy, changed all that with his gun. Roosevelt was his prey, but Cermak—seated next to the president in an open car—became his unintended victim.

On Wednesday, March 8, Cermak's bronze casket was greeted at the Twelfth Street station by somber-faced men in black coats, as the broad-shouldered city he had called home pulled down its shades and prepared to mourn its fallen son.

An escort drawn from the Democratic County Central Committee, the city council, the mayor's cabinet, and the various city departments marched behind the black hearse as it made its way from the station to the Cermak home, a modest two-story brick structure at 2348 South Millard Avenue.

There the mayor's cronies gathered around his coffin, offering words of comfort to the bereaved family (a widower since 1928, Cermak was survived by three daughters). There, too, the people of the neighborhood, many of whom remembered Cermak as a hard-working precinct captain, gathered to pay their respects. Touched by the crowds that came, the family kept the house open to visitors through the night.

On the second day the casket was taken to City Hall, where during the next twenty-four hours more than seventy-five thousand came, forming lines four, then two, abreast and then walking singly down flower-bedecked aisles past the casket, a wreath of roses, carnations, and orchids resting on it. A single light shone on the slain mayor's ashen but serene face, visible under a glass cover. Several women fainted, many wept openly, and some tried to throw themselves on the casket.

At 10 A.M. the next day an open Army caisson drawn by six black horses carried the casket to the Chicago Stadium amid the sound of carillons, bugles, and muffled drums and past crowds of about five hundred thousand. Marching in the procession were thirty thousand mourners, led by marshals, police and fire units, various infantry groups, veterans, state legislators, commissioners, the band of the then predominantly Czech Harrison High School, and a delegation of fifty-two silk-hatted men representing different nationalities.

At the stadium the casket, flanked by an honor guard of seven soldiers, was set in the middle of a cruciform garden of flowers. With some twenty-three thousand people in attendance, nonsectarian rites were held by a minister, a priest, and a rabbi. Then for a full minute at noon, as taps was played, the whole city paused in silent tribute. Transportation stopped, business in the State Street stores ceased, and in the city's hotels telephones rang unanswered, elevator services halted, and guests in the lobbies stood quietly, their heads bared.

Later that afternoon fifty thousand people gathered for burial services at Bohemian National Cemetery, 5300 North Crawford Avenue (now Pulaski Road), where the casket, draped with the flags of the United States and Chicago, rested during the ceremony on a velvet-covered stone in front of the family mausoleum.

The three-day tribute later led Cermak's biographer Alex Gottfried to remark, "In death Cermak was honored more than in life." As the city's first foreign-born and non-Irish or Anglo-Saxon mayor, he was often the butt of ethnic jokes ("Where's your pushcart, Tony?"), and his lack of personal warmth stood in sharp contrast to the rabble-rousing, bigger-than-life ways of William Hale Thompson, his predecessor.

But in his own quiet way Cermak got things done, forging a new coalition that brought together the city's various ethnic and interest groups and giving the people during his two short years in office decent and efficient government. Already admired for his humanitarianism and courage, Cermak in his martyr's death well deserved the funeral that has been called one of the most spectacular ever seen in Chicago.

DISASTERS AND EVENTS

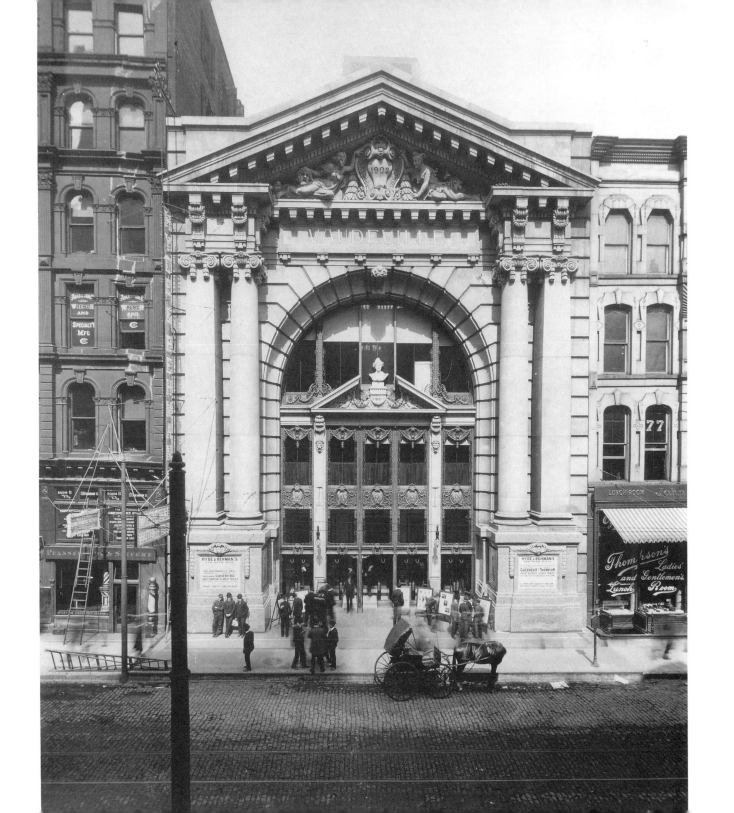

Iroquois Theater building, circa 1905 (photo by Branes-Crosby. Chicago Historical Society, ICHi–19138). A devastating fire broke out at the Iroquois Theater on a cold December afternoon in 1903, claiming more than five hundred victims, many of them children. Within a few years the theater reopened under a new name, Hyde and Behman's New Music Hall. Later the Oriental Theater (now demolished), one of the last of the Loop's grand movie palaces, stood here.

THE SHIPWRECK OF THE *LADY ELGIN*

The news was devastating. The *Lady Elgin,* a one-thousand-ton sidewheel excursion steamer carrying about four hundred people, had sunk in Lake Michigan off Winnetka after being rammed by the schooner *Augusta* on a stormy September night.

As dawn broke, wreckage could be seen from the bluffs above the beach. Survivors clung to scattered debris as waves crashed over their heads, but many were carried away by a strong undertow. The final death toll of 297 made the shipwreck the greatest disaster in the recorded history of Lake Michigan.

The trip began innocently enough. The passengers—most of them Irish members of the Union Guard, a Milwaukee paramilitary organization, on a fundraising trip to Chicago and back—were in good spirits as the *Lady Elgin* headed back north shortly after midnight on September 8, 1860. Fog shrouded the lake, a heavy rain was falling, and lightning flashed overhead. But inside the steamer, protected from the weather, couples danced to the strains of Irish airs.

Shortly after 2 A.M. the dimly lit schooner *Augusta,* headed for Chicago with a load of Michigan lumber, crashed into the *Lady Elgin,* her bow slashing the steamer amidships. Unaware of the extent of the damage, the *Augusta*'s skipper, Captain D. M. Malott, swung his ship alongside her and, peering through the darkness, offered assistance. "Shall I stand by?" he shouted through his megaphone in the howling wind. Captain Jack Wilson of the *Lady Elgin* reportedly replied, "No. Proceed on your course." Another account, though, suggests that Malott, hearing no response, concluded that no serious damage was done and sailed away.

Assessing the situation, Wilson first tried to plug the hole in his ship with mattresses stripped from their bunks and then had the two hundred head of cattle in the hold driven overboard—but in vain.

As word of the disaster spread, area residents rushed to the scene on foot, on horseback, and in carriages. There were many gallant attempts to rescue the victims. Edward W. Spencer, a divinity student at Garrett Biblical Institute, was one of the first to arrive. Diving repeatedly into the frigid, stormy water, he saved seventeen lives. The feat, however, so overtaxed him that he had to drop out of school and retire in frail health to Colorado.

In the early morning light some fifty survivors, including Wilson, were seen hanging on to what was once the *Lady Elgin*'s hurricane deck. But the deck disintegrated less than three hundred feet from shore as hundreds of bystanders watched helplessly. Only thirty in that group reached safety.

Inquests found Wilson, who died trying to save others, and his crew without blame but mildly censured the second mate of the *Augusta* for failing to notify Malott as soon as the *Lady Elgin* was sighted, twenty minutes before the collision. A minority report by two jurors, however, reprimanded the captain and crew of the *Lady Elgin* for "insufficiency of the lookouts," citing a law that required two full-time lookouts for ships of the *Lady Elgin*'s class.

The shipwreck helped to reform U.S. maritime law. Uniform lighting and passage codes were imposed on all vessels, even the smallest. At least one historian, Charles M. Scanlan, speculated that because many of those who perished with the *Lady Elgin* were the cream of Milwaukee's Irish population, that city, barring the disaster, might have been predominantly Irish, not German. And the tragic story acquired a life of its own, spread far and wide by the sentimental song "Lost on the *Lady Elgin*." Written by a Chicago printer named Henry C. Work, the song was heard in theaters and saloons, in homes and street corners across the land and remained popular through the Civil War years.

As for the *Augusta* and her crew, they, too, later perished in storms in the Great Lakes—the *Augusta* after it had been renamed the *Colonel Cook*; Malott and crew when they were manning another ship, the *Mahor*.

The saga of the *Lady Elgin* continues to this day. In 1989, diver Harry Zych discovered remnants of the famous ship off the waters of Waukegan. He sought to claim ownership of the ship's contents, even going so far as to establish the Lady Elgin Foundation. Meanwhile, the state insisted it was only proper that the remains belong to the people of Illinois. After a four-year legal battle, the state was rewarded ownership of the wreck in September 1993.

Meanwhile, several weeks earlier, on August 11, 1993, the last piece of the puzzle was solved when another diver discovered the missing stern of the ship off Wilmette. The *Lady Elgin*, it seemed, had no more secrets to divulge.

# THE *EASTLAND:* TRAGEDY IN THE CHICAGO RIVER

Oh the ship, she's rolled o'er on the river's muddy floor
Eight hundred thirty-five would not survive.
With a fatal list to port, led the captain to report
That the *Eastland* she would sail the lakes no more.

"The *Eastland,*" Tom and Chris Kastle[1]
(Privateer Publishing © 1985)

One of the greatest disasters in Chicago history occurred on July 24, 1915, on the placid Chicago River, when more than eight hundred people aboard the *Eastland* lost their lives in shallow water only a few feet from the river's edge.[2]

On an overcast Saturday morning some nine thousand workers of the Western Electric Company were looking forward to their annual company outing to Michigan City, Indiana. Because it had so many employees, Western Electric had arranged for them to be transported by several steamers, departing at various intervals. The ships were the *Theodore Roosevelt*, the *Petoskey*, the *Racine*, the *Rochester*, and the *Eastland*. Ultimately, more than two thousand people would board the *Eastland*.

The *Eastland* was moored just west of the Clark Street bridge. The vast majority of the employees were Polish and Bohemian workers. Many came early to avoid the crush, boarding the steamer and carrying with them an assortment of baskets, boxes, and other packages. Although the mood was festive, some people had sensed that the *Eastland* would be too crowded and had moved to another steamer, the *Theodore Roosevelt*, which was scheduled to depart one-half hour later.

The tragic events that followed happened in quick succession. As the *Eastland* prepared to depart, the passengers began to congregate on the port side of the ship to view a passing tugboat and to wave good-bye to family and friends standing on the dock. When the engines were turned on, the boat started to tilt. Although the captain and crew tried their best to keep the ship upright, the weight of the passengers on the port side doomed the ship. As water from the Chicago River poured into the port windows and the open gangway doors, the ship rolled over on its side. It was precisely 7:23 A.M. when the *Eastland* capsized.

Amid screaming and shouting, passengers fell into the river. Many were rescued by bystanders. But the river's current and the subsequent panic led to the loss of many lives. Below deck passengers perished as water rushed into the hull. Others were crushed to death.

Several hundred people, mostly from the upper deck, survived by scrambling over the *Eastland's* starboard rail and frantically hung on for dear life. People, still inside, could be heard pounding on the walls until a hole was cut on the exposed side of the ship and they were rescued. Some bystanders stood helplessly on the dock or in nearby excursion vessels. Other people threw boxes and various objects that would float to the passengers who found themselves flailing about in the river. Fire department tugboats responded immediately, as did Coast Guard vessels and private boats.

Word of the disaster spread quickly. Chicago hospitals sent doctors and nurses—anyone who could help—to the scene. The decks of the *Theodore Roosevelt* and, across the river, the Reid-Murdoch warehouse were turned into a temporary hospital and morgue. Later, the much larger Second Regiment Armory on Washington Boulevard served the same purpose.

People gathered on the bridges and along the river docks to view the grisly rescue work. By late afternoon, the crowd numbered in the thousands. For the most part, they were quiet and respectful, too shocked or numb to speak, able only to look on in

THE EASTLAND DISASTER.
CHICAGO. JULY, 24 - 1915.

Eastland disaster, 24 July 1915 (Chicago Historical Society, ICHi–02033).
More than eight hundred people died when the *Eastland* capsized in
the Chicago River.

muted and horrific helplessness. Meanwhile, relief work continued for the better part of a week or more, involving hundreds of people. Emergency morgues were set up around the downtown area. Free inoculations to prevent typhoid were given.

Headlines proclaimed the tragedy in stark black-and-white letters. A total of 835 people lost their lives; ironically, all of the crew members survived.[3] An overwhelming majority of the victims were young people, many children. The western suburbs were hardest hit, since most of the employees lived in Cicero. Twenty-two families, for example, perished, and some 660 families lost at least one member, according to Great Lakes historian Dwight Boyer.

The inevitable investigations began, many of them involving heated discussions with unions. The Chicago Federation of Labor, for example, had warned as much as one year earlier that a tragedy was waiting to happen because the excursions leaving Chicago were often overcrowded. Others charged the federal government, which was responsible for steamboat inspections, with gross criminal negligence, and hundreds filed claims against the *Eastland* and its owners.

In August 1915, an Illinois grand jury indicted the four head officers of the Saint Joseph-Chicago Steamship Company, the *Eastland*'s owners, as well as the ship's captain and chief engineer. A further charge of manslaughter was issued against the president of the Indiana Transportation Company, which chartered the vessel to Western Electric. Federal indictments followed in September.

But the charges met a dead end in early 1916, when a federal district judge determined that the accident occurred outside federal jurisdiction and that the evidence failed to establish probable cause. Insisting that "the dead cannot be restored to life," he then dismissed all charges of criminal negligence.

The final court decision on the *Eastland* tragedy occurred years later, in August 1935, when the U.S. Circuit Court of Appeals upheld a district court ruling that the Saint Joseph-Chicago Steamship Company was not responsible for the 835 deaths.[4] Rather, the court ruled that the company was liable only to the extent of the salvage value of the vessel "and that the responsibility was traced to an engineer who neglected to fill the ballast tanks properly."

On December 15, 1915, the courts disposed of the *Eastland* at public auction to Edward A. Evers. Evers eventually sold the steamer to the government to be converted into a gunboat. Redesigned and renamed the *U.S.S. Wilmette*, the steamer served the Great Lakes as a training ship for naval reserves. Finally, in 1946, the government sold the former *Eastland* for scrap.

Notes

1. "The *Eastland*" appears on *Helm's Alee!* (Sextant Music) by Tom and Chris Kastle.

2. Another Great Lakes tragedy involved the "Christmas Tree Ship." The Christmas Tree Ship was a familiar sight in Chicago harbor, and generations of Chicago children looked forward to seeing the ship, with its firs tied to its masts, every Christmas season. From the late nineteenth century until 1935, the Schunemann family of Michigan would load their ship with Christmas trees and make the journey to Chicago in the dead of winter. In November 1912, however, tragedy struck when one of the Christmas ships, the *Rouse Simmons*, went down with its entire crew in Wisconsin waters. A recording of Lee Murdock's "The Christmas Ship" appears on the singer's *Folk Songs of the Great Lakes Region* (Depot).

3. Eight hundred twelve bodies had been recovered and identified; an additional twenty-three people died later. Other sources say 844 people perished.

4. Some argue that drastic safety measures imposed on passenger ships as a result of the sinking of the British ship *Titanic* in 1912 led to the *Eastland* tragedy. Steamship operators believed that a law ordering lifeboats for every passenger would create top-heavy ships, making them likely to capsize and almost guaranteeing disaster. See George W. Hilton, *Eastland: Legacy of the Titanic* (Stanford, Calif.: Stanford University Press, 1995).

Select historic sites

- *Eastland plaque.* Overlooking the Chicago River at LaSalle Street and Wacker Drive, a small plaque commemorates the 835 people who lost their lives on that fateful day in July 1915.

THE IROQUOIS FIRE

It all started with a small piece of burning paper and a spark of light. Hundreds of children and mothers had gathered at the Iroquois Theater on the bitterly cold winter afternoon of December 30, 1903, to enjoy a holiday musical, *Bluebeard, Jr.*, starring comedian Eddie Foy. Before the day was over, almost six hundred people would perish. The Iroquois fire claimed more casualties than any other in the city's history.[1]

Billed as "absolutely fireproof," the Iroquois had opened only one month earlier—on November 23, 1903.[2] Such a boast was based more on idle wishes than fact, since the theater was not equipped with either an alarm signal or an automatic sprinkling system.

The sold-out matinee was filled with mothers and their children—almost two thousand people. In a prophetic statement before the show, one anxious mother, already late for the performance, walked up a marble staircase with her child and observed, "Gee, what a long stairway to come down in case of fire."

Bluebeard, Jr., was, by all accounts, an extravagant production. Originating at London's Theatre Royal in Drury Lane, it featured a cast of 275 and stunning special effects, including a complex light show and "fairies" that floated over the audience on trolley wires. The first half went smoothly. During the second act, however, something went terribly wrong. Gas lights had apparently ignited a flimsy curtain backstage. A spark of light appeared on one side of the stage. When the audience became noticeably agitated, Foy emerged from the wings to reassure them that everything was under control. "Please keep your seats," he pleaded. "Don't get excited. There's no danger. Take it easy. You'll get out." The theater lights came on. Meanwhile, the orchestra continued to play as the stagehands tried to lower the "fireproof" asbestos curtain. But it wasn't fireproof after all. It stuck halfway and caught fire. By that time, no amount of assurance by Foy or anyone else could

calm the frightened crowd. Loud music by the orchestra was soon drowned out by hysterical screams.

Everything happened so fast. Someone apparently opened a stage door and a rush of wind, fanning the flames, swept heat, smoke, gases, and sheets of fire over the petrified audience. One survivor recalled, years later, the haunting image of turning and seeing people's heads silhouetted against the wall of flames that engulfed the stage and reached as high as the ceiling.

People ran for the exits in hysterics. One escape door was locked; the others could be opened only from the inside. Hundreds suffocated; others were asphyxiated while still seated. Children were separated from their parents in a mad rush to get to the exit doors. Other youngsters were trampled underfoot. Exits that were open were covered by draperies, making it impossible to see in the darkened theater. Worse, the exit signs were unlit. Hundreds died within minutes; as many as two hundred victims were found piled high at one stairway.

Some escaped through the stage door. There are stories of children being picked up and passed along, from hand to hand, over the heads of adults into the safety of the street or of others managing to escape through the crush of people in the lobby.

Then it was over. All that remained was an eerie silence.

On the sidewalks, newsboys hawked the daily paper: "Read all about the great fire!" Horse-drawn wagons and streetcars clogged State Street and disbelieving people, many in a hushed state of shock, stood motionless outside in the frigid air. Bodies were placed on long tables in a restaurant next door to the theater.

The city was stunned. Mayor Carter Harrison II announced that there would be no official New Year's Eve celebrations. Nightclubs were closed.

As always in tragedies of such enormity, there were heroes. An elevator boy, already badly burned, wrapped his hands and head in wet towels and made sure that every one of the female cast members who were still in their backstage dressing rooms escaped safely. Unfortunately, one of the actresses, a young woman named Nellie Reed, was deathly afraid of elevators and insisted on taking the stairs. She was the only member who did not survive.

Another cast member, Frank Holland, still in full costume and makeup, miraculously made his way out of the theater unscathed. He walked down a nearby alley and into the crowds. Dazed, Holland felt somehow compelled to go to State Street until he found himself in front of a jewelry shop. From a back room, he saw a woman in hysterics. It took a moment or two before he realized it was his own mother. When she saw her son she almost fainted. Thinking he had perished in the flames, the poor woman thought she was seeing his ghost.

Nearly 600 people died in the theater and more than 30 succumbed within the following two weeks. Of the victims, 212 were children and 76 of them were under ten years of age. The youngest victim was two-year-old Margaret Dee.

The tragedy of the Iroquois fire led to changes in fire laws for public buildings; unfortunately, the price for such future safety came at a terribly high cost.

Notes

1. Somewhere between 250 to 300 people were killed during the Great Chicago Fire of 1871. The fire's destructive path destroyed the downtown area and much of the North Side. Further, 17,450 buildings were destroyed and 90,000 people were left homeless. For a complete history, see Robert Cromie, *The Great Chicago Fire* (Nashville, Tenn.: Rutledge Hill Press, 1994); and Ross Miller, *American Apocalypse: The Great Fire and the Myth of Chicago* (Chicago: University of Chicago Press, 1990).

2. The now-demolished Oriental Theater stood on the site of the Iroquois Theater on Randolph Street between State and Dearborn.

THE DAY THE TWISTER STRUCK

On a calm and bright Sunday in 1920, a tornado arose from the west and cut a deadly swath through Elgin, Melrose Park, Maywood, and the Northwest Side of Chicago before ending its ruinous journey in Evanston and Wilmette. It killed 103 people, 28 of them in the Chicago area. Melrose Park and Elgin suffered the most damage and casualties.

Palm Sunday fell on March 28 that year, and by noon most of those who had gone to church were already back at home, leisurely perusing their Sunday papers ($.07) for Easter sales (women's oxfords and pumps, $9.75; "hats for every occasion," $10.00; taffeta frocks, then quite popular, $50.00). Many were preparing or having lunch, as children, enjoying the unseasonably warm temperatures, played idly on the sidewalks. At one o'clock, when the sky suddenly turned black and a torrential downpour and hailstorm erupted, the tornado struck.

In Elgin the Reverend J. W. Welch of the First Congregational Church had just closed his sermon with these prophetic words: "Be prepared, for you know not when you will be called." As services ended, the congregation began filing out of the pews, but the fierce rain fell, forcing the parishioners to remain inside. Then a terrific roar punctuated by a sickening thud echoed through the village. The church roof had caved in, showering debris and broken beams upon the parishioners in the church and their children in the basement, where they had been attending Sunday school. Miraculously, only two women and one girl, twelve-year-old Isabel McConnachie, were killed.

Teenager Robert E. Shearin of Norwood Park was riding in a car along Milwaukee Avenue with fellow passenger William Dwyer when he saw the twister hit. "First we were pelted with hailstones as big as pigeon eggs," he told a *Chicago Tribune* reporter. "Then we were soaked in a deluge of rain. We saw a funnel-shaped cloud coming toward us and [we] stopped the machine," referring to their automobile. "Then the strangest sight I ever expect to see met our eyes. We saw shingles flying off roofs. Chickens carried high up in the air. Telephone poles snapped off. Houses shook and collapsed. Birds were flung down in the road with such force that their lives were crushed out."

Amid the turmoil, a few heroes emerged, including one that lived up to its reputation as man's best friend. The McGuinness family lived in Dunning, on the far Northwest Side. Virtually a prairie in those days, the area was one of the hardest hit. Houses on four city blocks were stripped from their foundations and hurled through the air. At Dunning Hospital terror-struck patients screamed uncontrollably as they jumped off their beds and ran wildly through the corridors. At the McGuinness residence on Nottingham Avenue, Rover, a black-and-white German shepherd, darted into the wind-wracked house to find Mrs. McGuinness pinned under heavy beams. In the darkness her anguished screams mingled with the sounds of crashing objects and the wind's unearthly moaning. Rover tugged at the tangled debris until he finally pulled Mrs. McGuinness to safety.

Others were not so lucky. Most died where they sat (in the presumed safety of their living rooms) or ate (a two-year-old was crushed to death by a dining room table). Many were missing for days, and others were left homeless. Parents called out in the wind for lost children. Flung about on the ravaged, wreckage-strewn landscape were the everyday items of life, a surrealistic inventory of the mundane, worthy of a Salvador Dali painting: a piano, its legs up in the air; gas stoves and heaters; iceboxes; kitchen utensils; living room furniture; a frying pan, a steak still in it; a baby buggy; a bloodstained pillow; a dead horse; a picture of Jesus with a palm frond inserted in the frame.

Army, National Guard, and Reserve units patrolled the streets with orders to shoot looters, if necessary. Local chapters of fraternal orders raised funds for the homeless, and the Red Cross provided temporary shelter. Relief trains brought food, clothing, medical supplies, and skilled help to those in need.

It took a few minutes for the death wind suddenly to come and just as quickly go. The sun soon reappeared, as if nothing had happened, and an eerie calm ensued. Yet Nature's arbitrary blow cost twenty-eight Chicago-area residents their lives, injured hundreds more, destroyed thousands of homes, churches, theaters, banks, and other businesses, wreaking more than $10 million in damages. It was one Palm Sunday few would ever want to see again.

THE DAWN OF THE ATOMIC AGE

They came to conduct an experiment, this group of forty-two scientists who gathered on December 2, 1942, in a heavily guarded laboratory under the west stands of the now-demolished Stagg Field on the University of Chicago campus. At precisely 3:25 P.M. that day they achieved the first controlled nuclear chain reaction—and led the world into the Atomic Age.

The head of that group was physicist Enrico Fermi, born in Rome in 1901 to an Italian railroad official. Called by some the most gifted Italian scientist since Galileo, Fermi was essentially a self-taught scholar whose groundbreaking neutron studies at the University of Rome won him the Nobel Prize in physics in 1938. That same year he and his family fled Mussolini's regime and immigrated to the United States. In 1939 Fermi became a professor of physics at Columbia University in New York.

It was a critical time in world history. As Nazi Germany flaunted its military prowess, the Allies felt an urgent need to conduct nuclear research. On November 8, 1940, the United States awarded forty thousand dollars to Columbia University scientists, including Fermi, to conduct atomic research, the first contract of its kind. The following year the government expanded the program and named Arthur Holly Compton, dean of the University of Chicago's physical science department, its director. Compton then placed Fermi in charge of the experiments.

By November 1942, the group had put together a nuclear reactor—a beehive structure consisting of graphite blocks with chunks of uranium embedded in them. The objective was to produce under controlled conditions a self-sustaining fission, or break-down, of—and thus the release of the energy in—the nuclei of uranium atoms.

On December 2, after some false starts and a break for lunch, Fermi and his group resumed their efforts. At 3:20 Fermi gave an order to make an adjustment and made some calculations. Five minutes later he ordered another adjustment and said, "This is going to do it." After a final calculation Fermi, grinning broadly, quietly announced, "The reaction is self-sustaining." A ripple of applause broke the silence.

To celebrate the historic event, one of the scientists opened a bottle of Chianti, and each one present sipped the red wine silently, lost in the private thoughts of the moment. Compton then sent a coded telephone message to President James B. Conant of Harvard University:

The Italian navigator has landed in the New World.

"How were the natives?" asked Conant. "Very friendly," came Compton's reply.

With that milestone accomplished, Fermi moved to Los Alamos, New Mexico, to work on the development of the atomic bomb. On July 16, 1945, the first atomic bomb was exploded in a test at Alamogordo Air Base, New Mexico, and not long afterward President Harry S. Truman ordered the bombings of Hiroshima and Nagasaki. The following year, in 1946, Fermi returned to the University of Chicago as professor in the newly created Institute of Nuclear Physics, later renamed the Enrico Fermi Institute for Nuclear Studies.

Fermi devoted the rest of his years to the study of solid-state, nuclear, and high-energy nuclear physics. A dynamic speaker, his lectures usually attracted standing-room-only crowds. Yet his needs were few, recalled a colleague: "chalk, a blackboard and an eager student." On November 28, 1954, at age fifty-three and still at the peak of his scientific career, the architect of the Atomic Age died of stomach cancer.

Select historic sites

- *Nuclear Energy.* South Ellis Avenue between Fifty-sixth and Fifty-seventh Streets. An eerie work of art by noted English sculptor Henry Moore, *Nuclear Energy* is a permanent reminder of the promise and danger that science can create. The sculpture, in the shape of a mushroom cloud and a human skull, commemorates the first self-sustaining, controlled nuclear chain reaction. Ironically, this most serious of human endeavors took place in a squash court under the bleachers of then Stagg Field. It is now the site of the Regenstein Library.

FIRE AT THE LASALLE HOTEL

Built in 1909, it was called "the most comfortable, modern and safest hotel west of New York City." The LaSalle Hotel, a twenty-two-story structure at LaSalle and Madison Streets, with its ornate walnut-paneled lobby and rooftop garden, was the city's most famous, especially during the pre–World War II years. It was a favorite of the country's elite. The likes of Bertha Palmer—wife of the famous merchant, Potter Palmer—and other "ladies of fashion" loved to dine in its sumptuous Blue Fountain Room. And for many years the state Republican Party kept its headquarters there.

But shortly after midnight on June 5, 1946, a devastating blaze swept through the supposedly fireproof building, reducing its magnificent lobby to a charred cavern, taking the lives of sixty-one people and leaving more than two hundred injured.

The fire, the worst hotel blaze in the city's history, started in an elevator shaft in the Silver Lounge on the ground floor. A former Marine, several guests, and some hotel employees tried to extinguish the flames with seltzer water, but the intense heat soon drove them from the lounge and into the street. Three explosions then shook the Madison Street entrance, and the flames and billowing smoke quickly spread through the mezzanine and to the upper floors.

Many of the guests panicked, but others kept calm and managed to escape to safety. Reportedly as a husband and wife who were trapped on the eighteenth floor leaned out a bathroom window to breathe the clear night air, the wife absentmindedly applied lipstick as they waited to be rescued. Joseph Hearst, who had just returned from China as a *Chicago Tribune* war correspondent, and his wife survived by wrapping wet towels around their faces and finding their way to a fire escape.

In a rash move that could have cost him his life, an orchestra leader dashed back to his dressing room to rescue his thirty-five-hundred-dollar violin. He was later seen wading through water from the fire hoses to salvage musical arrangements valued at several thousand dollars.

Sailors Robert Might and Joseph O'Keefe and three civilians dragged at least twenty-seven people to safety. Two guests came upon a man, a legless amputee, lying unconscious in a hallway and carried him down seven flights of stairs. Anita Blair of El Paso, Texas, twenty-three and blind, calmly donned robe and slippers and followed her seeing-eye dog, Fawn, to a window and down eleven flights on a fire escape.

Lieutenant Colonel Ralph P. Weaver of Kansas City, however, stayed in his room, not emerging until the next morning, unharmed, cleanly shaven, and crisply dressed.

Others were not so fortunate. By 5:30 A.M., City Hall, a few doors away, had been converted into a makeshift first-aid station and morgue where the injured received attention and forty-two of the sixty-one men, women, and children who died were laid out in neat rows.

Most of the deaths were caused by asphyxiation. Many of the victims succumbed because they opened the doors of their rooms, in effect fanning the flames and, disastrously for them, allowing dense smoke to enter.

According to fire marshal John L. Fenn, the fire broke out at 12:15 A.M., but the first alarm was not sounded until 12:35, a precious twenty-minute delay that allowed the blaze to spread. Some investigators said the fire was caused by faulty electrical wiring in a wall of the lounge; others said gas, leaking into the lounge area from newly installed pipes in an adjacent alley, might have been to blame.

Many fire-related regulations now taken for granted grew out of the proposals made in the aftermath of the LaSalle Hotel fire. Radio station executives recommended that all firefighting units be equipped with two-way portable radios (only three fire department vehicles were so equipped). Further, a special mayoral committee proposed that instructions on what to do in case of fire be posted in every hotel room and that every public building constructed of combustible materials be required to have either a sprinkler system or automatic fire alarms. And from an aldermanic group came the idea of a twenty-four-hour emergency system that would assign fire-duty guards to various hotels and other public buildings.

Surviving the fire, the LaSalle Hotel lived on for many more years. Not until July 1976 did it eventually close its fabled doors, and the building was demolished shortly thereafter.

THE ARTS

Glickman's Palace Theatre poster, 1925–26, promoting three plays, "Day and Night," "Hard to Be a Jew," and "The Green Fields," performed by Vilna Troupe, a well-known Yiddish theater company from Lithuania (courtesy Irving Cutler). Elias Glickman, a Russian-born Jewish actor and director, opened Glickman's in 1919 in a building that formerly housed the power facility of the West Chicago Street Railway Co. It was the largest of the legitimate Yiddish theaters of the Maxwell Street area. Glickman's closed in 1931.

Shooting on the Selig Polyscope lot, 1914 (Chicago Historical Society, Daily News Collection, DN–62405). The likes of Charlie Chaplin, Gloria Swanson, Tom Mix, and Ben Turpin made Chicago the film capital of the world dur-

ing the early years of this century. Originally located in Rogers Park, the Selig studio moved in 1907 to larger facilities at Irving Park Road and Western Avenue.

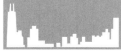

THE CELLULOID DREAM FACTORY

Before Hollywood captured the popular imagination, Chicago enjoyed a brief reign as film capital of the world, from 1907 to 1917.[1] Two of the leading studios were Essanay Film Manufacturing Company and Selig Polyscope Company, and they attracted the top actors and actresses of the day, including Gloria Swanson, Francis X. Bushman, Wallace Beery, Lewis Stone, and a young Englishman named Charlie Chaplin.

The new industry also lured some of the country's finest writers to Chicago. Journalist Ring Lardner and humorist George Ade wrote for Essanay, where Louella Parsons, a cub reporter from downstate Illinois, supervised the scriptwriting department; Frank Baum of *The Wizard of Oz* fame found success at Selig.

Chicago's movie industry began around 1895, when William N. Selig, a magician by trade, bought one of Thomas Edison's newly created Kinetoscopes and opened what reputedly was the country's first motion picture studio on Peck Court. Meeting quickly with success, Selig then built a larger studio at Irving Park Road and Western Avenue.

Soon afterward, George Spoor, the manager of the Waukegan Opera House who in 1895 had invested sixty-five dollars in the production of a movie projector designed by a local mechanic and went on to establish a chain of movie theaters, had a chance meeting with actor and director Gilbert "Bronco Billy" Anderson. On February 5, 1907, Essanay—a play on the initials of Spoor and Anderson—was born.

Their first release, "An Awful Skate, or The Hobo on Rollers," starred Essanay's only actor, cross-eyed comedian Ben Turpin, who, according to historian Charles A. Jahant, for a weekly sum of fifteen dollars also swept the floors.

Concentrating on slapstick and light domestic comedies, Essanay invested some $1 million to construct various buildings in Chicago (as well as in California and New York) before consolidating its operations in larger quarters on West Argyle Street. It also published *The Essanay News*, a four-page weekly newspaper that kept the growing movie community abreast of the latest studio developments. Demand was so great for Essanay productions that the company had to increase the number of new releases to six a week.

As movie audiences became more sophisticated, so did their appetite for realism. It became unthinkable for movie directors to film only within the confines of their studios, and both Essanay and Selig followed the trend to location shooting. Ironically, Selig was one of the first film companies to shoot in California.

But other locations were also used. According to Jahant, a Selig entourage once went down to Florida, along with a shipment of cheetahs and elephants, to film a series of jungle pictures and pirate adventures. Another time a large Selig contingent of Indians, cowboys, and cowgirls, complete with steers and bucking broncos, traveled to Oklahoma, where they sought technical advice from a United States marshal named Tom Mix. As the screen's first cowboy star, Mix subsequently appeared in more than two hundred Selig westerns between 1910 and 1917.

With success came recognition from the city's elite. Essanay's "The Crimson Wing," written by Chicago socialite Hobart C. Chatfield-Taylor, was filmed in the homes and on the grounds of some of the city's wealthiest citizens. As part of his campaign for reelection in 1915, Mayor Carter H. Harrison II had Essanay photographers take photos of him as he went through a workday.

Chicago's success as a celluloid dream factory was fed by the availability of investment capital, the quick delivery of prints from its central location, and, above all, its plentiful talent. The city was a big theater town that supported a steady stream of stage and vaudeville shows.

Outside competition, however, soon undermined the city's dominance as a film center. A 1915 United States Supreme Court decision affirming the legality of antitrust laws and effectively disbanding the distribution arms of the Chicago studios left them vulnerable to assaults from the new studios in Hollywood. And when most of their own talent departed for the warmer climate of southern California, the lights went out for the city's once proud and thriving indigenous film industry.

Notes

1. During the 1930s more than two dozen film studios operated what came to be known as "film exchanges." These exchanges supplied movie theater exhibitors with the nuts and bolts of the film industry, from coming-attraction trailers and movie projectors to billboards and canopies. "Film Row" was located along Wabash and Michigan Avenues from Roosevelt Road to West Sixteenth Street. For a description of the buildings still standing from that era, see *AIA Guide to Chicago*, edited by Alice Sinkevitch (San Diego, Calif.: Harcourt Brace and Company, 1993), 142.

THE GLORY DAYS OF YIDDISH THEATER

They came in the last two decades of the nineteenth century, some fifty thousand of them, their possessions in a small bundle, the most they could carry with them as they fled the brutal pogroms in Eastern Europe. Poor in worldly wealth but rich with the traditions of their Jewish faith and rural homeland, many of these immigrants settled in the crowded, cheap-rent neighborhood around Maxwell Street on the Near West Side.[1]

Here these Russian and Polish Jews, unable to speak English and bewildered by life in the bustling New World, sought the security of familiar sights and sounds: Jewish peddlers, hawking their goods in Yiddish from two-wheeled pushcarts; kosher butchers and poultry stores; matzo bakeries; Hebrew schools and synagogues; and all kinds of Old World shops, where bearded men in long black coats haggled and argued over copies of local Yiddish newspapers.[2]

It was the Yiddish theater, however, that provided the warmest and most reassuring sense of home. Yiddish, the language of Central and Eastern European Jews and their descendants around the world, was the mother tongue, a reminder of the way things used to be.

Following a trend that saw as many as forty Yiddish theater companies flourishing across the country by the 1920s, the first Chicago Yiddish theater group, its name now buried in obscurity, opened in 1887 at 716 West DeKoven Street. By the turn of the century, the most prominent of the Chicago companies were the Metropolitan Theatre at Jefferson Street near Roosevelt Road and the Standard at Halsted and Adams Streets. Attention later shifted to the Empire and the Haymarket Theaters on Madison Street near Halsted and then to the Glickman's Palace on Blue Island Avenue near Roosevelt and the Lawndale Theatre on Roosevelt near Pulaski Road. There were also dozens of vaudeville houses and nickel shows. In the late 1930s it was the Douglas Park Theatre at

Kedzie and Ogden Avenues that became the center of a loyal following, and it was there, during the late 1940s, that its Yiddish production of Lillian Hellman's *The Little Foxes*, starring the noted Yiddish actress Dina Halpern, set attendance and long-run records.[3]

Typical fare of the Yiddish theater included Jewish classics, farces, and melodramas. Brassy musicals about nice Jewish boys meeting nice Gentile girls (or vice versa) were extremely popular, but the repertoire also included original drama and adaptations of works by Shakespeare and the German dramatist Johann Schiller.

But, as drama critic Harold Clurman once said, "Yiddish theater was more than mere entertainment; it was Jewish culture." Speaking to its audiences in a language they understood and recreating for them a distant, fondly remembered world, the theater fostered a close, special kinship between actor and patron.

Yiddish performers were often flamboyant personalities who were as colorful offstage as the characters they portrayed onstage. Stars would denounce one another both onstage and off. Seasoned actors advised greenhorns to go along with the director during rehearsals but to do what they wished during performances. The plays themselves were largely improvised and peopled with such clearly identifiable stereotypes as the greedy landlord, the noble peasant, or the oppressed worker.

A typical program might present a Russian show, a Tolstoy or Dostoyevski interpretation, or a comedy by the prominent Yiddish playwright Sholom Aleichem. So many shows were performed on any given day that the actors were not expected to memorize their lines, frequently relying instead on prompters.

Many stars of the Yiddish stage—both here and in New York—later translated their success to Broadway, in the movies, and on television—among them Halpern, Molly Picon, Leo Fuchs, Irving Jacobson, and Tony Curtis.

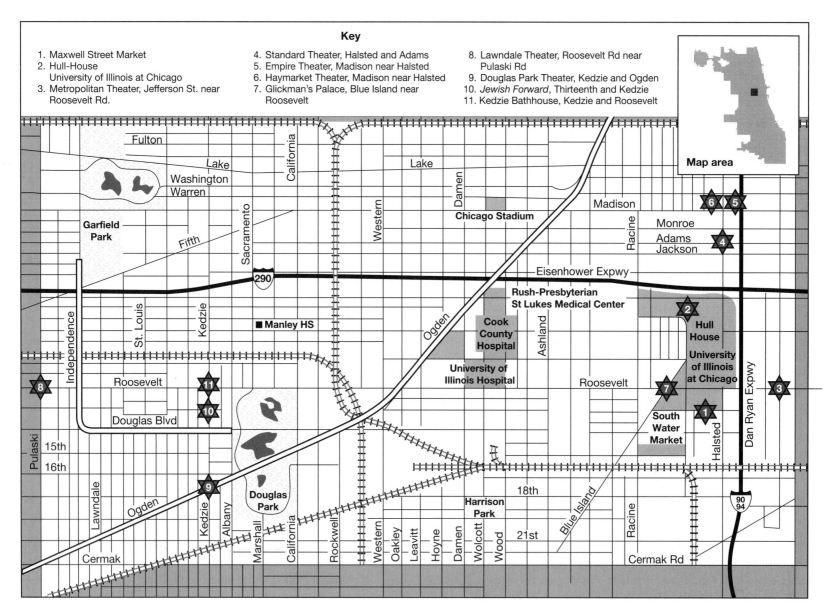

Key

1. Maxwell Street Market
2. Hull-House
   University of Illinois at Chicago
3. Metropolitan Theater, Jefferson St. near Roosevelt Rd.
4. Standard Theater, Halsted and Adams
5. Empire Theater, Madison near Halsted
6. Haymarket Theater, Madison near Halsted
7. Glickman's Palace, Blue Island near Roosevelt
8. Lawndale Theater, Roosevelt Rd near Pulaski Rd
9. Douglas Park Theater, Kedzie and Ogden
10. *Jewish Forward*, Thirteenth and Kedzie
11. Kedzie Bathhouse, Kedzie and Roosevelt

Map area

Map 10 Historic Jewish sites

Maxwell Street, 1906 (photo by Charles R. Clark, Chicago Historical Society, CRC–1431). Vendors hawking their wares in the Maxwell Street neighborhood. Maxwell Street was a world unto itself, with its own cultural and social institutions, bakeries, kosher butchers, secondhand stores, sweatshops, and bookstores. Yiddish was the language of the streets and of the home. There were Yiddish schools, Yiddish publishing houses, and Yiddish theaters. In the 1920s, 1930s, and 1940s, many Jewish families left congested Maxwell Street behind, moving farther west and northwest to Wicker Park, Humboldt Park, Logan Square, and North Lawndale. In the 1940s and 1950s, Albany Park and Rogers Park were popular choices for an increasingly large number of Jews.

From Chicago came Muni Weisenfreund, who started out, barely seventeen, at his father's Yiddish theater on Roosevelt Road near Halsted Street and went on to became the famed Paul Muni, who played a gamut of movie roles from Emile Zola to "Scarface" to Benito Juarez.

When quotas imposed after World War I restricted the flow of Yiddish-speaking immigrants into the United States and as the children and grandchildren of the first Jewish immigrants became assimilated into the American mainstream, the Yiddish theater became largely a thing of the past. Valiant efforts were made, in Chicago and elsewhere, to revitalize the art form, but in vain. When the language waned, so did the theater. The last of the Yiddish theaters, Douglas Park Theatre, closed in 1951. The Yiddish Theatre Association, founded by Danny Newman and Dina Halpern in 1960, provided Chicago audiences with an annual professional production for another decade.

Notes

1. In 1994 Maxwell Street, Chicago's thriving outdoor market and local institution for more than a century, moved from its historic location along Halsted Street south of Roosevelt Road to Canal Street between Fifteenth Place and Roosevelt Road to make way for the expansion of the University of Illinois at Chicago campus. For a verbal and pictorial portrait of Maxwell Street's last days, see David Whiteis, "The Last Sunday: A Farewell to Maxwell Street," *Chicago Reader,* September 2, 1994, 8–9, 24–27.
2. Another Jewish institution on the Near West Side was the Jewish People's Institute (JPI), the forerunnner of today's Jewish Community Centers, at 3500 Douglas Boulevard. Originally called the Chicago Hebrew Institute, the JPI offered cultural and arts programs, English language classes, and social activities.
3. Publicist Danny Newman calls *Anna Lucasta*, a runaway hit in 1949 that starred his late wife Dina Halpern, the "biggest in the entire history of Yiddish theatre in Chicago . . ." See Beatrice Michaels Shapiro, *Memoirs of Lawndale* (Chicago: Chicago Jewish Historical Society, 1991), 46.

Museums

- *Spertus Museum*. 618 South Michigan Avenue, Chicago 60605; 312-922-9012. Hours: Sunday–Thursday, 10 A.M.–5 P.M.; Friday, 10 A.M.–3 P.M. Admission: Adults, $3.50; children, senior citizens, and students, $2; Friday, free. Houses paintings, sculpture, and artifacts spanning thirty-five hundred years of Jewish history. The Zell Center for Holocaust Studies offers weekday and weekend courses and programs. The Asher Library contains a vast collection of books, periodicals, videos, sound recordings, and archival material.

Organizations

- *Chicago Jewish Historical Society*. 618 South Michigan Avenue, Chicago 60605; 312-663-5634. Established in 1977 to preserve, collect, and share the history of the Jewish community of Chicago. Gathers and maintains written, oral, and photographic records; publishes historical overviews; sponsors lectures; and offers tours.
- *Chicago YIVO Society*. 141 West Jackson Boulevard, Suite 1910A, Chicago 60604. YIVO is the Yiddish acronym for Yiddish Scientific Institute. Committed to preserving and promoting the culture of Eastern European Jewry.

THE TUNESMITHS
OF CHICAGO'S "TIN PAN ALLEY"

A rich cacophony of sounds drifted out through the open windows as singers, songwriters, and pianists, alone or in groups, worked feverishly down narrow corridors and behind cramped cubicles, humming melodies, spewing lyrics, testing chords, and swapping ideas. As the musical babel swirled in the air, it would mix freely with the city noises rising from the streets below. That was the way it was during a typical day at the factory—the mythical factory called "Tin Pan Alley" that for years produced the nation's popular songs.

As the name for a group as well as a district that produced popular music, Tin Pan Alley flourished not only in the Broadway area of New York City but also in Chicago, in a downtown section on Randolph Street roughly between State and Clark Streets.[1]

The term *tin pan* was entertainment slang for a cheap, tinny piano, and the tunes it designated were melodic yet simple, their lyrical content spun from the headlines of the day or centered on the old standbys of love, hearth, and country. The latest fads and ethnic stereotypes were also popular subjects.

In the Chicago version of Tin Pan Alley, countless publishers, composers, and lyricists worked in the Randolph Building, the Garrick Theatre Building, and others.

By its heyday in the 1920s, Tin Pan Alley could boast nearly fifty popular music publishers in the city. They were among the more than three hundred music publishers that flourished here between 1850 and 1930, including Van & Schenck on East Jackson Boulevard, H. M. Higgins on South Clark and West Randolph Streets, Will Rossiter on West Lake Street, Leo Friedman on North Dearborn Street, and Root and Cady, one of the oldest firms, on North Clark Street.

Chicago first emerged as a major center for the publication of popular songs in the 1890s. The low cost of the upright piano, the status symbol of the burgeoning middle class, contributed to the popularity of sheet music. The rise of vaudeville, which served as a showcase for popular tunes of the day, further spurred the growth.

"Down by the Old Mill Stream" (1910), "When You're Smiling, the Whole World Smiles with You" (1928), "My Blue Heaven" (1927), "Let Me Call You Sweetheart" (1910), and "It's a Long, Long Way to Tipperary" (1912)—these were just some of the national hits that originated in Chicago. Other hits, such as Fred Fisher's "Chicago (That Toddling Town)" (1922), carried the city's spirit across the nation.

New songs were always in constant demand, and a new type of salesman, or "plugger," promoted these songs, driven by the rewards of a million-dollar business. During the sheet-music era, a medium-sized hit sold six hundred thousand copies, a smash hit as many as six million, and the success or failure of songs depended on their pluggers' skill.

Brash, fast-talking, and flashy dressers, many of the pluggers were immigrants or children of immigrants from middle and central Europe. Excluded from the Anglo-Saxon-dominated fields of banking, medicine, and law, they flocked to the more free-spirited world of entertainment, where talent and ideas were more important than accent or breeding. Irving ("God Bless America") Berlin, for one, who was born Israel Baline in Russia, started out as a plugger.

Competition among pluggers was fierce. Those from Chicago promoted their songs around the country by persuading popular vaudeville performers to include them in their acts, enticing them with limousine services and promises of gifts and money. (Al Jolson reputedly was given a racehorse as a gift.) Also called "boomers" because they had to be able to sing, pluggers infiltrated theaters, political rallies, saloons, even lavatories—in short, anywhere a captive audience could be found. Jack Robbins, one of

"Gen. Sherman and his Boys in Blue," Civil War sheet music (courtesy Chicago Public Library, Harold Washington Library Center, Special Collections Division). One of many song sheets published by Chicago's burgeoning Tin Pan Alley industry. Sentiment and patriotism were perennial crowd pleasers. This song had both.

the city's more innovative pluggers, was said to have donned farmer's clothing, jumped on a haywagon, and driven down a busy Chicago street singing "It's an Old Horse That Knows Its Way Home" to amused crowds.

Chicago's Tin Pan Alley also produced seasonal songs, most notably "Rudolph, the Red-Nosed Reindeer." The legendary Rudolph was created in 1939 by a young Montgomery Ward copywriter, Robert May, who wrote a Christmas story patterned after Dr. Clement Moore's *A Visit from St. Nicholas* for a store holiday giveaway. In 1949 Alley tunesmith Johnny Marks put the tale to music and sent a demonstration copy to Gene Autry. Autry's recording sold two million copies in that year alone and quickly became a Christmas classic.

But the growth of motion pictures and the introduction of radio soon left behind the Model T, the raccoon coat, the upright piano—and the Tin Pan Alley legacy. Popular music became more sophisticated, more literate. A new breed of songwriters with a new set of standards—including Jerome Kern, George Gershwin, and Cole Porter—emerged. And in 1961, when the old Garrick Theatre Building was razed, one of the last physical reminders of Chicago's piano-pumping, finger-snapping Alley men faded into the past.

Notes

1. In addition to the Randolph Street entertainment district, Chicago also had "Music Row." "Music Row" was located on Wabash Avenue south of Adams Street. In the late 1890s music industry businesses, such as the W. W. Kimball Company and Lyon and Healy, began to occupy the new commercial buildings along Wabash Avenue. In 1993–94 DePaul University celebrated the rebirth of "Music Row" with the renovation of the former Goldblatt building at 333 South State Street and the opening of the Chicago Music Mart at DePaul Center, a unique shopping mall that houses music retailing stores, such as Baldwin Piano and Organ Company, and the Old Town School's Music Store. The stores surround a 250-seat performance atrium.

THE NIGHT *SALOME* SHOCKED THE TOWN

You'd think it would take a lot to offend a city as brash and gruff as Chicago. But the city sure took offense when, to open the Chicago Opera Company's inaugural season in 1910, a flamboyant red-haired young woman named Mary Garden took the stage as the star of Richard Strauss's one-act opera, *Salome.*

Garden caused a genuine civic uproar with her lusty performance, drawing horrified condemnation in particular for her interpretation of a pivotal scene. That was when soldiers brought in the severed head of John the Baptist, which the bejeweled performer, singing as if in a frenzy, then proceeded to kiss passionately.

That was clearly too much for "puritanical" Chicago. The opening night audience was reported to have left the show "silent and shocked." Virtually every critic, clergy, and street corner philosopher professed—in public, at least—to have been distressed by it all. Editorials, even poems, were composed to denounce the show and its star. According to the *Chicago Tribune,* opera patrons were "oppressed and horrified. But of any real enjoyment, there was little or no evidence."

At the behest of Arthur Burrage Farwell, president of the Chicago Law and Order League, police chief Roy T. Steward agreed to attend the following night's performance to see for himself. His critical assessment: "It was disgusting. Miss Garden wallowed around like a cat in a bed of catnip. If the same show was produced on Halsted Street, the people would call it cheap, but over at the Auditorium they say it's art." Farwell himself did not see the show, but apparently trusting Steward's judgment, he issued a statement calling Garden "a great degenerator of public morals."

Salome was scheduled for four performances, but despite three sellout shows, an edgy board of directors, fearful of any blemish that might sully their fledgling company's pristine reputation, can-

celed the final performance, thereby saving Mary Garden from further attacks.

Garden, however, was no stranger to controversy. Born in Aberdeen, Scotland, in 1877, she came as a child to the United States and as a teenager played in amateur productions in Chicago. A wealthy socialite who heard her singing one afternoon in a local church choir was so taken by her sweet, clear voice that she agreed to finance the young singer's studies in Paris.

By the time Garden returned to Chicago in 1910 to launch the Chicago Opera Company's initial season, she came not only with a French maid, a valet, and a diamond ring from a lovesick Turkish flame but also international renown as a diva. She was by then a seasoned trouper who had given many performances in various European opera houses.

And with her continental flair, quick wit, and devastatingly biting tongue, Garden couldn't help but make news. Devoted fans called her the Sarah Bernhardt of opera; detractors saw her as a temperamental prima donna, ruled by favoritism and subject to caprice.

Indeed, Garden's glibness once almost cost her her life. During a charity benefit at the Chicago Stock Exchange, a "dreadful-looking man with long gray hair" came up from behind and tried to shoot her. Fortunately, a police officer, reacting quickly, was able to wrestle the revolver away from the man before he could fire it. When asked why he tried to harm the diva, the would-be assassin replied coldly, "She talks too much."

In 1921 Garden was named director—or, as she preferred, "directa"—of the Chicago Opera Company. She sang, selected the operas, supervised the performers, and feuded with various cast members. During her stormy one-year tenure, several leading players resigned, and a few others came close to having nervous breakdowns. Unperturbed, she signed up a huge roster of new talent, hiring twice as many of them as the company needed and promising them more money than she could afford to spend.

Soon after she became director, she began receiving anonymous threats in the form of letters—and of knives and other weapons, such as a box of bullets that came with an ominous note: "There should be 12 bullets in this box. Count them. There are only 11. The 12th bullet is for you."

Garden's productions during her term as director were artistic winners, but the season ended with a hefty $1,100,000 deficit for the company. She resigned her post, saying, "I am an artiste, and I have decided that my place is with the artists, not over them." Still, she had no regrets. "If it cost a million dollars, I'm sure it was worth it."

For twenty years, Mary Garden dominated Chicago opera. She gave her last performance in 1931 and after formally retiring from the stage in 1934, returned to Aberdeen. There on her native soil she quietly passed away in 1967, an ocean and many years removed from the fame and controversy that once swirled around her.

THE LITTLE THEATER MOVEMENT

Long before Steppenwolf, Lookingglass, Bailiwick, and other off-Loop theater companies captured the imagination of Chicago theatergoers, an earlier generation of artists was offering an alternative to the mainstream fare of vaudeville, musicals, and melodrama popular at the time. Staging intimate productions in such small spaces as rooms in the Fine Arts Building on Michigan Avenue,[1] storefront studios in Jackson Park, or salons in the homes of wealthy patrons, they spawned a movement that came to be known as "little theater." To one critic it was the "most important chapter yet written in the history of the art theater movement in this country."

Chicago early in the century was already an important drama center. It had a large pool of local talent and many large theaters that attracted big-name entertainers like Fanny Brice and the Ziegfeld Follies, Al Jolson, John Barrymore, Helen Morgan, W. C. Fields, Will Rogers, Eddie Cantor, Billie Burke, and Sarah Bernhardt. But a few rebels thought the theater had grown too safe and predictable and needed a change. According to some sources, the little theater movement began at Jane Addams's Hull-House in 1901, when Laura Dainty Pelham formed the Hull House Players, an amateur group that presented classic Greek drama; Ibsen, Shaw, and Galsworthy; and contemporary efforts by local playwrights, including Ben Hecht and Kenneth Sawyer Goodman.

Soon other avant-garde little theaters began cropping up: the Players' Workshop on Fifty-seventh Street, the Playshop Theater in the Edgewater Beach Hotel, the Romany Club, the Ravinia Workshop, Grace Hickox Studios, and Jack and Jill Theatre.

In the Fine Arts Building itself, there were various attempts to nurture a little-theater movement. Drama teacher Anna Morgan staged works by George Bernard Shaw in her studio while producer-director Donald Robertson produced plays in the building's Music Hall—including the first Midwestern productions of Ibsen, according to historian Perry R. Duis.

The most renowned was Maurice Browne's Chicago Little Theatre, which was founded in 1912. Browne was an intense young Englishman with a background in poetry and publishing who came to Chicago in 1911 in romantic pursuit of Ellen Van Volkenburg, a society girl he had met in Italy. Inspired by the visiting Irish Players of Dublin's Abbey Theatre, Browne decided to form his own troupe. In this he found support from Lady Gregory, one of the founders of the Abbey Theatre; and from Van Volkenburg, who wanted an outlet for her acting talents and who had many wealthy friends to help fund the venture.

Following Lady Gregory's advice to use not professionals, but amateurs—"shopgirls, schoolteachers, counter-jumpers"—Browne staged his productions in a tiny theater of less than one hundred seats on the fourth floor of the Fine Arts Building. The company's first production, William Butler Yeats's *On Baile's Strand,* was presented on November 12, 1912. The Little Theatre produced revivals of Greek tragedies, the work of contemporary playwrights, and modern classics. Productions included Euripides' *The Trojan Women* and *Medea,* Ibsen's *Hedda Gabler,* Shaw's *Mrs. Warren's Profession,* a joint production (with the Washington Square Players) of John Millington Synge's *Deirdre of the Sorrows,* and various experimental works, such as *Grotesques,* a modern drama by Chicago playwright Cloyd Head; and the adventurous *Chicago Little Theatre Passion Play,* a Christmas pageant performed in mime.

For several years the Little Theatre attracted the cream of the city's literary crop, with Browne playing the genial host. A tiny tearoom was adjacent to the theater. Aside from the plays, there were Tuesday afternoon discussions, Wednesday night lectures, and a Sunday open house that attracted a diverse group of notable visitors,

Contemporary theater paraphernalia (photo by Jill Mark Salyards). A new generation of theater companies emerged in the 1970s and 1980s as an antidote to the numbing conformity of commercial theater. Today, ensembles such as Steppenwolf and the up-and-coming Lookingglass continue to create exciting theater.

including author Theodore Dreiser, Sara Allgood of the Irish Players, and Ben Reitman, the so-called king of the hoboes.

By 1915, however, some members had left the Little Theatre, apparently angered by Browne's unrealistic demands (he liked to rehearse nine hours a day, seven days a week, according to one account). Some thought the offerings had become too esoteric to attract a steady audience. Quarrels with the management of the Fine Arts Building aggravated the situation.

The curtain finally fell on Browne's Little Theatre in 1917, as it eventually did on the little theater movement itself. During its brief five-year existence, the Chicago Little Theatre produced forty-four plays, of which twenty-five were American premieres. Some critics have faulted the little theaters for being mere dabblers in the arts and not producing any really great plays. Others forcefully disagree. Maurice Browne was an innovator in many ways. He promoted the ensemble style of acting and the imaginative use of lighting and sets. His Little Theatre influenced avant-garde theater across the country, having a profound impact, for example, on such seminal American theater groups as the Provincetown Players and the Washington Square Players, both in New York. Whatever your opinion there can be little doubt that the Little Theatre can still be seen as a vibrant forerunner of today's lively off-Loop theaters.

Notes

1. The building, originally called the Studebaker, was constructed in 1885 and converted to the Fine Arts Building in 1898. The manager, Charles C. Curtiss, felt that the building's construction—the second through tenth floors had soundproofed and fireproofed studios, shops, and offices—made it perfect for the arts. The tenth floor in particular was specifically designed with artists in mind. Curtiss's vision was not as risky as it sounds. The Tree Studios building at State and Ontario had opened in 1892 and already proved that renting to artists could be profitable.

(For a listing of Fine Arts Building residents during its heyday and today, see the appendix.)

SILENCING A MOVIE CLASSIC

It has been called the greatest film ever made and, allowing for inflation, ranks as one of the biggest moneymakers of all time. Yet from the day of its release in 1915, D. W. Griffith's Civil War opus, *The Birth of a Nation,* has aroused controversy. Harvard president Dr. Charles W. Eliot claimed the picture perverted "white ideals," and black educator Booker T. Washington damned it in letters to newspapers.

In Chicago Jane Addams was "painfully exercised over [its] exhibition." Police and city officials several times tried to prevent its showing on grounds that it incited racial hatred with its portrayal of blacks as villains and Ku Klux Klansmen as heroes. Indeed, some critics blamed it for the 1919 race riots on the South Side.

The censorship of motion pictures was not, of course, new to Chicago. As early as 1907 nickelodeons, "the 5-cent theaters," were condemned by *Chicago Tribune* readers as being "without a redeeming feature to warrant their existence." Chicago then had 116 nickelodeons, eighteen five-cent vaudeville houses, and nineteen penny arcades. "These theatres cause, directly or indirectly, more juvenile crime coming into my court than all other causes combined," wrote an angry judge.

Birth of a Nation was first shown in Chicago in 1915 under an agreement with Mayor Carter Harrison II. In 1916 Epoch Film Corporation, which produced the film, obtained a temporary injunction against a 1907 city ordinance that barred the showing of any movie without a permit from the chief of police. But in 1917 the city, led by Alderman Robert R. Jackson of the Third Ward, passed a law that essentially banned the film from Chicago screens.

In 1924 the producers tried again, booking *Birth* at the Auditorium Theatre for a two-week run at the then-unheard-of price of two dollars a ticket. "Positively will be shown," boasted

an advertisement. But in the audience during the first showing sat police Captain Charles R. Larkin, three sergeants, Judge John Rooney of the Municipal Court, and Rooney's assistant. As the film reached its climax, the officials rose from their seats and ordered the movie stopped. The theater lights flashed on, arousing protests from the capacity crowd, and Judge Rooney, holding court in the lobby, signed a warrant for the arrest of the theater operators, Nathaniel Galben and Jay Webb. Ironically, the judge personally thought that the movie was artistically good. "It was a great picture," he said. "I do not think it would hurt reasonable men and women to see it, [but] it might incite others."

Despite four canceled showings and amid threats of more cancellations from the police and counter-threats by the movie people to sue the city for damages amounting to five thousand dollars per day, the movie continued to be shown—and broke all previous attendance records.

But the film's problems in Chicago were far from over. In 1939 twenty-four African-American citizens from the South Side asked Mayor Edward J. Kelly to ban the movie, then showing at the Admiral Theater on Lawrence Avenue, because of its negative image of blacks. Kelly agreed. "The picture should be banned," he said. "I don't approve of censorship, but any show that incites racial hatred should be stopped." So on October 1, 1939, Lieutenant Harry Costello, head of the police department's movie censorship bureau, ordered that the film be pulled. Legally, the city's corporation counsel, Barnet Hodes, held that the 1916 injunction prohibiting police to act against the film, though upheld by the courts in 1924, did not apply to the movie's current version, a new release with synchronized sound. The following May, Judge Donald S. McKinlay disagreed and ruled that the movie could be shown again in the city—but only in one theater at a time.

Birth of a Nation, filmed over a nine-week period at a cost of under one hundred thousand dollars, has grossed millions, launched the careers of Lillian Gish and Donald Crisp, and pioneered such cinematic innovations as close-ups, fade-outs, and fade-ins. Despite its racist view, it is is still studied in film classes across the country, admired not for its morality but for its techniques. Embellished further with an authentic musical score, it was re-released in July 1970 and shown at the Wilmette Theater. There the movie, for the first time in its turbulent history, enjoyed a quiet run in the Chicago area.

 HOME OF THE BLUES

In 1955 a down-and-out blues singer from St. Louis walked into the Chess Records office on South Michigan Avenue and played a country-tinged song called "Ida Red." Renamed "Maybelline," the song made Chuck Berry one of rock 'n' roll's earliest stars and become the Chess label's first national hit.[1]

Ironically, "Maybelline" also marked the beginning of the end for Chess. The Chicago record company had originally found success selling "race records," African-American music aimed strictly at African Americans. Promoted through catalogs and sold primarily in the so-called race market—the urban African-American neighborhoods mainly of the Chicago area; Gary, Indiana; St. Louis, Missouri; Memphis and Nashville, Tennessee; and Shreveport, Louisiana—these records seldom enjoyed substantial distribution on either the East or West Coast, nor did they receive any radio airplay. A record that sold sixty thousand copies was considered a hit. But the market was lucrative enough for Chess and other independent labels.

Chess was the creation of Leonard and Phil Chess, Polish-born Jews who came in 1928 to Chicago, where they established a string of liquor stores and then several bars on the South Side. Their biggest bar, the Macomba Lounge at Thirty-ninth Street and Cottage Grove Avenue, often featured Billy Eckstine and Ella Fitzgerald along with lesser-known jazz and blues artists. Sensing that an audience existed for this kind of music, the Chess brothers formed Aristocrat Records in 1947, changing its name in June of 1950 to Chess.

In the beginning Chess was strictly a two-man operation. The two brothers did everything from finding the talent to producing the records to packing orders. Leonard Chess, who had a keen entrepreneur's ear for what he knew would sell, became a familiar figure on the South Side in the 1950s, haunting the taverns and dives, tape recorder in hand. During the early days of the label, the company moved from various storefront locations on the South Side until late 1956, when Chess moved to a two-story building at 2120 South Michigan Avenue.

Every three months or so Leonard would travel south to sell records from the backseat of his car and, more important, make contacts. On one occasion he did a live, or "in the field," recording of bluesman Arthur Crudup performing "That's Alright, Mama," the song Crudup was best known for and which a young Elvis Presley later recorded for Sun Records. The Sun label was owned by Sam Phillips, through whom Leonard was able to sign up some of the best blues talent in Memphis.

Chess also recorded some of the greatest Chicago blues performers—Muddy Waters, Howlin' Wolf, Robert Nighthawk, Johnny Shines, Little Walter Horton, Willie Dixon, Otis Rush, and Buddy Guy. Even the Rolling Stones once used its facilities—in 1964—to record on the group's own label. But the company at heart remained a family-run operation. The brothers worked closely with the artists, visited their homes, and occasionally paid their hospital bills. Relationships were sometimes turbulent, sometimes strained, but there was always a genuine respect between artist and producer.

Muddy Waters was Chess Records's first and biggest star. Formerly of Clarksdale, Mississippi, Waters drove a truck by day delivering venetian blinds in the Chicago area and at night played the smaller clubs and house parties. Noticed by a local talent scout in late 1948, he cut his first record for the Chess brothers that year. His first recording on the Chess label, however, was "Rollin' Stone/Walkin' Blues."[2] It also introduced the distinct "Chess sound," a big, booming echo effect partly created by rigging a mike at one end of a sewer pipe and a speaker at the other.

For years Chess was the dominant company in the local recording business. But Chuck Berry and his ebullient paean to young love introduced a new sound, a sound that blurred distinctions between country and blues and rock and broke racial and cultural barriers. Ultimately, it also made the race record, the Chess mainstay, obsolete.

Although the Chess brothers were known for their musical acumen, their judgment sometimes faltered. When a financially strapped Sam Phillips offered them the chance to buy the recording rights to Elvis Presley and the entire Sun Record contingent, they turned him down. Having just signed Berry as well as Bo Diddley—another energetic performer—they failed to see, much less grasp, that great opportunity. Little did they realize that a full-fledged musical revolution was right around the corner, to be led by a young white singer from Tupelo, Mississippi, who with a sneer of the lip and the snap of a guitar would bring the blues to its knees.

Later attempts to diversify with forays into avant-garde and progressive rock proved unsuccessful. Shortly after Leonard Chess died in October 1969, brother Phil left the firm to run radio station WVON, and Chess Records was sold to and absorbed by a New York recording company. MCA Records acquired the Chess catalog in 1986. On June 7, 1990, the former Chess studios were dedicated as an official Chicago historical landmark.

Notes

1. Chuck Berry recorded four of his seven top ten hits at the Chess studios, including "Johnny B. Goode" and "Rock 'n' Roll Music." See Commission on Chicago Landmarks report, "Chess Records Office and Studio," July 1989.
2. The first record on the Chess label was Gene Ammon's "My Foolish Heart" in 1950.

Select historical sites

- *Chess Records Office and Studio.* 2120 South Michigan Avenue, Chicago. A Chicago blues historical landmark that served as the label's headquarters from 1956 to 1967. Willie Dixon's widow Marie Dixon purchased the Chess building in 1993 and then donated it to the not-for-profit Blues Heaven Foundation. The foundation has mounted a $500,000 restoration project. Plans call for the building to house a museum, gift shop, educational center, and recording studio.
- *Theresa Needham Blues Center.* 4801 South Indiana Avenue, Chicago. For more than thirty years, Theresa Needham ran Theresa's Tavern in the basement of this South Side six-flat and made it into one of the great blues hangouts in the city's history. A community group is hoping to convert the blues landmark into an educational center for the blues.
- *Vee-Jay Records.* 1449 South Michigan Avenue, Chicago. Location of what was once the largest African-American owned record label in the country.

VISITORS AND OTHER STRANGERS

Harry Houdini and friend in Chicago, circa 1924 (courtesy Jay Marshall). Houdini, the master magician, always claimed that he accomplished his celebrated feats by "natural means." Consequently he spent considerable time campaigning against deceptive mediums and spiritualists, exposing fakery wherever possible. Here he is shown with Anna Clark Benninghofen (left), a reformed spirit medium, who is holding a "spirit trumpet" through which voices of the dead were said to communicate.

RUDY, OSCAR, AND SARAH'S
ADVENTURES IN THE WINDY CITY

Chicago after the Great Fire of 1871 and before the 1933 Century of Progress Exposition was a favorite spot for visitors—entertainers, literary figures, dignitaries, social scientists, and philosophers—from elsewhere in the nation and abroad. To them, particularly the Europeans, the young, brash city was the last urban vestige of a disappearing Wild West mentality.

Not all visitors were favorably impressed, however, to judge from accounts recorded by Bessie Louise Pierce in her 1933 book, *As Others See Us*. English poet and novelist Rudyard Kipling, for one, found little to praise. The language of the business community was everywhere, he observed—on the street, in the finest hotels, even in the churches. The Palmer House was "crammed with people talking about money and spitting about everywhere." Attending a church service—"a circus, really"—he noted how a silver-tongued preacher addressed his flock as if presiding over a grand auction, proclaiming that Judgment Day would not be the end of the world because "God don't do business that way." Summing up, Kipling concluded: "This is the first American city I have encountered. Having seen it, I urgently desire never to see it again. It is inhabited by savages."

Oscar Wilde, the Irish poet and dramatist, was equally vitriolic. Local newspapermen did not take kindly to this foppish visitor who came to town wearing knee breeches and long silk stockings and disparaging everything he saw, from Chicago newspapers ("comic but never amusing") to Chicago landmarks ("Your Water Tower is a castellated monstrosity with pepperboxes stuck all over it"), and, indeed, the entire city ("too dreary for me").

Others were mesmerized by the city's frenzied pace: young men in dark clothes and derby hats rushing up and down crowded streets, past the slow-moving streetcars and into and out of the giant monoliths that reached high toward the sky.

"Everybody is in such a hurry that if a stranger asks his way, he is apt to have to trot along with his neighbor to gain the information, for the average Chicagoan cannot stop to talk," wrote Julian Ralph, an author and journalist from, of all places, New York. The busiest time of the day, wrote Ralph, was the hour from 5:30 to 6:30 P.M., when the "famous tall buildings of the city vomit their inhabitants about the pavements."

After watching the action in the Board of Trade building, one visitor wrote, "Everywhere else but in Chicago, people seem to be lively but sensible; here they seem to be maniacs." The great French actress, Sarah Bernhardt, remembered Chicago as a city where "men pass each other without stopping, with knitted brows, with one thought in mind: the end to attain."

Chicagoans were exceedingly proud of their city, another visitor wrote. One resident was quoted as saying that Chicago was the greatest wholesale lumber market in the world, contained the greatest market for hide and leather, and distributed more automobiles than any other city. The proud native then announced, "Chicago's destined to be the most important city in the world."

Yet the city was praised also for its grandiose architecture, its noble parks, its elegant mansions, and its independent-minded and well-dressed women. Chicago women could take care of themselves, and "all true Chicago men," wrote one visitor, encouraged this.

To most visitors, the city, despite its scenic location on the lake, hardly ever appeared to be pretty or gracious. But its sheer physical size, its "dreadful and magnificent" stockyards, and its "fearfully busy downtown corners" fascinated and astonished the outsiders. Many also saw it as a land of extremes—too violent, too noisy, too dirty, too rich, too poor.

Capturing the paradox of the city, English journalist George Warrington Steevens proclaimed, "Chicago, queen and guttersnipe of cities, cynosure and cesspool of the world!" To which a fellow Englishman, William Archer, countered, "It is the young giant among the cities of the world, and it stands but on the threshold of its destiny." Strong sentiments, but, for the Chicago of that period, nothing less would have done.

 VALENTINO

With his swarthy good looks and elegant bearing, Rudolph Valentino was the greatest matinee idol of the silent screen. During the height of the Valentino craze, one glimpse of his melancholy gaze as his lithe figure came onto the big screen brought his female admirers to the brink of hysteria, many of them fainting right in their seats. The men, too, fell under his spell, leading the *Chicago Tribune* to express its concern. "When," the paper asked rather harshly in an editorial, "will we be rid of all these effeminate youths, pomaded, powdered, bejeweled and bedizened in the image of Rudy—that painted pansy?"

At the peak of his popularity, on August 23, 1926, the great Valentino died unexpectedly in New York City of a perforated ulcer, sending the world into shock and grief.

Unaware until just hours before his death that his condition was truly serious, Valentino told his doctor, "I'm looking forward to going fishing with you next month." But soon afterward, at 8 A.M., he fell into a coma, and four hours later he was dead.

News of his death flashed across the screens of local movie theaters, causing "general consternation and occasional hysteric outbursts of grief among some of the patrons," the *Tribune* reported. Fans telephoned newspaper offices and film companies to verify the news. Balaban & Katz's downtown headquarters was swamped with calls from distraught patrons. The chorus of one Loop revue interrupted its rehearsal and faced east in silence for two minutes in honor of the dead actor. Many still couldn't believe the news. Ugly rumors spread that Valentino had been poisoned by a jilted lover.

In New York, a riot nearly ensued when a mob of sixty thousand, mostly girls and women, tried to get a glimpse of the actor's body lying in state at Campbell's Funeral Parlor. Despite the presence of mounted police officers, there was much screaming and shoving. Many in the crowd fainted or were trampled under the horses' hoofs. More than one hundred were injured.

Several days later, members of Chicago's Italian-American community formed the Rudolph Valentino Memorial Association. At a service held at the Trianon Ballroom on Sixty-second Street and Cottage Grove Avenue, Chicago Civic Opera singer Kathryn Browne sang two of the actor's favorite songs, "Rock of Ages" and "Lead, Kindly Light."

Only three years earlier Valentino, during a personal appearance, had danced in the very same ballroom before a large adoring crowd. At that time the Trianon was the most expensive and elaborate dance hall in the city. The women came dressed to kill in long flowing gowns, low-necked sleeveless outfits, and lace dresses. The men wore their best wide-bottomed trousers and patent-leather dancing shoes. Amid sighs of "Ooooooo, Ruuuuuudolph" from the smitten females, a gracious Valentino said, "I thank you. I am grateful for this reception of just an ordinary man."

En route from New York to its final resting place in Hollywood, Valentino's body, on the Lake Shore Limited, arrived at the LaSalle Street station at 5 P.M. on September 3, 1926. To avoid a repeat of the mob scenes in New York, local authorities had deployed a force of police officers to keep order at the station. As the funeral train pulled into the station, some of the grieving fans managed to break through the police lines and run onto the tracks. Most of the crowd, however, stood patiently under the drizzling rain, unable to catch even a glimpse of the casket but content to be there to offer their last respects to their fallen idol. Only representatives from the Rudolph Valentino Memorial Association, bearing a floral tribute, and a group of reporters were permitted to board the train.

Born Rodolfo Guglielmi in the village of Castellaneta, Italy, Valentino came to the United States in 1913 as a gardener but instead found work as a vaudeviller dancer in New York. He played in several musical comedies and soon drifted into movies in bit parts as a dancer or a villain. Suddenly rising to stardom in

1921 in *The Four Horsemen of the Apocalypse,* Valentino then became the heartthrob of millions in such movies as *Blood and Sand, The Sheik,* and *The Son of the Sheik.*

The Valentino mystique lives on, though not with the same intensity that was fueled by his untimely death and led, among other things, to talk of putting a statue in his honor in Grant Park. In 1977 dancer Rudolf Nureyev played the ill-fated star on the big screen in *Valentino,* and the following year a section of Irving Boulevard in Hollywood was renamed Rudolph Valentino Street.

A CITY FALLS UNDER HOUDINI'S SPELL

orn Ehrich Weiss in Appleton, Wisconsin, to an impover-
ished rabbi from Budapest, Hungary,[1] he won fame
throughout the world as Harry Houdini, the greatest illu-
sionist and escape artist of the twentieth century. The president of
the British College of Psychic Science called him "one of nature's
profoundest miracles," and no less than Sir Arthur Conan Doyle
believed he had supernatural powers. But as he thrilled the world
with his exploits, Houdini also worked hard and often exposed
mind readers and mediums—individuals who claimed to have a
link to the spirit world—as charlatans and frauds. Some of his
most celebrated attempts against them took place in Chicago.

By the turn of the century, the spiritualist movement, marked
by a fervid belief in communication with the dead, had gained
acceptance among all classes of people. It had also become rife
with hucksters eager to make a fast buck. Mediums attracted sold-
out crowds across the country. One Chicago firm, Ralph E.
Sylvestre & Company, catered to the psychic market with such
offerings as slate-writing secrets, rope-escape kits, and telescopic
rods that caused ghostly apparitions to appear over the heads of
those attending séances.

Visitors to Chicago who came for the 1893 World's Columbian
Exposition also flocked to the city's numerous "spirit" parlors.
Typical of the opportunistic hustlers was Zan Zic, a stage magician
who, according to Milbourne Christopher in *Houdini: The Untold
Story*, professed to be able to conjure up souls of the departed—
for a price, of course—and cure poor vision with "spirit" mud.
Tragedy resulted when one of these clients, an elderly German
gentleman, died of heart failure upon seeing and actually touching, he believed, his long-departed wife.

Houdini waged a vigorous campaign to expose unscrupulous
mediums and spiritualists. While in town to perform at the Princess
Theater in the mid-1920s, he and his staff investigated some forty of

these mediums. One of his most publicized "raids" occurred in the
South Emerald Avenue home of Minnie Reichart, who, according to
Christopher, claimed to have the power to evoke the spirit of Chief
Blackhawk and have him speak and sing songs such as "Yes, Sir,
That's My Baby" and "Nearer My God to Thee" through a trumpet.

During a séance in a pitch-black room, as Reichart's Chief
Blackhawk was purportedly communicating through his trumpet,
the flash of a camera suddenly lit the room, fired by a photographer from the *Chicago American* who had sneaked into the room
with other members of Houdini's team. The next morning in the
American, under the headline "Picture Bares Fraud," there was a
photograph of Reichart "at work," holding a trumpet to her lips.

Angered by Houdini's denunciations, Herbert O. Breedlove, a
self-proclaimed Chicago medium and mind reader, filed a criminal
libel suit, claiming that Houdini's crusade made it impossible for
him to communicate with his spirits and, consequently, cost him a
considerable amount of business. Judge Francis Borelli heard the
case in a crowded courtroom on South Clark Street, where the
atmosphere was so intense that one man fainted and Breedlove
himself collapsed in his chair.

After Breedlove regained his composure, the judge asked him if
he could summon up spirits in the courtroom. Breedlove shook his
head and flatly said, "No. You see, the environment is not right."
Then Houdini, taking the stand, offered one thousand dollars to
Breedlove or any other medium or mind reader who could tell the
nickname his father had given him as a child. A nervous silence fell
over the courtroom. Breedlove stared at the ceiling, perhaps pon-
dering the question but more likely realizing his case was lost. All
charges against Houdini were then dropped.

By 1918 Houdini was starring in silent films while continuing to
perform in stage shows on the vaudeville circuit. A frequent and
popular figure in Chicago, he baffled the Chicago Police Department

Harry Houdini (1874–1926) (courtesy Jay Marshall). Houdini flirted with death throughout his life. But on Halloween 1926 he succumbed to peritonitis and a ruptured appendix, brought on by several blows to his abdomen.

with such feats as freeing himself from handcuffs and leg irons while in a locked cell and escaping from a water-torture cell while standing on his head with his ankles bound with clamps. "For years there has not been a sensation [such] as Houdini," said the *Chicago Daily News,* "which is not likely to be extinguished by the army of imitators, of apes, of envious fakers."

Houdini, however, agreed to an experiment in spiritualism by promising to try to communicate with his wife after his death. He died, appropriately enough, on Halloween, October 31, 1926,[2] but despite the numerous séances that have been held since then, especially on Halloween, to give him a chance to make contact, not a word has been heard—yet—from the Great Houdini.

Notes

1. Houdini's place of birth remains a matter of conjecture. Some say he was born in Appleton; others say he was born in Budapest, Hungary, and brought to America as a small boy. His most recent biographer, for example, claims that no record of his birth in Wisconsin exists. See Ruth Brandon, *The Life and Many Deaths of Harry Houdini* (New York: Random House, 1994), 13.

2. Considerable controversy continues to surround the mysterious circumstances of Houdini's death. Houdini always took great pride in his top physical condition and insisted, if properly prepared, he could sustain any blows to his midsection. After performing at the Princess Theater in Montreal earlier in the week, Houdini lectured at McGill University on Friday, October 22, 1926. A McGill student came backstage and asked the magician, who by this time was exhausted from touring, whether punches to the stomach would hurt. Without allowing time for a response, the student began pounding Houdini below the belt. Despite being in considerable discomfort, he continued to perform until unbearable pain forced him to enter a Detroit hospital, where his appendix—by this time it had turned gangrenous—was promptly removed. But it was too late. Despite the best efforts of all involved, Houdini died on Halloween. Ibid., 287–94.

Museums

- *Houdini Historical Center.* 330 East College Avenue, Appleton, Wisconsin; 414-733-8445. Hours: Tuesday–Saturday, 10 A.M.–5 P.M., Sunday, noon–5 P.M., Monday, 10 A.M.–5 P.M. during June, July, and August. Admission: $3; children under 18, $1.50. Located on the second floor of the Outagamie Museum, the center contains Houdini paraphernalia (handcuffs, straitjackets, and other assorted props), displays on Houdini's career, Houdini films, and pamphlets on Houdini's life in Appleton.

THE FAB FOUR START A FIRE

They were the biggest thing to play Chicago since Elvis Presley came to town—four young Liverpool lads who crossed an ocean to conquer America with their wit, charm, and good-natured cheekiness. When they arrived in September 1964, they were greeted by thousands of screaming teenagers, most of them girls, who had started converging at the airport since the early morning hours.

At 4:30 P.M. their four-engine plane landed and pulled up not at the main passenger terminal but, as part of a crowd-control plan, at the Butler Aviation terminal at West Sixty-third Street and South Cicero Avenue. Many fans tried to scale the fence surrounding the area as they jostled to get a closer look at their heroes while a contingent of Chicago police officers strained to maintain order.

Paul McCartney was the first Beatle to emerge from the plane. Giving a perfunctory wave to the crowd that by this time was a mass of hysterically screaming humanity, he was quickly led by a police escort to a waiting limousine. Next came George Harrison, followed by John Lennon, and Ringo Starr. Within minutes, after the foursome had posed briefly for some photos, they were whisked away, and it was all over at the airport. Yet many fans, mesmerized by the glimpse they had caught of their idols, stayed around long after the last of the limousines had left.

All this, if he was to be believed, seemed strange to special events director Colonel Jack Reilly, who professed to see nothing special in this first visit to the city by the already-famous rock 'n' roll group. When two members of the Chicago Beatles Fan Club wrote to Mayor Richard J. Daley to ask if they could present the Beatles with a symbolic key to Chicago at a special welcoming ceremony, Reilly replied, "The Beatles will be one more group of entertainers who are interested in nothing more than they will have a bunch of customers at the box office."

Onstage that evening at the International Amphitheatre, the Beatles could hardly be heard above the constant screaming of an estimated crowd of thirteen thousand that had to be kept in check by three hundred police officers, 150 fire fighters, and two hundred Andy Frain ushers. But it hardly mattered. It was an event, after all, much more than a concert.

The Beatles came back on August 20, 1965, to perform at Comiskey Park, where they attracted an even bigger crowd of some fifty thousand fans. They came again on August 5, 1966, this time amid a swirl of controversy.

Earlier that year Lennon was quoted in the London *Evening Standard* as saying that the Beatles were more popular than Jesus. "Christianity will go," he reportedly said. "I needn't argue about that. We are more popular than Jesus now."

The reaction around the world was severe. In the United States about thirty-five radio stations in fifteen states said they would no longer play Beatles records, and several radio stations in the South sponsored Beatles bonfire parties at which listeners were invited to burn their Beatles records. Concerned, Beatles manager Brian Epstein cut short his vacation in Europe and flew to New York to cool the flames.

In the middle of their fourteen-city, four-week American tour, the Beatles held a press conference in Chicago's Astor Towers Hotel. There a contrite and somber Lennon admitted he had made a mistake. "I was not saying we were greater or better," he said. It was billed in some quarters as "the public apology of the year."

That night the Beatles played their third—and final—concert in Chicago. After 1966 they gave up live performances altogether and retreated to the sanctuary of the recording studio. Three years later, on December 31, 1970, the Beatles partnership was officially dissolved in High Court in London.

SPORTS, FAIRS, AND RECREATION

Ferris wheel on the Midway, World's Columbian Exposition of 1893 (photo by C. E. Waterman. Chicago Historical Society, ICHi–02440). Invented and constructed by Pittsburgh engineer George W. Ferris, the Ferris wheel was 250 feet in diameter and contained thirty-six cars that could hold sixty people each. A single trip, which included two revolutions, cost fifty cents and lasted twenty minutes. The Ferris wheel remained in Jackson Park until 1895, when it was dismantled and moved to private property near Clark Street and Diversey Avenue. In 1904 it resurfaced at the St. Louis Fair. Two years later it was scrapped.

THE GRAND ILLUSION:
THE WORLD'S COLUMBIAN EXPOSITION OF 1893

In 1893 Chicago played host to the world.[1] The World's Columbian Exposition opened on May 1, 1893, and everyone was invited. Those who came saw two cities—one real, one an illusion: a growing and increasingly vibrant metropolis and a dream city of shimmering white buildings that seemed to float on water.

The exposition earned the nickname of "White City." In order to promote a sense of unity and harmony, Daniel H. Burnham, the fair's director, decided that all of the fair's buildings should be designed in a similar style using the same color—white.

Plans for the fair began a few years earlier. During the summer of 1886, a committee was organized in Congress to organize a world's fair. Soon a fierce rivalry developed among the chief competitors. Washington, D.C., and St. Louis were among the cities considered, but the real contest was between Chicago and New York. It was during this era that Chicago received its famous nickname of the Windy City. Coined by New York *Sun* writer Richard Henry Dana, the term referred not to the wind but to the so-called hot air coming from Chicago boosters.

New Yorkers felt there was no competition; that Chicago, even as late as 1893, was little more than a parochial Midwestern backwater. In truth, Chicago had grown considerably in the previous few decades, developing into a powerhouse industrially, commercially, and culturally.

Then, in mid-August 1889, a Chicago corporation was formed to explore the possibility of holding a world's fair in Chicago in 1892. By December 1889, an Exposition bill was introduced in the Senate. On April 25 of that year, President Benjamin Harrison signed the bill granting permission for Chicago to host the next world's fair. The World's Columbian Exposition of 1893 celebrated the four hundredth anniversary of Christopher Columbus's discovery of America, but the fair also honored the progress of American culture.

The actual planning of the fair, including fiscal responsibility, was placed under local jurisdiction for the most part. But final say, including the right to grant exhibition space, lay with a national commission, which, at times, pursued its own agenda.

By the summer of 1890, details were falling into place. Frederick Law Olmsted was hired as landscape architect, while Daniel Burnham and John Root were chosen as the fair's chief architects. Burnham hired mostly East Coast firms to create his vision: a shimmering city, clad in white, that would both impress and delight everyone who saw it. Root didn't entirely agree with Burnham's concept—Root visualized a more modern and American city. What's more, the White City style sharply contrasted with Root's simple, unadorned Chicago school of architecture. Whereas the White City looked to European models for inspiration—critics sniffed that White City architects slavishly copied the past—the modern Chicago school looked to the future and to indigenous ideals for guidance.

Unfortunately, Root died of pneumonia on January 15, 1891, and it fell to Burnham to complete the project alone. He accepted full responsibility—both in design and construction—and forged ahead with his vision.

In February 1891, Jackson Park was chosen as the site for the fair. Although its northern fringes had already been under development, most of the park consisted of marshy land that was smothered with vegetation and rough growth.

The major buildings were constructed mostly of iron and timber sheds. The outside layer, or cladding, was made of a mixture of plaster, cement, and jute fibers, which was then covered with white paint, according to historian Stanley Appelbaum. This particular mixture had been invented in France and used at European fairs. Indeed, adds Appelbaum, a majority of the staff workers at the Chicago fair were French or Belgian.

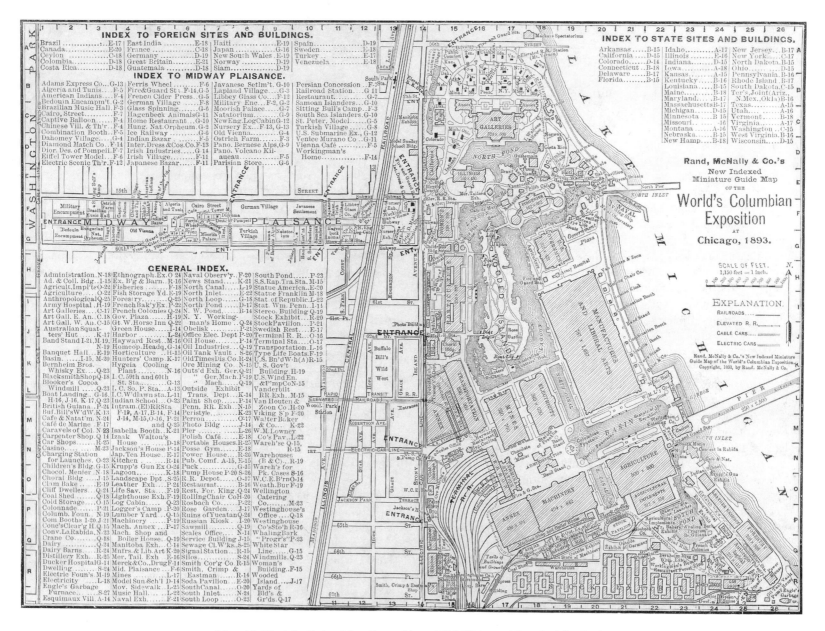

Map 11 World's Columbian Exposition, 1893 (Chicago Historical Society)

Unlike most of the buildings, the Palace of Fine Arts was made of sturdier material, since it was designed to house art from throughout the world. The Palace later changed its name to the Field Columbian Museum, and after much renovation, it reopened in 1933 as the Museum of Science and Industry.

Dedication day was planned on October 26, 1892. Actress Sarah Cowell LeMoyne read from the "Columbian Ode," a poem composed specifically for the fair by Root's sister-in-law and editor of *Poetry Magazine,* Harriet Monroe.[2]

In more ways than one, the Exposition functioned as a city within a city. It had its own police force (the Columbian Guard), restaurants and cafes, and a high level of sanitation and maintenance. Transportation consisted of an elevated electric railway on the fairgrounds themselves and on the water a round-trip gondola ride that cost fifty cents.

The visual highlight of the Exposition was the Court of Honor and its buildings, a series of white-colored buildings formed around a water basin. The fairgrounds were also dotted with sculptures and murals, many by prominent artists, including the Brooklyn-born Frederick William MacMonnies, then an up-and-coming sculptor; Daniel Chester French, and Edward Kemeys, among others.

The fair attracted numerous famous speakers and personalities and even included such novelty acts as Buffalo Bill Cody and Annie Oakley. Speakers included Carl Schurz and Frederick Douglass. Paul Laurence Dunbar read an original poem, and the Jubilee Singers performed spirituals. There were also various conferences and symposiums held. Speakers included John Dewey, Julia Ward Howe, historian Frederick Jackson Turner, Samuel Gompers, and Clarence Darrow.

Exhibits were also popular. Thomas Edison's Kinetoscope, a machine that showed motion pictures shorts, was a hit. Most people, though, when given half a chance, gravitated toward the Midway, a narrow strip of land connecting Washington and Jackson Parks and also designed by Olmsted. The Midway functioned as an amusement park. If the Exposition was art, the Midway was sheer entertainment. Many pleasures could be found along the Midway from re-creations of foreign villages, animal shows, rinks and toboggan slides, and A Street in Cairo. The latter consisted of camel and donkey rides, bazaars, and a dancer named "Little Egypt."

The high point of the Midway was the Ferris wheel. Invented by an engineer from Pittsburgh named George W. Ferris, the Ferris wheel delighted thousands of visitors. It contained thirty-six cars that could hold up to sixty people each. A fifty-cent ride bought two times round and lasted twenty minutes.

The influences of the Columbian Exposition on American architecture were profound; indeed, its legacy could be felt for many decades to come. Not everyone felt that the influences were entirely welcome. Louis Sullivan, in a famous remark, claimed that the World's Columbian Exposition, with its penchant for classical ideals, set American architecture back decades. To the general public, however, the White City was hardly old-fashioned. On the contrary, most people were overwhelmed by its beauty and elegance.

Even Burnham's prophetic Chicago Plan of 1907–1909 owes much to the spirit of the White City. If the White City led to the development of the "city beautiful" movement, then the Chicago Plan was nothing short of its manifestation.

The fair ended on a tragic note. In late October 1893, Mayor Carter Harrison I was shot in his Ashland Street mansion by a disgruntled citizen. Two days later the World's Columbian Exposition closed.

Notes

1. The other big fair in Chicago history was the 1933–34 Century of Progress. The fair took place on a landfill called Northerly Island, the present site of Meigs Field.
2. The World's Columbian Exposition was a mammoth undertaking. The fairgrounds consisted of nearly seven hundred acres. It contained a dozen or so major buildings, including the Agricultural Building, the Manufacturers Building, the Administration Building, the Machinery Hall, and the Palace of Fine Arts as well as nineteen foreign buildings and thirty-eight state buildings. In total, the number of buildings constructed for the fair amounted to approximately two hundred. Over 250 million people attended the fair during its May–October run.

AMOS ALONZO STAGG:
A MAN FOR ALL SEASONS

In the early days of college football, how you played the game was just as important as winning it. At least that was the philosophy of Amos Alonzo Stagg, the coach who gave the University of Chicago six Big Ten conference titles and five unbeaten seasons.

Some University of Chicago officials were concerned that competitive sports would lead students to neglect their studies, but President William Rainey Harper disagreed, maintaining that "the athletic field is one of the university's laboratories and by no means the least important one."

In 1892 Harper himself picked Stagg, a former divinity student from Yale, to be athletic director and associate professor, a departure from the practice of college coaches being hired by autonomous athletic associations.

A gifted athlete, Stagg believed that the chief function of sports was to build character. According to his "Ten Commandments," a good football player was, among other things, honest; helped "the other fellow"; refused to "complain, whine, knock or quit"; said a prayer each evening; and always behaved like "a sportsman and a gentleman."

At his very first practice, Stagg had to play quarterback because there were not enough students to fill all the positions. But within several years, the Maroons had become a formidable team with a large following. Anticipating the usual big crowd for a game, the *Chicago Tribune* felt compelled to warn fans to avoid stomping their feet in unison for fear that the stands—at what at first was called Marshall Field and later, in 1913, Stagg Field—would collapse under the pressure.

Stagg's honesty and integrity was legendary. In a 1909 game against Northwestern, Chicago got a lucky break by recovering a loose ball at the goal line for what should have been an easy touchdown. As the players lined up for the next play, Stagg motioned officials over and said, "Gentlemen, I happen to be on the rules committee, and I believe you have erred in giving us that touchdown. Chicago is not entitled to that score, as the impetus did not come from our team."

Stagg played a significant role in the growth of intercollegiate football. He was the first to award varsity letters ("The Order of the C"), and he invented the tackling dummy, put numbers on the back of football jerseys as a convenience for spectators, pioneered the forward pass, and reportedly introduced the onside kick, the short punt, the huddle, the fake punt, the place kick, the T-formation, and the fake pass—elements that are considered essential ingredients of today's game.

After forty-one years at Chicago, Stagg was forced to retire at age seventy. The administration, perhaps feeling a bit sheepish about relieving the legendary Stagg of his duties, offered him a noncoaching position in the public relations department at a higher salary. But insisting that he still had a few good years left in him, he accepted an offer to coach at the College of the Pacific in Stockton, California. When the University of Chicago dropped intercollegiate football in 1939, Stagg was still coaching, and in 1947 he joined his son at Susquehanna College in Pennsylvania, where he coached for another six seasons. Then he went to Stockton Junior College in 1953 as an adviser, where he finally retired in 1955.

Stagg wrote his memoirs in 1927, appropriately entitled *Touchdown*. He was a five-time member of the Olympic committee and the only man elected to the Football Hall of Fame as both a player and a coach. Sports was always more than a mere game to

him. If University of Chicago president Robert Maynard Hutchins dismissed athletics as an unnecessary distraction to the business of education, Stagg countered that sports, and football in particular, was a great builder of character.

By the time Stagg died in 1965 at age 102, the game that he helped develop had undergone massive changes. But to this day the "grand old man of the Midway" is still fondly remembered as one of the greatest figures in the history of the game.

Amos Alonzo Stagg (1862–1965). Stagg's career paralleled the development of intercollegiate football. As coach of the University of Chicago football team, Stagg won six Big Ten conference titles. The "grand old man of the Midway," as he was known, died at the age of 102.

Sports, Fairs, and Recreation

THE "FRIENDLY CONFINES"
OF AN EARLIER FIELD OF DREAMS

The fans, some twenty-one thousand of them, were in a festive mood as they braved the chilly winds of April 23, 1914, to welcome manager Joe Tinker and the Chicago Whales of the recently established Federal League to the team's spanking new home at Addison and Clark streets, Weeghman Park. Weeghman Park?

Weeghman Park was what later, in 1926, became Wrigley Field. (The Cubs then played in an old, run-down park at Polk Street and Lincoln, now Wolcott, Avenue on the West Side.) Built for the new club in 1914, "up to date in every particular" to show the National and American Leagues that the upstart Federal League meant business, it was named for Chicago restauranteur Charles Weeghman, who with coal magnate James Gilmore and others owned the Whales. In raiding the old teams to build up its roster, the new team failed to land such giants as Ty Cobb and Tris Speaker—their salaries were doubled to keep them from jumping to the "outlaw league"—but it did get Joe Tinker, the shortstop who had led the Cubs to a National League pennant in 1906, to be its manager.

When it played that inaugural game against the Kansas City Packers, the home team was known as the Chicago Federals, or Chi Feds for short. The name Whales came the following year. (Weeghman wanted to convey the idea that his team and the new league were "big.") It was a well-attended game. The windows and roofs of nearby buildings overflowed with spectators. Inside the park, the stands were packed with fans wearing Chicago Federal League caps and waving the league's pennants, both courtesy of the management.

Though Europe was at war and the United States deeply embroiled in an ugly conflict that threatened to explode into open conflict with Mexico—after an affront to American sailors in Tampico and to prevent a German ship from unloading munitions, President Woodrow Wilson had ordered the Navy to occupy the port of Veracruz—the mood of the nation was confident. Chicago, in fact, was "war mad," as veterans, politicians, and young men, even Boy Scouts, offered themselves for military service. Encouraged by the press, that kind of patriotic fervor became closely tied to the national pastime. "Baseball loyalty springs from the same fount as patriotism," said a headline in the *Chicago Tribune*'s sports section.

At the Weeghman Park opener one hundred members of the El Bravo Club, wearing colorful gold and red sashes, tried to stage a mock bullfight, a steer from the Union Stock Yard representing the Mexican leader, Victoriano Huerta. The steer, however, turned out to be a stubborn peacenik and refused to play its part.

Next on the field came a marching band followed by twenty Daughters of the Grand Army of the Republic carrying a huge American flag and then by members of both ball clubs. As the women hoisted the flag to the top of the flagpole at the far center field, fireworks erupted in the sky and the band played "Columbia, the Gem of the Ocean." Then followed the game, which the home team won, 9–1.

The Whales won the Federal League pennant in 1915 but folded that same year, as the once-promising league ran into financial troubles and, with America's entry into World War I becoming imminent, found it much harder to recruit from the diminishing pool of available players. When peace proposals came from the National and American Leagues, the Federal League teams sold back to them $385,000 worth of player contracts, allowing players to return to their former teams.

With no franchise in Chicago, Federal League owners initiated steps to purchase the Cubs, at that time owned by the Taft family of Cincinnati. They formed a syndicate of ten members, who each contributed fifty thousand dollars toward the venture. Joining them was financier J. Ogden Armour, who soon recruited William A. Wrigley, Jr., of the Wrigley chewing-gum empire.

Ironically, Wrigley had no special interest in baseball, but he posted an additional one hundred thousand dollars because he thought a baseball team should be locally owned. The syndicate then made an offer to the Tafts, spokesman Charles P. Taft eventually accepted it, and the deal was finalized on January 20, 1916. By 1919 Wrigley, who had been elected director, had majority control of the club. Thus did a man who had no personal interest in the game come to establish a Chicago baseball dynasty, and that, too, is how we now have Wrigley Field, not Weeghman Park.

AGAINST ALL ODDS:
THE BEARS WAGE A COMEBACK

On the bitterly cold afternoon of December 29, 1963, a little more than three years before the first Super Bowl game, forty-six thousand fans gathered in Wrigley Field to watch the underdog Chicago Bears play the New York Giants for the National Football League championship. An estimated fifty-five million fans across the country also watched the game on TV, and an additional twenty-six thousand—in what *Chicago Tribune* reporter George Strickler described as "an ambitious bit of commercialism"—enjoyed the game on closed-circuit TV in McCormick Place, the Coliseum, and the Amphitheatre. To Bears fans, it was a particularly special game because it was the last shot that Coach George Halas, then sixty-eight and near the end of his coaching career, had at another NFL title.

Despite his record as the "winningest" coach in football history, Halas on this cold winter day had something to prove—to himself, to his players, and, most of all, to his critics. Doomsayers were saying he was too old, that his best years were over, that he should retire. The Bears themselves had been written off by sports analysts even before the season began. They had won the first NFL championship in 1933 and repeated the feat in 1940, 1941, 1943, and 1946.[1] Since then, they had made it to the playoffs just once more, in 1956, and they lost that one badly, 47–7, to New York. This year the Bears would end up in the cellar, said the experts, who picked Detroit to win the league's western division and then vie with the eastern champs for the 1963 title. "It's getting to a now-or-never stage for the aging Halas players, and it won't be now," trumpeted one national publication.

Against all odds, the Bears won their division title. But despite compiling the best defensive record in the league, the team—led by quarterback Bill Wade and the likes of Bill George, Joe Fortunato, Larry Morris, Ed O'Bradovich, Doug Atkins, Willie Galimore, Johnny Morris, and Mike Ditka—still wasn't given much of a chance against its eastern division rival, the New York Giants.

The Giants, driving to the Bears' fourteen-yard line, scored first when quarterback Y. A. Tittle tossed a pass to Frank Gifford, who took it for a touchdown. Late in the first quarter, the Bears struck back with a sixty-one-yard interception by linebacker Larry Morris that set up their first touchdown, a quarterback sneak by Wade.

Again the Giants marched, getting all the way to the Bears' three-yard line. But they were checked and forced to settle for a field goal. A number of plays later, Larry Morris crashed into Tittle, and the quarterback, stunned, had to be helped to his feet. Bears fans, smelling victory despite trailing three points, cheered wildly as he was assisted off the field.

A determined Tittle, his knee heavily bandaged, came back to play in the second half but soon enough threw an interception to O'Bradovich, who ran it back to the Giants' fourteen-yard line. Wade then threw a short pass to tight end Ditka, who rumbled to the one. Two plays later, Wade jumped over for his second touchdown. The Bears led 14–10.

As Tittle threw pass after pass, the Bears continued to play strong, defensive ball. With a minute and a half left, the Giants, from their own fourteen, began a final drive to regain the lead and win the game.

Tittle to Aaron Thomas for ten yards.
Tittle to Thomas again for another eight.
Tittle to Joe Morrison for twelve.

The crowd grew tense. Halas paced on the sidelines as the clock ticked away: thirty-nine seconds to go.

Another Tittle pass, to Gifford, incomplete; twenty seconds left. Tittle again to Gifford, good for fifteen yards; first down on the Bears' thirty-nine.

Then came the crucial moment of the game. Tittle fell back, looked, and heaved a pass intended for Del Shofner in the end zone. But it was too high and too wobbly. "It had no authority. [Shofner] could not have gotten there in a taxi," wrote a *Tribune* reporter. Instead it was an alert Richie Petitbon who grabbed the ball for the Bears. End of drive and, with only two seconds left, end of game. As Tittle, tears of frustration streaming down his face, flung his helmet to the ground in disgust, the crowd exploded. The Bears, confounding the experts, had won it all!

The 1963 NFL championship was "Papa Bear" Halas's swan song, the last time he would coach his team to a title.[2] He retired at age seventy-three in May 1968, and died at age eighty-eight in 1983, less than three years before another generation of Bears, coached by '63 veteran Mike Ditka, crushed the New England Patriots 46–10 on January 26, 1986, in New Orleans to win Super Bowl XX.

Notes

1. Chicago won its first NFL title in 1921 as the Chicago Staleys. The name was changed to the Chicago Bears the following year. During the 1930s the Bears won two NFL championships—one an unofficial game in 1932 and its first official NFL championship game in 1933. So, depending on your interpretation, the Bears either won seven or nine championship games.
2. Halas made many firsts during his long career with the Bears. He commissioned, for example, the Bears' first fight song in 1922. The current fight song, the familiar "Bear Down, Chicago Bears" by songwriter Al Hoffman, dates back to 1941. See Richard Whittingham, *The Bears: A 75-Year Celebration* (Dallas, Tex.: Taylor Publishing, 1994), 87 and 91.

George Halas (courtesy Chicago Bears). Founder of the Chicago Bears football team, Halas (1895–1983) led the Bears to National Football League championships in 1933, 1940, 1941, 1943, 1946, and 1963. During his long career with the Bears, Halas accumulated some impressive statistics: 326 wins, 151 losses, 31 ties.

RIVERVIEW:
THE CLOSING OF A CHICAGO LANDMARK

Riverview was the last of Chicago's great amusement parks.[1] Located on a seventy-acre site on the Northwest Side and bounded by the north branch of the Chicago River, Western and Belmont Avenues, and Lane Tech High School, it was billed as the world's largest amusement park. In the days before shopping malls and home entertainment, there were few other outlets for diversion on Riverview's scale. For generations of Chicagoans, an outing at Riverview was the best way to spend a warm summer evening. It was cheap. It was fun. Best of all, it was exciting.

Riverview opened its doors on July 2, 1904. It employed more than one thousand workers and attracted more than two million annual visitors. The big sign at the main entrance seemed to say it all:

"Welcome to Riverview . . . Thrilling rides, attractions, freak show arcades, shooting galleries."

What would become Riverview began in the late 1800s as a private skeet-shooting club run by William Schmidt and his family on the banks of the north branch of the Chicago River. On Sunday Schmidt would invite neighbors to join him to shoot skeet and drink beer in a swampy area not even served by the streetcar. William's son, George, would later add some swings and rides for the sportsmen's wives and children.

Throughout its turbulent history, Riverview saw its share of controversies. In the 1920s, for example, gambling took place in the park, leading critics to attack it as the Monte Carlo of Chicago. In July 1934, Riverview was supposed to be the site of a bullfight. The bullfight, however, was stopped by the authorities and all involved—including two toreadors from Spain—were brought before a judge and charged with bullbaiting.

Riverview had between sixty and seventy rides. During its heyday it had nine wooden rollercoasters, including reportedly the only covered rollercoasters in the United States—the Silver Flash, the Blue Streak, and the Comet. One of the most popular rides—and, according to Riverview legend, the most dangerous—was the Bobs. Depending on whom you believe, the Bobs ran as slow as twenty-four miles per hour or as fast as ninety miles per hour.

There were other equally entertaining rides, such as the Pair-O-Chutes, which originally started as an observation tower called the Eyeful Tower. Stories about getting stuck on the chutes and gleefully mad operators with mayhem on their mind are part of Riverview legend. Other rides included the ornate Carousel (complete with seventy horses); the Tilt-a-Whirl; and the Shoot-the-Chutes.

Then there were the colorful midways—the Main Walk, the River Walk, and the Bowery. One of the best fun houses at Riverview, Aladdin's Castle, was presided over by the looming presence of a huge turbaned man with arresting eyes, pencil-thin mustache, and devilish smirk, as if to say, "Beware all who enter." One attraction, the Flying Turns, a rollercoaster without tracks, found its way to Riverview from the Century of Progress, according to some accounts. Other attractions included a roller rink, a picnic ground, a beer garden, a restaurant, and a dance hall, as well as parades and marching bands, special events, and various theme parades.

In those days amusement parks were not as politically correct or socially sensitive as they are today. So Riverview had its share of sideshow freaks: the woman with the features of a gigantic Georgia mule called the Mule-Faced Lady; the Armless Wonder; the Four-Legged Girl; and, more menacingly, the African Dip, in which African-American men were hired to taunt patrons into throwing balls at a target that would knock then them off balance and into a bucket of water. The Dip was discontinued in the late 1950s under pressure from the NAACP.

Crowds at Riverview amusement park (Chicago Historical Society, ICHi–00060). In the background looms two of Riverview's most popular attractions: Aladdin's Castle and the Pair-O-Chutes. Wide-eyed and bearded, Aladdin and his mischievous grin welcomed anyone who dared to roam his dark corridors and hall of mirrors. For most people, though, the Pair-O-Chutes parachute ride was the highlight of any visit to the amusement park. The drop from the 212-foot tower was an experience thrill seekers would not soon forget—the butterflies in the stomach and wobbly knees that it inevitably produced were just part of the fun.

In the early 1950s, Riverview was rated as the safest amusement park in the world, but this doesn't mean that the occasional tragedy did not occur, such as the time in the mid-1920s, when one of the Strat-O-Strat planes broke loose from its cables and flew across the Midway, over the fence, and into the Chicago River. According to the *Chicago Tribune*, eight people were killed in the 1920s and 1930s, including three in 1935 alone. Two people reportedly died at the park in the 1950s and two in the early 1960s. The biggest nonfatal accident occurred in 1937, when two trains on the Pippin roller coaster collided, injuring seventy-two people. The following year the coaster was renamed the Silver Streak and, finally, the Silver Flash.

The 1967 season ended uneventfully. So it came as a shock to everyone with the sudden announcement on October 3, 1967, that the grandson of the original owner, George A. Schmidt, had sold the popular amusement park to investor Edward F. Grimm for an estimated $3 million. Shortly after, Grimm sold the land to the Arvey Corporation for development as a light industrial park. Grimm apparently had no patience with sentimentality. "Where else can you find that much land on the North Side?" he asked. When the park closed, it had 120 rides, including six roller coasters. The rides were dismantled and auctioned off. Most, though, were demolished. It is now the site of a shopping center, a police station, and the DeVry Institute of Technology.

Over the years, speculation arose as to the reasons for Riverview's demise. There were reports of mounting violence, much of it racial in origin. Other stories emerged of sexual assaults, robberies, and general urban thuggery.

Riverview would never be confused with the safe and sterile "theme" parks of today. In truth, Riverview transcended age, gender, and economic status. It tried to be everything for all people. At times, it could be a bit seedy, sometimes dangerous, always unpredictable. That was part of its appeal. Riverview was, for better or worse, an urban amusement park. Anything could happen, and sometimes it did.

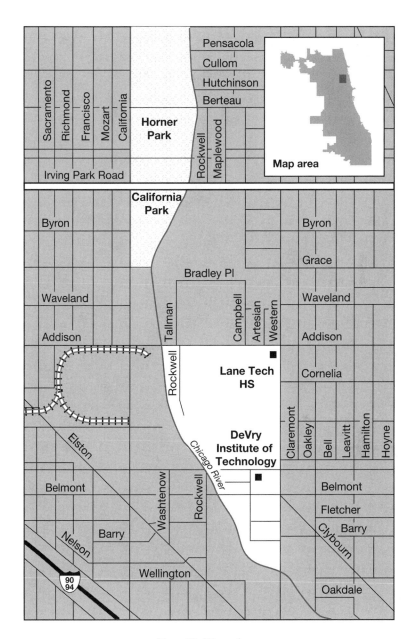

Map 12 Riverview

Sports, Fairs, and Recreation

Notes

1. Located at Sixty-third and Cottage Grove, White City was one of the most popular amusement parks in the city prior to World War I. Opening in 1905, it featured a roller coaster, a bowling alley, a roller rink, and two large dance floors. Plagued by fires, the park was placed in receivership in 1933 and condemned in 1939.

Engraving from a drawing, "Chicago in 1820" by Henry Rowe Schoolcraft from *History and Statistical Information Respecting the . . . Indian Tribes of* *the United States* (6 vols., 1853–56), part 4, 1856 (Chicago Historical Society, ICHi–15073).

 CHRONOLOGY OF CHICAGO HISTORY

1674 Father Jacques Marquette reaches the mouth of the Chicago River.

1779 (circa) Jean Baptiste Point du Sable settles in Chicago.

1803 Fort Dearborn is established.

1804 First permanent white resident (John Kinzie).

1804 Birth of first white child (Ellen M. Kinzie).

1812 Indians attack troops and their families at the Fort Dearborn Massacre.

1822 First baptism (Alexander Beaubien baptized by Rev. Stephen D. Badin).

1823 First marriage in Chicago (Dr. Alexander Wolcott and Ellen M. Kinzie).

1833 Chicago is incorporated as a town on August 10.

1833 Treaty of Chicago removes Native-American tribes in Chicago to west of the Mississippi.

1836 Ground broken for Illinois and Michigan Canal on July 4.

1837 The town of Chicago becomes the city of Chicago on March 4; William B. Ogden is elected the first mayor.

1837 First theater license in Chicago issued to Harry Isherwood and Alexander McKenzie.

1837 First city census taken (pop. 4,170).

1847 The *Chicago Tribune* is founded on June 10.

1848 The Chicago Board of Trade opens on April 3.

1848 Illinois and Michigan Canal opens.

1851 Northwestern University founded.

1856 Chicago Historical Society founded.

1860 In Chicago's first national political convention, Republican delegates meet at the Wigwam at Lake Street and Wacker Drive and nominate Abraham Lincoln as their presidential candidate.

1860 *Lady Elgin* sinks off Winnetka coast on September 7; 297 die.

1863 Two-year mayoral term begins.

1865 The Union Stock Yards open.

1871 Great Chicago Fire, October 8–10.

1884 Fine Arts Building opens.

1885 Construction begins on the Home Insurance Building, the world's first skyscraper.

1886 Haymarket Affair; seven police officers are killed.

1887 The Haymarket four—August Spies, Albert Parsons, Adolph Fischer, and George Engel—are executed on November 11.

1889 Hull House opens.

1889 Auditorium Theater is dedicated.

1891 University of Chicago founded.

1891 Theodore Thomas organizes Chicago Symphony Orchestra.

1892 Elevated train service begins.

1892 Newberry Library opens.

1892 Art Institute opens.

1893 World's Columbian Exposition opens on May 1.

1893 Governor John P. Altgeld pardons the three surviving Haymarket martyrs—Samuel Fielden, Oscar Neebe, and Michael Schwab.

1894 Pullman strike.

1897 The Chicago Public Library opens (now the Chicago Cultural Center).

1900 Everleigh Club, the city's most famous and notorious brothel, opens.

1900 The Chicago Sanitary and Ship Canal reverses the flow of the Chicago River.

1903 Fire breaks out at Iroquois Theater.

1904 Orchestra Hall opens.

1906 White Sox win World Series 4–2 against the Cubs in the Crosstown rivalry.

1907 Four-year mayoral term begins.

1908 Cubs win World Series.

1909 Daniel Burnham presents his *Plan of Chicago*.

1909 March 5. *Friday Literary Review* debuts in the pages of the *Chicago Evening Post* newspaper; often cited as the beginning of the Chicago Literary Renaissance.

1911 Everleigh Club closes.

1912 *Poetry: A Magazine of Verse* is published.

1914 Margaret Anderson establishes *The Little Review*, an influential literary magazine.

1914 Weeghman Park (now Wrigley Field) opens on April 23.

1915 The *Eastland* capsizes in the Chicago River on July 24, killing 835 people.

1916 June 7. Suffrage parade.

1917 White Sox win World Series.

1918 Goodman School of Drama opens.

1919 "Black Sox" scandal; White Sox players throw the World Series to St. Louis.

1919 Chicago race riots break out; fifteen whites and twenty-three African Americans die.

1920 Prohibition begins.

1924 In one of the more shocking crimes in the city's history, Nathan Leopold and Richard Loeb kidnap and murder fourteen-year-old Bobby Franks. Clarence Darrow acts as their attorney.

1924 Soldier Field opens on October 9.

1925 Tribune Tower opens on July 6.

1926 Roman Catholic International Eucharistic Congress held.

1927 Midway Airport, the city's first municipal airport, opens.

1929 Civic Opera House opens on November 4.

1931 Al Capone found guilty of income tax evasion and sentenced to eleven years in the federal penitentiary.

1933 Century of Progress opens on May 27.

1933 Prohibition, the "grand experiment," ends.

1938 Famed lawyer Clarence Darrow dies.

1941 *Chicago Sun* makes its debut.

1942 First self-sustaining nuclear reaction occurs at the University of Chicago on December 2.

1947 Chicago Transit Authority established.

1947 *Daily Times* merges with *Chicago Sun* to become the *Chicago Sun-Times*.

1947 Real estate developer Arthur Rubloff introduces his "Magnificent Mile" plan.

1953 First issue of *Playboy* is published.

1955 Richard J. Daley elected on April 5 to his first term as mayor.

1955 O'Hare Airport opens.

1958 Bill Veeck buys White Sox.

1965 First Chicago International Film Festival held.

1966 Dr. Martin Luther King, Jr., organizes marches to protest racial segregation from a West Side apartment.

1967 McCormick Place destroyed by fire.

1967 "Picasso" unveiled in Civic Center Plaza (now Daley Center).

1967 Riverview Park closes.

1968 Riots break out during the Democratic National Convention.

1968 Sir Georg Solti named conductor of the Chicago Symphony Orchestra.

1969 John Hancock Center completed.

1973 Sears Tower, the world's tallest building, opens.

1976 December 20. Richard J. Daley dies.

1976 Author Saul Bellow wins Nobel Prize in Literature.

1979 Jane Byrne first woman to be elected mayor.

1982 Joseph Cardinal Bernardin appointed Archbishop of Chicago.

1983 Harold Washington first African American to be elected mayor.

1986   Bears win the Super Bowl.

1989   Richard M. Daley, the son of Richard J., elected mayor.

1991   Bulls win National Basketball Association championship. They went on to capture the title two more times—in 1992 and 1993.

1992   Great Chicago flood.

CHICAGO'S MAYORS

1. William B. Ogden (1837–38); died 1877

2. Buckner S. Morris (1838–39); died 1879

3. Benjamin W. Raymond (1839–40) and (1842–43); died 1883

4. Alexander Lloyd (1840–41); died 1872

5. Francis C. Sherman (1841–42) and (1862–65); died 1870

6. Augustus Garrett (1843–44) and (1845–46); died 1848

7. Alson S. Sherman (1844); died 1903

8. John P. Chapin (1846–47); died 1864

9. James Curtiss (1847–48) and (1850–51); died 1860

10. James H. Woodworth (1848–49); died 1869

11. Walter S. Gurnee (1851–52); died 1903

12. Charles M. Gray (1853); died 1885

13. Isaac L. Milliken (1854–55); died 1889

14. Levi D. Boone (1855); died 1882

15. Thomas Dyer (1856–57); died 1862

16. John Wentworth (1857–58) and (1860–61); died 1888

17. John C. Haines (1858–60); died 1896

18. Julian S. Rumsey (1861–62); died 1886

19. John B. Rice (1865–69); died 1874

20. Roswell B. Mason (1869–71); died 1892

21. Joseph Medill (1871–73); died 1899

22. Lester Legrant Bond (1873); died 1903

23. Harvey D. Colvin (1873–76); died 1892

24. Thomas Hoyne (1875–76); elected but did not serve; died 1894

25. Monroe Heath (1876–79); died 1894

26. Carter H. Harrison I (1879–87) and (1893); died 1893

27. John A. Roche (1887–89); died 1904

28. DeWitt Cregier (1889–91); died 1898

29. Hempstead Washburne (1891–93); died 1918

30. George B. Swift (1893) and (1895–97); died 1912

31. John P. Hopkins (1893–95); died 1918

32. Carter H. Harrison II (1897–1905) and (1911–15); died 1953

33. Edward F. Dunne (1905–07); died 1937

34. Fred A. Busse (1907–11); died 1914

35. William Hale Thompson (1915–23) and (1927–31); died 1944

36. William E. Dever (1923–27); died 1929

37. Anton J. Cermak (1931–33); died 1933

38. Frank Corr (1933); interim mayor; died 1934

39. Edward J. Kelly (1933–47); died 1950

40. Martin H. Kennelly (1947–55); died 1961

41. Richard J. Daley (1955–76); died 1976

42. Michael Bilandic (1976–79)

43. Jane M. Byrne (1979–83)

44. Harold Washington (1983–87); died 1987

45. David Orr (1987); interim mayor

46. Eugene Sawyer (1987–89)

47. Richard M. Daley (1989–present)

Sources: Paul M. Green and Melvin G. Holli, eds. *The Mayors: The Chicago Political Tradition*. Rev. ed. Carbondale, Ill.: Southern Illinois University Press, 1995; Chicago Historical Society.

APPENDIX

A. Select Native-American Prehistoric Sites and Museums

Indian museums outside Chicago:

Black Hawk State Historic Site. 1510 Forty-sixth Avenue, Rock Island, Illinois 61201; 309-788-0177. Hours: 8:30 A.M.–noon and 1:00 to 4:00 P.M. daily; closed Monday and Tuesday December 1–February 28. Admission: Donation suggested.

Located on a wooded, rolling tract of 208 acres. Prehistoric Indians and nineteenth-century settlers once lived here. The site was occupied by Indians as far back as twelve thousand years ago. Beginning around 1730 and continuing for a century, the Sauk and Mesquakie Indians lived here, controlling parts of Illinois, Wisconsin, and Missouri and all of Iowa.

The village of Saukenuk was destroyed by the Americans in 1780 during the Revolutionary War. In 1804 the land was ceded to the U.S. government. Black Hawk, a pro-British Sauk warrior, refused to recognize the cession.

White settlers began to move into the area during the late 1820s. By 1831 the Sauk and Mesquakie tribes had been forced across the Mississippi River. The next year Black Hawk led fifteen hundred followers back into Illinois in an attempt to regain their lost land. Black Hawk was defeated at the Battle of Bad Axe in southern Wisconsin on August 2, 1832.

Located on the grounds of the historic site is the *Hauberg Indian Museum*. The collection of Dr. John Hauberg, a Rock Island philanthropist, contains artifacts, jewelry, and domestic items as well as dioramas using life-size figures. The museum interprets the culture of the Sauk and Mesquakie Indians. The museum also contains the *Black Hawk Forest* and *Dickson (Pioneer) Cemetery*.

Cahokia Mounds State Historic Site. P.O. Box 681, Collinsville, Illinois 62234; 618-346-5160. Hours: Open daily from 8 A.M. to dusk except New Year's, Thanksgiving, and Christmas days. Interpretative Center open from 9 A.M. to 5 P.M. Suggested donation: $2 adults, $1, 17 and younger.

Cahokia Mounds consists of the most sophisticated prehistoric Indian civilization north of Mexico. Cahokia was inhabited from about A.D. 700 to 1500. During its heyday, the city covered nearly six square miles and had a peak population of about twenty thousand. Scientists are not sure what happened to the Cahokians. Some attribute the population decline to a climate change; others to the triple threats of war, disease, and social unrest.

Cahokia Mounds contains a park of twenty-two hundred acres. The focal point of the village is *Monks Mound,* the largest Indian mound north of Mexico and the largest prehistoric earthen construction in North America. Built in several stages between A.D. 900 and 1200, Monks Mound covers more than fourteen acres and rises to a height of one hundred feet. *Woodhenge* is a reconstructed sun calendar consisting of forty-eight large, evenly spaced cedar log posts arranged in a 410-foot-diameter circle. Woodhenge is so named because of its functional similarity to England's Stonehenge and was probably used to mark the changing of the seasons. It was constructed around A.D. 1000. *Cahokia Mounds Interpretative Center* depicts daily life in a twelfth-century Indian village.

Dickson Mounds Museum. Lewistown, Illinois 61542; 309-547-3721. Hours: 8:30 A.M.–5:00 P.M. daily, except New Year's Day, Easter Sunday, Thanksgiving Day, and Christmas Day. The grounds are open until dusk from May 1 to November 1; after this date they close at 5:00 P.M. No admission fee.

The museum's purpose is to discover and preserve the heritage of the prehistoric American Indian. The property consists of 162 acres, including a number of prehistoric villages and burial mounds. Exhibits emphasize the daily life of the Mississippian culture (A.D. 900–1300). *Eveland Village Site,* a short walk or drive from the main building, consists of three early Mississippian structures.

Important Indian treaties affecting the Chicago area:

Treaty of 1795; Treaty of Greenville, August 3, 1795: signed by Little Turtle and General Anthony Wayne. Twelve tribes ceded southern Ohio and other locations, including six square miles at the mouth of the Chicago River, the future site of Fort Dearborn.

Treaty of 1816; St. Louis; August 24, 1816: The Potawatomi ceded a strip of land twenty miles wide that reached from Lake Michigan south to the Illinois River; the northern boundary, known as "The Indian Boundary Line," is located ten miles north of the Chicago River. The street that marks this boundary is now Rogers Avenue in the Rogers Park neighborhood. This treaty was important for another reason: It secured land for the building of the famous Illinois and Michigan Canal.

Treaty of 1829; Treaty of Prairie du Chien; Wisconsin; July 29, 1829: Government received land along the lakefront from Rogers Avenue north to Kenilworth, including Evanston and Wilmette.

Treaty of 1833; Chicago Treaty of September 26, 1833; the treaty brought together thousands of Indians to Chicago. This treaty led to the ultimate expulsion of the Potawatomi from their tribal lands. Held at the old council grounds, reportedly under an elm tree on the Far Northwest Side.

B. Select African-American Historical Sites

The following is a brief selection of prominent African-American historical sites in Chicago:

Original Providence Baptist Church. 515 North Pine Street 60644; 312-378-5676. Founded in 1863 on Hubbard Street as a station of the Underground Railroad, it is the oldest church on the West Side.

Jean Baptiste Pointe DuSable Home. 401 North Michigan Avenue 60611. Trading post site. DuSable was the first nonwhite settler in what is now Chicago. He arrived in the late 1770s and established a trading post at the portage between the Chicago and Des Plaines Rivers. Designated a National Historic Landmark in 1976.

Black Metropolis Trail. Created by the National Park Service, the trail centers around the vicinity of South State Street and Thirty-fifth Street, once a thriving community.

Chicago Daily Defender. 2400 South Michigan Avenue 60616; 312-225-2400. Has housed the *Chicago Daily Defender,* the city's leading African-American newspaper, since the 1950s.

Former site of old Illinois Central Gulf railroad station. Roosevelt Road and Michigan Avenue. The end of the journey for thousands of Southern blacks who rode the rails to Chicago between the two world wars.

Quinn Chapel A.M.E. Church. 2401 South Wabash Avenue 60616; 312-791-1846. This church was organized in 1847 and is the oldest African-American church in Chicago. The congregation was prominent in abolitionist and underground railroad activities. The present building dates back to 1892.

Olivet Baptist Church. 401 East Thirty-first Street 60616; 312-842-1081. Because Olivet Baptist was organized in 1850, it has been the parent church for many Baptist churches in Chicago. During the 1850s many of its parishioners assisted runaway slaves.

Ida B. Wells House. 3624 South Martin Luther King, Jr., Drive 60653. The home of the journalist and African-American activist Ida B. Wells. Designated a National Historic Landmark in 1974.

Margaret Goss Burroughs Home. 3806 South Michigan Avenue 60653. Burroughs founded the DuSable Museum in 1961 (originally named Ebony Museum of Negro History) in three rooms of this house, which dates from 1903. In the late 1930s it was converted to the Quincy Club, a social center that provided accommodations for African-American railroad workers.

Unity Hall. 3140 South Indiana Avenue 60616. Former headquarters of Alderman Oscar DePriest's People's Movement Club. The movement itself was established in 1917. The building stands as the site of the first major black political organization in the city.

***Chicago Bee* Building.** 3647–55 South State Street 60609. Erected by African-American entrepreneur Anthony Overton, the building housed his newspaper the *Chicago Bee,* which folded in the 1940s. It is the only surviving structure in an area once known as the "Black Metropolis."

Daniel Hale Williams House. 445 East Forty-second Street 60653. Dr. Daniel Hale Williams (1856–1931) was one of the founders of Provident Hospital and a pioneer in the field of heart surgery. He lived in this home from 1905 until 1929, which was designated a National Historic Landmark in 1975.

Oscar S. DePriest Home. 4536–38 South Martin Luther King, Jr., Drive 60653. DePriest (1871–1951) was the first African American to serve in the city council and the first African American elected to Congress. His home was designated a National Historic Landmark in 1965.

Robert S. Abbott House. 4742 South Martin Luther King, Jr., Drive 60615. Abbott (1870–1940) founded the *Chicago Daily Defender* in 1905. Once located in an affluent African-American community, the building is now a rooming house. It was designated a National Historic Landmark in 1976.

Provident Hospital. 500 East Fifty-first Street 60615; 312-572-2977. Founded in 1891 as an interracial hospital. Provident established the first training school for African-American nurses in the country. After much financial difficulty, Provident reopened in 1993.

DuSable Museum of African American History. 740 East Fifty-sixth Place 60637; 312-947-0600. As the oldest African-American history museum in the United States, it contains an extensive collection of books, photographs, and memorabilia of African-American history. Among its holdings: original slave documents; African woodcarvings, bronze castings, and ivory carvings; and films. Offers exhibitions, lectures, arts education classes, workshops, music, film, and visual arts performances.

Muddy Waters Home. 4339 South Lake Park 60653. The home of the great bluesman until he moved to suburban Westmont.

Oak Woods Cemetery. 1035 East Sixty-seventh Street 60637; 312-288-3800. Chartered in 1853; many prominent local African Americans are buried here, including abolitionist John Jones; banker Jesse Binga; civil rights leader Ida B. Wells; Mayor Harold Washington; athlete Jesse Owens; and the "father of gospel music," Thomas A. Dorsey.

New Regal Theatre. 1649 East Seventy-ninth Street 60649; 312-721-9301. Named after the original Regal Theatre that opened in 1928 but was demolished in 1973. Located on the former site of the Avalon Theatre and converted into a twenty-three-hundred-seat concert hall.

Carter G. Woodson Regional Library. 9525 South Halsted Street 60628; 312-747-6900. Woodson was a leading African-American scholar. Contains the Vivian Harsh Collection of Afro-American History and Literature. The library is named in honor of Vivian Harsh, the first African-American woman to head a branch of the Chicago Public Library.

Source: *Illinois Generations: A Traveler's Guide to African American Heritage*, a 40-page booklet published by the state of Illinois listing 102 African-American sites of historical interest.

C. Historical Jazz Clubs

Chicago was the jazz capital of the world during the 1920s. Although the music's popularity has waned off and on, it is still a potent force in the city today. The following is a list of some of the most historically significant clubs.

Apex Club. East Thirty-fifth Street between South Prairie and South Calumet Avenues
Owned by Julian Black, the manager of boxer Joe Louis. Catered to a wealthy—and white—clientele.
• Regulars: *Jimmie Noone, Earl Hines*

Beehive Club. East Fifth-fifth Street and South Harper Avenue
Popular Hyde Park club that opened in 1948. Closed in 1956.
• Regulars: *Art Hodes, Baby Dodds, Lester Young, and (when he was in town) Charlie Parker*

Blue Note Club. 3 North Clark Street
A legendary jazz club that flourished in 1940s and early 1950s under Franz Holzfeind.
• Regulars: *Muggsy Spanier, Sidney Bechet, Count Basie, Gene Ammons, Billie Holiday*

Cafe de Champion. 41 West Thirty-first Street
Owned by the African-American boxing champion Jack Johnson.

Club DeLisa. 5516 South State Street; 5521 South State Street
Opened during the Century of Progress Exhibition in 1933. The original

building was destroyed by fire in February 1941. It reopened two months later at a larger locale.
- Regulars: *Billy Eckstine, Jimmie Noone, Fletcher Henderson*

The College Inn at the Sherman Hotel. West Randolph and North Clark Streets
Featured the jazz-influenced dance music of Isham Jones and his Orchestra; also live radio broadcasts. Its downtown location made it popular with out-of-towners and tourists.
- Regulars: *Paul Whiteman, Bud Freeman, Fats Waller, Muggsy Spanier, Jimmy McPartland*

DeLuxe Club. 3503 South State Street
Flourished in the 1930s.
- Regulars: *Jelly Roll Morton, King Oliver*

Dreamland Cafe. 3518–20 South State Street; 4700 South State Street
Opened in early 1920s; closed in 1928 for violating prohibition laws. Reopened in 1933 at new location.
- Regulars: *Louis Armstrong, Baby Dodds, Johnny Dodds, Cab Calloway*

Elite Club. 3030 South State Street between Twenty-sixth and Thirty-first Streets
Flourished between 1910 and 1928.
- Jelly Roll Morton was the resident pianist

Friar's Inn. 343 South Wabash Avenue
Loop club that featured white performers, such as the New Orleans Rhythm Kings. Its whites-only policy eventually led to confrontations with African-American music unions.

Grand Terrace. 3955 South Parkway Boulevard (now Dr. Martin Luther King, Jr., Drive); 315–17 East Thirty-fifth Street
Opened in 1928. A combination of dancers and orchestra, buoyed by syndicate support, helped the club make it through the depression; mostly white clientele.
- Regulars: *Earl Hines, Count Basie, Fletcher Henderson, Billie Holiday*

* Green Mill. 4802 North Broadway
The Green Mill opened in 1907, making it the longest-running nightclub in Chicago. Under current owner Dave Jemilo, the Green Mill has become one of the best places to hear jazz in Chicago.

* Joe Segal's Jazz Showcase. North Clark Street; Rush Street; 636 South Michigan Avenue in the Blackstone Hotel
Established in the late 1940s and long a premier club for national talent. In early 1995 new owner, Maharishi Mahesh Yogi, planned to convert the Blackstone into a Heaven on Earth Inn, a holistic living and transcendental center.

London House. 360 North Michigan Avenue
Dinner club that opened in 1951 and flourished well into the 1970s.
- Regulars: *Oscar Peterson, George Shearing*

The Macomba. East Thirty-ninth Street and South Cottage Grove Avenue
Owned by Leonard and Phil Chess, founders of the legendary Chess Records.
- Regulars: *Louis Armstrong, Lionel Hampton, Ella Fitzgerald*

* New Regal Theater. Seventy-ninth Street and Stony Island Avenue
Housed in the former Avalon Theater. Today it presents national talent.

Pekin Theater. 2700 South State Street
Nightclub and theater that featured vaudeville and cabaret acts and early jazz acts. Jazz historian William Howland Kenney called the Pekin "the most important South Side Chicago club and musical theater before 1910 . . ."

Plantation Cafe. 338 East Thirty-fifth Street at Grand Boulevard
A black-and-tan club (black entertainment that catered to blacks and whites) that opened in October 1924. Controlled by Al Capone, it offered all-night dancing and drinking.
- Regulars: *King Oliver's Dixie Syncopators*

Regal Theater. 4719 South Parkway Boulevard (now Martin Luther King, Jr., Drive)
Built in Moorish style.
- Regulars: *Louis Armstrong, Duke Ellington, Count Basie, Lionel Hampton, Woody Herman*

Rick's Café Americain. 910 North Lake Shore Drive
Modeled after its namesake in the film *Casablanca*. Opened in 1976.
- Regulars: *Oscar Peterson, Teddy Wilson, Bill Evans*

Savoy Ballroom. South Parkway Boulevard and East Forty-seventh Street
Large, commercial dance hall that opened in November 1927, renovated in 1938, and closed in 1948.

- Regulars: *Carroll Dickerson, Fletcher Henderson, Duke Ellington, Count Basie, Dizzy Gillespie, Ella Fitzgerald, Gene Krupa*

Sunset Cafe. 315–17 East Thirty-fifth Street at South Calumet Avenue Opened August 1921. One of the most popular of the black-and-tan clubs on the South Side. Run by the Capone syndicate. Closed in 1937 and taken over by the Grand Terrace.
- Regulars: *Carroll Dickerson, Louis Armstrong, Earl Hines*

Three Deuces. 222 North State Street
Opened in 1930s.
- Regulars: *Roy Eldridge, Art Hodes, Jimmy McPartland, Baby Dodds, Johnny Dodds*

For further information on Chicago jazz clubs and jazz life, see William Howland Kenney, *Chicago Jazz: A Cultural History, 1904–1930* (New York: Oxford University Press, 1993); and Dempsey J. Travis, *An Autobiography of Black Jazz* (Chicago: Urban Research Institute, 1983).

* Clubs still operating.

D. Residents of the Fine Arts Building

Life on the tenth floor of the Fine Arts Building was a lively mixture of art and friendship, involving an endless cycle of music recitals, special shows, and exhibitions. Lorado Taft, the famous sculptor and a tenth-floor resident, and his large extended family of friends became so close that they soon established a summer art colony at Eagle's Nest, in Oregon, Illinois.

Here is a sample listing of some of the Fine Arts' most illustrious residents during its heyday. Many had their offices and studios on the fabled tenth floor:

Alliance Francaise. Promoter of French art and culture.

Artists' Guild. Professional organization of artists.

Browne Bookshop. Operated by Francis Fisher Browne, editor of *The Dial.* Located on the main floor between 1907 and 1912.

Castle Square Opera Company. Performed operas in English.

Caxton Club. Famous book club.

Chicago Literary Club. Discussed contemporary literature.

Chicago Little Theatre. Operated by Maurice Browne and his wife, Ellen Van Volkenburg, between 1912 and 1917.

Chicago Musical College. Annex.

Chicago Public School Art Society. Promoted art instruction in the schools.

Ralph Clarkson. Portrait painter.

Cordon Club. Professional organization of women prominent in the arts.

William W. Denslow. Commercial artist who collaborated with L. Frank Baum. Their best-known collaboration: *The Wizard of Oz.*

The Dial. Respected literary journal founded in 1880.

Fine Arts Shop. Cooperative shop run by members of the Artists' Guild.

Fortnightly of Chicago. Women's organization.

Irish Linen Shop. Fabrics and laces.

The Jarvie Shop. Operated by the Glasgow-born metalsmith Robert R. Jarvie and his wife, Lillian Gray.

Kalo Shop. Silver work.

The Little Review. In Room 917 Margaret Anderson edited this important literary magazine. The name is a play on Maurice Browne's Chicago Little Theatre.

The Little Room. Refers to a social gathering that met in the tenth floor of Ralph Clarkson's studio where, beginning in 1892, people in the arts met on a regular basis after the Friday afternoon concerts of the Chicago Symphony Orchestra. The members included sculptor Lorado Taft, cartoonist John McCutcheon, writers Hamlin Garland and Henry Blake Fuller, architect Howard Van Doren Shaw, and commercial artists Frank X. and Joseph C. Leyendecker. The Leyendeckers coordinated the painting of murals on the tenth floor, eight of which were completed.

John T. McCutcheon. Cartoonist.

Anna Morgan. Drama teacher who presented in her studio the first American performances of works by George Bernard Shaw and Henrik Ibsen.

Poetry: A Magazine of Verse. The durable poetry journal spent its first four years in Ralph Seymour's studio.

Rose Bindery. Bookbindery.

Saturday Evening Post. Chicago offices of the national magazine.

Ralph Fletcher Seymour. Designer and publisher.

Sherwood Music School. Annex.

Studebaker Theater.

Lorado Taft. Sculptor.

Frank Lloyd Wright. The famous architect rented a studio on the tenth floor for a brief time in 1908. He designed Francis Fisher Browne's bookshop.

The Fine Arts Building continues to be a lively place for the arts, as evidenced by the following arts-related businesses:

Apollo Chorus; Artists Guild of Chicago; Bein and Fushi (rare violins, violas, cellos, and bows); Booksellers Row; Jane Jordan Browne (literary agent); The Center for Voice; Chicago Drama League; Chicago Music Alliance; Chicago Music Studio; Chicago Youth Symphony; City Lit Theater Co.; Creative Writing School; Dancespace; Fine Arts Theatre; Harrington Institute of Interior Design; His Majesties Clerkes; Jazz Institute of Chicago; Lorado Studios (drawing, oil painting, and watercolor classes); Newman Rare Books; Performing Arts Chicago; Performers Music; Rain Dog Books; William Shatner School of Acting; and many more.

E. Chicago Landmarks

The following 106 individual landmarks and 27 districts were designated by the City Council of Chicago as of November 29, 1994:

1. *Jessie and William Adams House.* 9326 South Pleasant Avenue (1900–01); architect: Frank Lloyd Wright.

2. *Jane Addams Hull-House and Dining Hall.* 800 South Halsted Street (1856 and 1905; reconstruction 1967); architect (house) unknown; dining hall: Pond and Pond.

3. *All Saints Church and Rectory.* 4550 North Hermitage Avenue (1883); John C. Cochrane.

4. *Alta Vista Terrace.* 3800 north of North Alta Vista Terrace (1050 west), between Irving Park Road and Addison Street (1900–1904).

5. *American System-Built House.* 10410 and 10541 South Hoyne Avenue (1917); Frank Lloyd Wright.

6. *Arlington and Roslyn Place District.* 400 block of Arlington and Roslyn Places, between Clark Street and Lakeview Avenue.

7. *Astor Street District.* Astor Street between North Avenue and Division Street.

8. *Auditorium Building.* 430 South Michigan Avenue (1889); Adler and Sullivan.

9. *Emil Bach House.* 7415 North Sheridan Road (1915); Frank Lloyd Wright.

10. *Myron Bachman House.* 1244 West Carmen Avenue (1947–48); Bruce Goff.

11. *Brewster Apartments.* 2800 North Pine Grove Avenue (1893); Enoch Hill Turnock.

12. *Ransom R. Cable House.* 25 East Erie Street (1886); Cobb and Frost.

13. *Calumet-Giles-Prairie District.* Located between Thirty-first and Thirty-fifth Streets.

14. *Carson Pirie Scott & Co. Building.* 1 South State Street (1898–99; 1902–4); Louis Sullivan.

15. *Chapin and Gore Building.* 63 East Adams Street (1904); Richard E. Schmidt and Hugh Garden.

16. *James Charnley House.* 1365 North Astor Street (1892); Adler and Sullivan, Frank Lloyd Wright.

17. *Chess Records Office and Studio.* 2120 South Michigan Avenue (1911; 1956–57); John S. Townsend, Jr., and Jack S. Wiener.

18. *Chicago Board of Trade Building.* 141 West Jackson Boulevard (1930); Holabird and Root.

19. *Chicago Public Library Cultural Center.* 78 East Washington Street (1897); Shepley, Rutan, and Coolidge.

20. *Chicago Theater.* 175 North State Street (1921); Rapp and Rapp.

21. *City Hall-County Building.* Bounded by LaSalle, Clark, Randolph, and Washington Streets (1905–8; 1909–11); Holabird and Roche.

22. *Henry B. Clarke House.* 1855 South Indiana Avenue (ca. 1836); architect unknown.

23. *Edwin M. Colvin House.* 5940 North Sheridan Road (1909); George W. Maher.

24. *Cortland Street Drawbridge.* 1440 West Cortland Street (1902); John Ernst Ericson.

25. *Courthouse Place.* 54 West Hubbard Street (1893); Otto H. Matz.

26. *Dearborn Street Station.* 47 West Polk Street (1885); Cyrus L.W. Eidlitz.

27. *Delaware Building.* 36 West Randolph Street (1872–74); Wheelock and Thomas.

28. *Francis J. Dewes House.* 503 West Wrightwood Avenue (1896); Adolph Cudell and Arthur Hercz.

29. *Stephen A. Douglas Memorial.* Thirty-fifth Street and Cottage Grove Avenue (1881); Leonard W. Volk.

30. *East Lake Shore Drive District.* Consisting of the Drake Hotel, 999 North Lake Shore Drive, 179–99 East Lake Shore Drive, and Lincoln Park south of Lake Shore Drive.

31. *Eighth Church of Christ, Scientist.* 4359 South Michigan Avenue (1910–11); Leon E. Stanhope.

32. *Melissia Ann Elam House.* 4726 South Martin Luther King, Jr., Drive (1903); Henry L. Newhouse.

33. *Mathilde Eliel House.* 4122 South Ellis Avenue (1886); Adler and Sullivan.

34. *Field Building.* 135 South LaSalle Street (1934); Graham, Anderson, Probst, and White.

35. *Fine Arts Building.* 410 South Michigan Avenue (1885; 1898); Solon S. Beman.

36. *First Baptist Congregational Church.* 60 North Ashland Avenue (1869–71); Gurdon P. Randall.

37. *First Church of Deliverance.* 4315 South Wabash Avenue (1939; 1946); Walter T. Bailey; Kocher, Buss, and DeKlerk.

38. *Fisher Building.* 343 South Dearborn Street (1896); D. H. Burnham and Company.

39. *Five Houses on Avers Avenue District.* 1942, 1950, 1952, 1958, and 2102 South Avers Avenue (1892–94); Frederick B. Townsend.

40. *Getty Tomb.* Graceland Cemetery, Clark Street and Irving Park Road (1890); Louis Sullivan.

41. *John J. Glessner House.* 1800 South Prairie Avenue (1886); Henry Hobson Richardson.

42. *Walter Burley Griffin Place District.* 104th Place between Wood Street and Prospect Avenue.

43. *Abraham Groesbeck House.* 1304 West Washington Boulevard (1869); architect unknown.

44. *Harris and Selwyn Theaters.* 180–90 North Dearborn Street (1922); C. Howard Crane and H. Kenneth Franzheim.

45. *Heald Square Monument.* Michigan Avenue and Wacker Drive (1941); Lorado Taft and Leonard Crunelle.

46. *Isidore H. Heller House.* 5132 South Woodlawn Avenue (1897); Frank Lloyd Wright.

47. *Charles Hitchcock House.* 5704 West Ohio Street (1871); architect unknown.

48. *Holy Trinity Orthodox Cathedral and Rectory*. 1121 North Leavitt Street (1903); Louis Sullivan.

49. *Hutchinson Street District*. West Hutchinson Street from North Marine Drive to Hazel Street.

50. *Charles D. Iglehart House*. 11118 South Artesian Avenue (1857); architect unknown.

51. *Immaculata High School and Convent Buildings*. 640 West Irving Park Road and 4030 North Marine Drive (1922; 1955–56); Barry Byrne.

52. *Jackson Boulevard District*. Jackson Boulevard between South Ashland Avenue and South Laflin Street.

53. *Jackson Park Highlands District*. Bounded by Sixty-seventh Street on the north, Seventy-first Street on the south, Cregier Avenue on the west, and Jeffrey Boulevard on the east.

54. *Jackson/Thomas House*. 7053 North Ridge Boulevard (1874); architect unknown.

55. *Jewelers' Building*. 15–17 South Wabash Avenue (1881–82); Adler and Sullivan.

56. *K.A.M.-Isaiah Temple*. 1100 East Hyde Park Boulevard (1924; addition 1926); Alfred Alschuler.

57. *Keck-Gottschalk-Keck Apartments*. 5651 South University Avenue (1937); George, Fred, and William Keck.

58. *John F. Kenna Apartments*. 2214 East Sixty-ninth Street (1916); Barry Byrne.

59. *Sidney A. Kent House*. 2944 South Michigan Avenue (1883); Burnham and Root.

60. *Kenwood District*. Bounded by Forty-seventh Street, Blackstone Avenue, Fifty-first Street, and Drexel Boulevard.

61. *King-Nash House*. 3234 West Washington Boulevard (1901); George W. Maher.

62. *Krause Music Store*. 4611 North Lincoln Avenue (1922); William Presto, Louis Sullivan.

63. *Bryan Lathrop House*. 120 East Bellevue Place (1892); McKim, Mead, and White.

64. *Lexington Hotel*. 2135 South Michigan Avenue (1892); Clinton J. Warren.

65. *Longwood Drive District*. West side of Longwood Drive and east side of Seeley Avenue between 98th and 110th Streets.

66. *Albert F. Madlener House*. 4 West Burton Place (1902); Richard E. Schmidt and Hugh Garden.

67. *Manhattan Building*. 431 South Dearborn Street (1891); William LeBaron Jenney.

68. *Marquette Building*. 140 South Dearborn Street (1893–95); Holabird and Roche.

69. *McCormick Row House District*. Bounded by Belden and Fullerton Avenues, Halsted Street, and the elevated tracks.

70. *Metropolitan Missionary Baptist Church*. 2151 West Washington Boulevard (1901); Hugh Garden.

71. *Michigan Avenue Bridge and Wacker Drive Esplanade*. Bridge and bridge houses (1920) Edward Bennett; esplanade (1926) Bennett and Young.

72. *Mid-North District*. Bounded by Fullerton Avenue, Clark Street, Armitage Avenue, and Lincoln Avenue.

73. *Allan Miller House*. 7121 South Paxton Avenue (1915); John S. Van Bergen.

74. *Monadnock Block*. North half of 53 West Jackson Boulevard (1889–91) by Burnham and Root; south half of building at northwest corner of Van Buren and Dearborn Streets (1891–93) by Holabird and Roche.

75. *Navy Pier*. Grand Avenue and Streeter Drive at Lake Michigan (1916); Charles Sumner Frost.

76. *New Regal Theater*. 1641 East Seventy-ninth Street (1926–27); John Eberson.

77. *Samuel M. Nickerson House.* 40 East Erie Street (1883); Burling and Whitehouse.

78. *Noble-Seymour-Crippen House.* 5624 North Newark Avenue (1833 and 1868); architect unknown.

79. *North Kenwood District.* Five-square-block area surrounding South Berkeley Avenue and Forty-fifth Street and other buildings. Bounded by Forty-third and Forty-seventh Streets, Cottage Grove Avenue, and the Illinois Central railroad.

80. *North Pullman District.* Two square blocks bounded by 104th and 106th Streets, Corliss and Maryland Avenues, and four square blocks bounded by 106th and 108th Streets, Cottage Grove and Langley Avenues, and including 623 East 108th Street and 10800 South Langley Avenue.

81. *Northwestern University Settlement House.* 1400 West Augusta Boulevard (1901); Pond and Pond.

82. *Oakland District.* Bounded by East Thirty-sixth Street, South Cottage Grove Avenue, East Forty-third Street, and Lake Michigan.

83. *Old Chicago Water Tower District.* Chicago and Michigan Avenues (1869); W. W. Boyington. In 1981 boundaries changed to include Seneca Park and the fire station of Engine Company No. 98 (1904); C. F. Hermann.

84. *Old Colony Building.* 407 South Dearborn Street (1894); Holabird and Roche.

85. *Old Edgebrook District.* Bounded by Devon, Caldwell, Lehigh, and Central Avenues, the north branch of the Chicago River, and the south right-of-way of Prescott and McClellan Avenues.

86. *Old Town Triangle District.* Bounded by Lincoln Avenue, North Avenue, and the former Ogden Avenue right-of-way.

87. *Oliver Building.* 159 North Dearborn Street (1907; 1920); Holabird and Roche.

88. *On Leong Merchants Association.* 2216 South Wentworth Avenue (1926–27); Michaelsen and Rognstad.

89. *Page Brothers Building.* 177–91 North State Street (1872); John M. Van Osdel.

90. *Peoples Gas Irving Park Neighborhood Store.* 4839 West Irving Park Road (1926); Herman V. von Holst and George Grant Elmslie.

91. *Perkins, Fellows, and Hamilton Office and Studio.* 814 North Michigan Avenue (1917); Perkins, Fellows, and Hamilton.

92. *Pilgrim Baptist Church.* 3301 South Indiana Avenue (1890–91); Adler and Sullivan.

93. *Powhatan Apartments.* 4950 South Chicago Beach Drive (1927–29); Robert DeGolyer and Charles Morgan.

94. *Prairie Avenue Historic District.* Prairie Avenue between Eighteenth Street and Cullerton Avenue.

95. *Quinn Chapel.* 2401 South Wabash Avenue (1892); Henry F. Starbuck.

96. *Stephen A. Race House.* 3945 North Tripp Avenue (1874); architect unknown.

97. *John Rath House.* 2703 West Logan Boulevard (1907); George W. Maher.

98. *Reid, Murdoch and Company Building.* 320 North Clark Street (1914); George C. Nimmons.

99. *Reliance Building.* 32 North State Street (1890; 1894–95); Burnham and Root; D. H. Burnham & Co.

100. *Frederick C. Robie House.* 5757 South Woodlawn Avenue (1909); Frank Lloyd Wright.

101. *Robert W. Roloson Houses.* 3213–19 South Calumet Avenue (1894); Frank Lloyd Wright.

102. *Rookery Building.* 209 South LaSalle Street (1885–88); Burnham and Root.

103. *Rosehill Cemetery Entrance.* 5800 North Ravenswood Avenue (1864); W. W. Boyington.

104. *Saint Ignatius College Prep Building*. 1076 West Roosevelt Road (1869; 1874); Toussiant Menard; John P. Huber.

105. *Schoenhofen Brewery Powerhouse and Administration Building*. Eighteenth Street and Canalport. Powerhouse (1902): Richard Schmidt and Hugh Garden; administration building (1886): Adolph Cudell.

106. *Carl Schurz High School*. 3601 North Milwaukee Avenue (1910); Dwight H. Perkins.

107. *Second Presbyterian Church*. 1936 South Michigan Avenue (1874; 1900); James Renwick; Howard Van Doren Shaw.

108. *Seven Houses on Lake Shore Drive District*. 1250, 1254, 1258, 1260, 1516, 1524, and 1530 North Lake Shore Drive.

109. *James A. Sexton School*. 160 West Wendell Street (1882); architect unknown.

110. *Site of the first self-sustaining controlled nuclear chain reaction*. East side of South Ellis Avenue between Fifty-sixth and Fifty-seventh Streets. Site of Henry Moore's *Nuclear Energy* sculpture (1971).

111. *Site of Fort Dearborn*. Area at intersection of Michigan Avenue and Wacker Drive (1803–37).

112. *Site of Haymarket Tragedy*. Between Desplaines, Randolph, and Lake Streets.

113. *Site of the origin of the Chicago Fire of 1871*. Dekoven and Jefferson Streets. Location of commemorative sculpture *Pillar of Fire* by Egon Weiner (1971).

114. *South Pullman District*. Bounded by 111th and 115th Streets, Langley and Cottage Grove Avenues (1880–94); Solon S. Beman.

115. *South Side Community Art Center*. 3831 South Michigan Avenue (1892–93; 1940); Gustav Hallberg; Hin Bredendieck and Nathan Lerner.

116. *Lorado Taft Midway Studios*. 6016 South Ingleside Drive (ca. 1890–1929; 1929; 1964); architect unknown; Otis Floyd Johnson; Edward D. Dart.

117. *Thalia Hall*. 1215–25 West Eighteenth Street (1892); Frederick Faber and William F. Pagels.

118. *Theurer/Wrigley House*. 2466 North Lakeview Avenue (1896); Richard E. Schmidt.

119. *Thirty-five East Wacker Drive Building*. 35 East Wacker Drive (1927); Giaver and Dinkelberg.

120. *Three Arts Club*. 1300 North Dearborn Street (1914); Holabird and Roche.

121. *Tribune Tower*. 435 North Michigan Avenue (1922–25); Hood and Howells.

122. *Charles Turzak House*. 7059 North Olcott Avenue (1938–39); Bruce Goff.

123. *Union Stock Yard Gate*. Exchange Avenue at Peoria Street (ca. 1875); Burnham and Root.

124. *Uptown Theater*. 4816 North Broadway (1925); Rapp and Rapp.

125. *Villa District*. Bounded by Addison Street, Avondale Avenue, Pulaski Road, and Hamlin Avenue.

126. *Waller Apartments*. 2840–58 West Walnut Street (1895); Frank Lloyd Wright.

127. *Joseph Jacob Walser House*. 42 North Central Avenue (1903); Frank Lloyd Wright.

128. *Washington Park Court District*. 4900–45 South Washington Park Court and 417–39 East Fiftieth Street.

129. *Washington Square District*. Consisting of Washington Square Park; Newberry Library, 60 West Walton Street; and 915–29 North Dearborn Street.

130. *Whistle Stop Inn*. 4200 West Irving Park Road (1889); architect unknown.

131. *Wicker Park District*. Bounded by Caton Street, Bell and Leavitt Streets, Potomac Avenue, and the Milwaukee/O'Hare elevated right-of-way.

132. *John Wingert House.* 6231 North Canfield Avenue (1854 and later additions); architect unknown.

133. *Woman's Athletic Club.* 626 North Michigan Avenue (1928); Philip B. Maher.

Sources: Commission on Chicago Landmarks; Alice Sinkevitch, ed., *AIA Guide to Chicago* (San Diego, Calif.: Harcourt Brace & Company, 1993).

F. Lyrics

"The Illinois and Michigan Canal"

Words and music by Kevin O'Donnell
(© 1987 Arranmore Music)

It took singer-songwriter Kevin O'Donnell six or seven months to research the song. He wrote it, though, in one night. "Songs of emigration," says O'Donnell, "speak about the trauma and heartache of leaving the homeland."

On a hill behind the chapel, in the parish of Saint James
are weather-worn and tangled graves with mostly Irish names.
These faded flagstone monuments bear witness to a dream
that a 150 years ago no one could have foreseen.

In a young town called Chicago on the plains of Illinois
the I & M Commission brought in desperate men and boys
to have them build a great canal and change the rivers' flow
and wed the Great Lakes' waters with the Gulf of Mexico.

They came from ports in Galway, Howth, and Baltimore
on a promise of more money than they'd ever known before.
To carve a new beginning in a land of liberty,
they said goodbye and sailed across the sea.

Refrain:

So, bid farewell to famine, it's off to Americay
to work as a navigator for 90 cents a day.

And hope to dig a fortune by the time they reach LaSalle
on the Illinois and Michigan Canal.

Ten thousand Irish navvy's reached out across the land
and picked their way through the mud and clay and moved it all
by hand.
While the tyrant canal foreman worked poor "Paddy" without pay,
as he dreamed about his family in a country far away.

For empty-handed promises were all they came to know,
with food and tools in short supply and money running low.
Though many tried, thousands died, longing to be free
out where the blue stem prairie grasses grew as far as you could see.

Then the coming of the railway made their efforts obsolete
and it ran along her banks before the digging was complete.
The locks were finally opened and they tallied up the cost
with no mention of how many lives were lost.

Refrain

Now, gone are the locks and boatyards, the barges and the scows
and the clapboard shacks of "Corktown" where the navvy's used
to house.
From Bridgeport to LaSalle and every town along the way,
only remnants of this great canal can still be seen today.

Neglected through the ages, her water will not flow.
Where mule teams pulled river boats, now wild poplar grow.
Where canalling was a way of life that I might have tried myself,
it's now buried in the pages of some book upon a shelf.

And in the corner of that graveyard in the parish of Saint James,
lies a noble Irish navvy who helped pioneer these plaines.
Who fled the great oppression just to build himself a home.
Now, it's the only piece of sod he'll ever own.

Refrain and repeat

"Lost on the *Lady Elgin*"

The sentimental lyrics of "Lost on the *Lady Elgin*" were set to music by the printer and songwriter Henry C. Work (1832–84). The song was popular in many a Midwestern household during the last century. Work, an ardent abolitionist who composed songs for the Chicago publishing firm of Root and Cady, wrote many Civil War classics, including "Kingdom Come" and "Marching through Georgia" (See Rev. Edward J. Dowling, S.J., "Red Stacks in the Sunset," *Journal of the Illinois State Historical Society* XL, 2 [June 1947]: 179).

> Up from the poor man's cottage,
> Forth from the mansion's door,
> Reaching across the waters,
> Echoing 'long the shore;
> Caught in the morning breezes,
> Borne on the evening gale,
> Cometh a voice of mourning—
> A sad and solemn wail.
>
> Chorus:
>
> > Lost on the *Lady Elgin*,
> > Sleeping to wake no more;
> > Numbered with that three hundred
> > Who failed to reach the shore.
>
> Oh! 'Tis the cry of children
> Weeping for parents gone;
> Children who slept at evening,
> Orphans, awoke at dawn.
> Sisters for brothers weeping,
> Husbands for missing wives,
> Such were the ties dissevered,
> In those three hundred lives.
>
> Staunch was the noble steamer,
> Precious the freight she bore,
> Gayly she loosed her cable,
> A few short hours before.
> Grandly she swept our harbor,

> Joyfully rang the bell,
> Little thought she ere morrow,
> 'Twould toll so sad a knell.

"The *Eastland*"

Words by Tom and Chris Kastle
Tom and Chris Kastle are local singer-songwriters who specialize in the music of the Great Lakes.

> They came down to the dock, all in their Sunday best
> But the picnic turned a bitter twist of fate.
> They were bound to set sail, ran to the port[1] side rail
> And the ballast[2] could not hold the shifting weight.
>
> > Oh the ship, she's rolled o'er on the river's muddy floor
> > Eight hundred thirty-five would not survive.
> > With a fatal list to port,[3] led the captain to report
> > That the *Eastland* she would sail the lakes no more.
>
> Now she was a tender ship from the moment she slid down
> As a crank[4] she was known the lakes around.
> For her draft[5] was cut in two and she'd not obey the crew;
> True balance for her never could be found.
>
> > Oh the ship, she's rolled o'er on the river's muddy floor
> > Eight hundred thirty-five would not survive.
> > But the crew all stayed alive for they scrambled o'er the side
> > To gain their safety there upon the shore.
>
> Some say it was the captain's fault, some say the owner's greed
> Some say the engineers were all to blame.
> But inspectors on the take, they caused a "big mistake"
> And all of them were silent in their shame.
>
> > Oh the ship she's rolled o'er on the river's muddy floor
> > Eight hundred thirty-five would not survive.
> > Those below slowly died, while the water rushed inside
> > And the cryin' and the screams were heard no more.

Oh the ship, she's rolled o'er on the river's muddy floor
Eight hundred thirty-five would not survive
With that fatal list to port left the papers to report
That the *Eastland* she would sail the lakes no more.
Yes, the *Eastland* she would sail the lakes no more.

1. Port: left side of a ship.
2. Ballast: a heavy substance used to give a ship stability.
3. List to port: to tilt to the port side.
4. Crank: a ship that is difficult to handle or is known to easily tip.
5. Draft: the depth of water a ship draws, especially when loaded.

ANNOTATED BIBLIOGRAPHY

Much of the basic material for these essays came from *Chicago Tribune* newspaper files. Also helpful were the publications of the Commission on Chicago Historical and Architectural Landmarks. Whenever possible, I've tried to supplement the material with additional research. For the serious student of Chicago history, however, there is no better introduction to the city's past than the pages of *Chicago History,* the magazine of the Chicago Historical Society.

The following selections are offered as a guide for further study.

GENERAL

Chicago is fortunate enough to have a fair number of good general history books. The following titles are highly recommended: A.T. Andreas, *History of Chicago: From the Earliest Period to the Present Time.* 3 vols. (Chicago: A. T. Andreas, 1884–86); Emmet Dedmon, *Fabulous Chicago* (New York: Atheneum, 1981); Kenan Heise and Michael Edgerton, *Chicago: Center for Enterprise.* 2 vols. (Woodland Hills, Calif.: Windsor Publications, 1982); Harold M. Mayer and Richard C. Wade, *Chicago: Growth of a Metropolis* (Chicago: A. T. Andreas, University of Chicago Press, 1969); Bessie Louise Pierce, *A History of Chicago.* 3 vols. (New York: Knopf, 1937–57). In *Creative Chicago: From* The Chap-Book *to the University,* Henry Regnery (Evanston, Ill.: Chicago Historical Bookworks, 1993) explores the city from a cultural perspective. A fun and informative encyclopedia of Chicago history is Kenan Heise and Mark Frazel, *Hands on Chicago: Getting Hold of the City* (Chicago: Bonus Books, 1987). Another worthy reference guide is Richard Lindberg, *Passport's Guide to Ethnic Chicago: A Complete Guide to the Many Faces & Cultures of Chicago* (Lincolnwood, Ill.: Passport Books, 1993). Other worthwhile guides include Ira J. Bach and Mary Lackritz Gray, *A Guide to Chicago's Public Sculpture* (Chicago: Chicago University Press, 1983); Mary Alice Molloy, *Chicago Since the Sears Tower: A Guide to New Downtown Buildings,* 3rd rev. ed. (Chicago: Inland Architect Press, 1992); James L. Riedy, *Chicago Sculpture* (Chicago: University of Illinois

Press, 1981); and Franz Schulze and Kevin Harrington, *Chicago's Famous Buildings,* 4th rev. ed. (Chicago: University of Chicago Press, 1993).

EARLY DAYS

Last of the Potawatomi: The Treaty That Gave It All Away

For a comprehensive guide to local Indian history, past and present, see David Beck, *The Chicago American Indian Community 1893–1988: Annotated Bibliography and Guide to Sources in Chicago* (Chicago: NAES College Press, 1988); and *Indians of the Chicago Area*, compiled by Terry Straus (Chicago: NAES College Press, 1990). James A. Clifton explores early Indian history with "Billy Caldwell's Exile in Early Chicago," *Chicago History* 6, no. 4 (winter 1977–78): 218–28; and "Chicago, September 14, 1833: The Last Great Indian Treaty in the Old Northwest," *Chicago History* 9, no. 2 (summer 1980): 86–97. For Chicago during the Fort Dearborn period, see Allan Eckert, *Gateway to Empire* (Boston: Little, Brown, and Co., 1982). The Black Hawk War was an important episode in Illinois history. See Lloyd H. Efflandt, *The Black Hawk War, Why?* (Rock Island, Ill.: Rock Island Arsenal Historical Society, 1986); and Donald Jackson, ed., *Black Hawk: An Autobiography* (Urbana, Ill.: University of Illinois Press, 1990). Alexander Robinson plays a prominent role in Thomas McGowen's *Island within a City: A History of the Norridge-Harwood Heights Area* (Harwood Heights, Ill.: Eisenhower Public Library District, 1989). The best general history of Indian Chicago remains Milo Quaife's *Chicago and the Old Northwest, 1673–1835* (Chicago: University of Chicago Press, 1913). For a history of the Potawatomi, see R. David Edmunds, *The Potawatomis: Keepers of the Fire* (Norman, Ok.: University of Oklahoma Press, 1978).

The Canal That Brought the World to Chicago

Michael P. Conzon and Kay J. Carr, eds., *The Illinois & Michigan Canal National Heritage Corridor: A Guide to its History and Sources* (DeKalb,

Ill.: Northern Illinois University Press, 1988) contains various essays on aspects of the corridor's natural and human history. John M. Lamb explores the story of the I & M Canal in two works: *I & M Canal: A Corridor in Time* (Romeoville, Ill.: Lewis University, 1987); and John M. Lamb, "Early Days on the Illinois & Michigan Canal," *Chicago History* 3, no. 3 (winter 1974–75): 168–76. In 1993 Canal Corridor Association produced a handsome and informative map, "Historical Map & Guide to the Illinois & Michigan Canal National Heritage Corridor" (Canal Corridor Association, 1993), which describes surviving buildings and other sites of interest along the trail.

Along the Viking Trail: Magnus Andersen's Journey in the New World

For a description of the *Viking*'s journey, see A. A. Dornfeld, "The *Viking* in Lincoln Park," *Chicago History* 3, no. 2 (fall 1974): 111–16. The Viking Ship Restoration Committee has produced an informative pamphlet, *The Viking Ship: A Voyage of Courage and Hope* (Evanston, Ill.: Viking Ship Restoration Committee, 1985). For a general history of the Viking age, see Johannes Brøndsted, *The Vikings*, trans. Kalle Skov (London: Pelican Books, 1965). The magnificence of the Viking ship is examined in Ian Atkinson, *The Viking Ships* (New York: Cambridge University Press, 1979). Norwegian immigrant life in Chicago is the subject of Odd S. Lovoll, *A Century of Urban Life: The Norwegians in Chicago before 1930* (Norwegian-American Historical Association, 1988). For a Scandinavian perspective of the Columbian Exposition, see by the same author "Swedes, Norwegians, and the Columbian Exposition of 1893," in *Swedes in America: New Perspectives*. Series 6. Edited by Ulf Beijbom (Växjö, Sweden: The Swedish Emigrant Institute, 1993), 185–94.

Yankees and Copperheads: The Revolt at Camp Douglas

There aren't many full-length treatments of Civil War Chicago. Theodore J. Karamanski addresses that shortage quite nicely in *Rally 'Round the Flag: Chicago and the Civil War* (Chicago: Nelson-Hall Publishers, 1993). George Levy describes Camp Douglas from the prisoners' point of view in *To Die in Chicago: Confederate Prisoners at Camp Douglas 1862–1865* (Evanston, Ill.: Evanston Publishing, 1994). See also Garry Freshman, "Chicago in the Civil War," *Chicago Reader*, August 27, 1982.

Scotia's Children: Scottish Societies in Chicago

For a discussion of Robert Fergus, see Paul Angle, "Robert Fergus," *Chicago History* 2, no. 1 (fall 1948) and Henry Regnery, *Creative Chicago:*

From The Chap-Book *to the University* (Evanston, Ill.: Chicago Historical Bookworks, 1993). Rowland Berthoff offers a spirited view of the Scottish-American agenda in "Under the Kilt: Variations on the Scottish-American Ground," *Journal of American Ethnic History* 1, no. 2 (spring 1982): 5–34.

For descriptions of Scottish communities in northern Illinois, see Daniel G. Harvey, *The Argyle Settlement in History and Story* (Beloit, Wis.: Daily News Publishing Co., 1924) and Thomas C. Macmillan, "The Scots and their Descendents in Illinois," *Illinois State Historical Society Transactions*, 1919.

For a general discussion of Scottish immigration to the United States, see Ian Charles Cargill Graham, *Colonists from Scotland: Emigration to North America, 1707–1783* (Ithaca, N.Y.: 1956). A more thorough—and recent—study is David Dobson, *Scottish Emigration to Colonial America, 1607–1785* (Athens, Ga.: University of Georgia Press, 1994) and Jim Hewitson, *Tam Blake and Co.: The Story of the Scots in America* (Edinburgh: Canongate Press, 1993). Bernard Aspinwall in *Portable Utopia: Glasgow and the United States 1820–1920* (Aberdeen: Aberdeen University Press, 1984) explores the special connection between Scotland's largest city and America. An older work, recently reprinted, is D. MacDougall, *Scots and Scots' Descendants in America* (Baltimore, Md.: Genealogical Publishing Company, 1992). Finally, in *A Dance Called America: The Scottish Highlands, the United States, and Canada* (Edinburgh: Mainstream Publishing, 1994), James Hunter offers a personal and moving account of one Highlander's North American sojourn.

RADICALS, REFORMERS, AND ECCENTRICS

Following the North Star: Dare and Doing along the Underground Railroad

General histories of the Underground Railroad include Larry Gara, *The Liberty Line: The Legend of the Underground Railroad* (Lexington, Ky.: University of Kentucky Press, 1961); and Wilbur Henry Siebert, *The Underground Railroad from Slavery to Freedom* (Chicago: Johnson Publishing Co., 1967). Glennette Tilley Turner offers a look at a specific area of Underground Railroad sites in *The Underground Railroad in Du Page County, Illinois* (Wheaton, Ill.: Newman Educational Publishers, 1986). An unusual guidebook is Charles Blockson, *Guide to the Underground Railroad* (New York: Hippocrene Books, 1994), which is national in scope.

Patrick Cronin and the Clan-na-Gael

For a history of Irish nationalism in Chicago, see Michael F. Funchion, *Chicago's Irish Nationalists, 1881–1890* (New York: Arno Press, 1976). The history of the Irish in Chicago is explored in Melvin G. Holli and Peter d'A. Jones, eds., *Ethnic Chicago* (Grand Rapids, Mich.: William B. Eerdmans Publishing, 1984); and Lawrence McCaffrey, Ellen Skerrett, Michael F. Funchion, and Charles Fanning, *The Irish in Chicago* (Urbana, Ill.: University of Illinois Press, 1987). Paul Luning examines the Clan-na-Gael, the murder of Dr. Cronin, and the issue of Irish loyalty to the United States in "Irish Blood," *Chicago History* 22, no. 3 (November 1993): 20–37.

Haymarket

A great deal has been written about the Haymarket Affair. Recommended titles include Bruce C. Nelson, *Beyond the Martyrs: A Social History of Chicago's Anarchists 1870–1900* (New Brunswick, N.J.: Rutgers University Press, 1988). Dave Roediger and Franklin Rosemont, eds., *The Haymarket Scrapbook* (Chicago: Charles H. Kerr Publishing Co., 1986) is an anthology of writings on and about Haymarket. Carolyn Ashbaugh offers an incisive biography of an important figure in Haymarket history in *Lucy Parsons, American Revolutionary* (Chicago: Charles H. Kerr Publishing Co., 1976). In *The Haymarket Tragedy* (Princeton, N.J.: Princeton University Press, 1984), Paul Avrich concludes that the bomb-thrower emerged from within Chicago's anarchist movement. Other titles include Philip Foner, ed., *Autobiographies of the Haymarket Martyrs* (Chicago: Charles H. Kerr Publishing Co., 1976); and William J. Adelman, *Haymarket Revisited* (Chicago: Illinois Labor History Society, 1976). The summer 1986 issue of *Chicago History* (15, no. 2) is devoted to contemporary interpretations of the Haymarket Affair. Especially useful for putting the tragedy in its historical perspective are Bruce C. Nelson, "Anarchism: The Movement Behind the Martyrs," 4–19; and Carl S. Smith, "Cataclysm and Cultural Consciousness: Chicago and the Haymarket Trial," 36–53. In "Who Threw the Bomb?" *Chicago Tribune Sunday Magazine,* April 27, 1886, Edward Baumann identifies the likely bomb-thrower, a Hegewisch farmer and little known socialist in radical circles named George Meng. See also Harold Henderson, "1886: A Look Back at the Affair of Haymarket Square," *Chicago Reader,* April 25, 1986.

The Eccentric "Captain" of Streeterville

For a biography of George Streeter, see E. G. Ballard, *Captain Streeter Pioneer* (Chicago: Emery Publishing Service, 1914). See also K.C. Tessendorf, "Captain Streeter's District of Lake Michigan," *Chicago History* 5, no. 3 (fall 1976): 152–60.

Frances Willard and the Battle against "Demon" Alcohol

The definitive biography is Ruth Bordin, *Frances Willard: A Biography* (Chapel Hill, N.C.: University of North Carolina Press, 1986).

A Town Called Pullman

A good, all-purpose history is Stanley Buder, *Pullman: An Experiment in Industrial Order and Community Planning* (New York: Oxford University Press, 1967). See also Almont Lindsey, *The Pullman Strike* (Chicago: University of Chicago Press, 1942). Robert S. Fogarty examines the communitarian impulse in *All Things New: American Communes and Utopian Movements, 1860–1914* (Chicago: University of Chicago Press, 1990). Although Pullman figures only tangentially in his story, *All Things New* is nevertheless a fascinating study of the utopian vision in American society.

Jane Addams: Activist, Reformer, Pacifist

For personal perspectives on Hull-House, see Jane Addams, *Twenty Years at Hull-House* (New York: Macmillan, 1910); *The Second Twenty Years at Hull-House* (New York: Macmillan, 1930); and Allen F. Davis and Mary Lynn McCree, eds., *Eighty Years at Hull-House* (Bloomington, Ind.: Indiana University Press, 1969).

For a biography of Jane Addams, see Allen F. Davis, *American Heroine: The Life and Legend of Jane Addams* (Oxford: Oxford University Press, 1973). For an examination of the social settlement movement, see *Spearheads of Reform: The Social Settlements and the Progressive Movement, 1890–1914* (New York: Oxford University Press, 1971).

Lend Me Your Ears: The Orators of Bughouse Square

Frank Beck in *Hobohemia* (West Rindge, N.H.: Richard R. Smith Publishers, 1956) offers a personal look at bohemian life in Chicago. Roger A. Bruns in *The Damndest Radical: The Life and World of Ben Reitman, Chicago's Celebrated Social Reformer, Hobo King, and Whorehouse Physician* (Urbana,

Ill.: University of Illinois Press, 1987) presents a thoughtful and entertaining look at a complex man. Reitman also features prominently in Suzanne Poirier, *Chicago's War on Syphilis, 1937–40: The Times, the* Trib, *and the Clap Doctor* (Urbana, Ill.: University of Illinois Press, 1995), an account of the controversy surrounding the Chicago Syphilis Control Program in the 1930s. For descriptions of Bughouse Square and other aspects of bohemian life, see Lee Sustar, "When Speech Was Free (and Usually Worth It)," *Chicago Reader*, October 21, 1983; Harvey Zorbaugh, *The Gold Coast and the Slum* (Chicago: University of Chicago Press, 1929); and Alson J. Smith, *Chicago's Left Bank* (Chicago: Henry Regnery, 1953).

Towertown: Bohemia on the Prairie

Steven Watson in *Strange Bedfellows: The First American Avant-Garde* (New York: Abbeville Press Publishers, 1991) includes a chapter on Chicago's lively bohemian scene in the years before the outbreak of World War I. Other authors have studied the period more in-depth. In addition to Smith and Zorbaugh, they include Dale Kramer, *Chicago Renaissance: The Literary Life in the Midwest 1900–1930* (New York: Appleton Century, 1966) and Kenny J. Williams, *A Storyteller and a City: Sherwood Anderson's Chicago* (DeKalb, Ill.: Northern Illinois University Press, 1988).

Floyd Dell and Margaret Anderson were among the more flamboyant members of the Chicago Literary Renaissance of the early twentieth century. Like many self-proclaimed bohemians, they kept journals. Anderson, in fact, wrote several autobiographies. See especially Margaret Anderson, *My Thirty Years War: An Autobiography* (New York: Covici, Friede Publishers, 1930) and Floyd Dell, *Homecoming: An Autobiography* (New York: Farrar, 1933). A recent biography of Dell is by Douglas Clayton, *Floyd Dell: The Life and Times of an American Rebel* (Chicago: Ivan R. Dee, Inc. Publisher, 1994). "Martie," a charming profile of Anderson by Don Darnell, appears in the *Chicago Tribune Magazine,* 20 January 1991, 20–23. The Newberry Library houses the Floyd Dell Papers, which consist of miscellaneous correspondence, autobiographical information, articles, and poems as well as notebooks, clippings, photos, documents, and family letters. A portrait of Dell by artist B. J. O. Nordfelt is displayed in the fourth floor reading room. Dell looks typically raffish with his scarf, hat, canes, and glove.

A later generation of bohemians emerged during the 1950s. The so-called Beat Generation borrowed elements from their predecessors. They professed an interest in poetry and theater, for example, but, in general, expressed contempt for mainstream society and its values. A seminal journal of that era was *Big Table,* edited by Paul Carroll, which formed when the University of Chicago suppressed the winter 1959 issue of *Chicago Review,* the student literary magazine, for containing offensive literature by beat writers. For a description of Carroll and his battle against censorship and the subsequent beat invasion of Chicago, see Gerald Brennan, "Big Table," *Chicago History* 17, nos. 1 and 2 (spring–summer 1988): 4–23.

THE LITERARY BEAT

Deadlines and Coffins:
The Not-So-Discreet Charm of the Whitechapel Club

Harry Hansen offers fond reflections of the Whitechapel Club and other literary groups in *Midwest Portraits: A Book of Memories and Friendships* (New York: Harcourt, Brace, 1923). For an examination of the role the city played in literature, see Carl S. Smith, *Chicago and the American Literary Imagination, 1880–1920* (Chicago: University of Chicago Press, 1984). For a colorful portrait of life at a Chicago daily newspaper during the Front Page era, see George Murray, *The Madhouse on Madison Street* (Chicago: Follett Publishing, 1965).

Cliff Dwellers Club:
Lowbrow and Highbrow Meet on Michigan Avenue

Henry Regnery offers a brief history in *The Cliff Dwellers: The History of a Chicago Cultural Institution* (Evanston, Ill.: Chicago Historical Bookworks, 1990).

Encyclopaedia Britannica: Origins of a Chicago Institution

The standard history of *Encyclopaedia Britannica* is Herman Kogan, *The Great EB: The Story of the Encyclopaedia Britannica* (Chicago: University of Chicago Press, 1958). See also Roald Haase, *The Story of Encyclopaedia Britannica* (Chicago: Encyclopaedia Britannica, n.d.) and Robert Davis, "Rule, Britannica," *Chicago Tribune Sunday Magazine*, December 9, 1984. In recent years, the Chicago institution has been having considerable trouble keeping pace with electronic advances. From 1992–95 *Britannica* reportedly lost more than $22 million in sales. For an up-to-date accounting of the company's financial woes, see Jeannette De Wyze, "Britannica Bytes," *Chicago Reader,* June 16, 1995.

The Golden Tongue of Mr. Dooley

There are a number of worthwhile books on Finley Peter Dunne and his era. See Elmer Ellis, *Mr. Dooley's America: A Life of Finley Peter Dunne* (New York: Alfred A. Knopf, 1941); Charles Fanning, ed., *Mr. Dooley and the Chicago Irish: An Anthology* (New York: Arno Press, 1976); Charles Fanning, *Finley Peter Dunne and Mr. Dooley: The Chicago Years* (Lexington, Ky.: University of Kentucky Press, 1978); and Barbara C. Schaff, *Mr. Dooley's Chicago* (Garden City, N.Y.: Anchor Press/Doubleday, 1977).

Jerry DeMuth looks at Chicago journalism from a peculiarly humorous perspective in *Small Town Chicago: The Comic Perspective of Finley Peter Dunne, George Ade, Ring Lardner* (Port Washington, N.Y.: Kennikat Press, 1980).

Schlogl's: Chicago's Literary Round Table

For a profile of Henry Blackman Sell and Schlogl's, see Virginia Gardner, "A Literary Editor Reminisces: Henry Blackman Sell," *Chicago History* 3, no. 2 (fall 1974): 101–10. Much has been written about the Chicago Literary Renaissance. The best overall history is Dale Kramer, *Chicago Renaissance: The Literary Life of the Midwest 1900–1930* (New York: Appleton-Century, 1966). See also Bernard Duffey, *The Chicago Renaissance in American Letters, A Critical History* (East Lansing, Mich.: Michigan State College Press, 1954); and Anthony Grosch, "H. L. Mencken and Literary Chicago," *Chicago History* 14, no. 2 (summer 1985): 4–9, 18–25. Similarly, a fair amount of renaissance figures have written down their recollections of the era. See Harry Hansen, *Midwest Portraits: A Book of Memories and Friendships* (New York: Harcourt, Brace and Company, 1923); Ralph Fletcher Seymour, *Some Went This Way: A Forty-Year Pilgrimage among Artists, Bookmen and Printers* (Chicago: R. F. Seymour, 1945); and Vincent Starrett, *Born in a Bookshop: Chapters from the Chicago Renascence* (Norman, Okla.: University of Oklahoma Press, 1965). In *Creative Chicago: From The* Chap-Book *to the University* (Evanston, Ill.: Chicago Historical Bookworks, 1993), Henry Regnery devotes several chapters to literary history, discussing such important purveyors of the written word as Robert Fergus, an early Chicago printer and publisher; Herbert Stone, publisher of *The Chap-Book;* Francis Browne, editor of *The Dial;* Harriet Monroe, editor of *Poetry* magazine; and three Chicago writers: Henry Fuller, Hamlin Garland, and Theodore Dreiser.

The *Seed:* Voice of the Flower Children Generation

There is no general history of the underground press in Chicago, but a former Northwestern University professor, Abe Peck, examines the history from a national perspective in *Uncovering the Sixties: The Life & Times of the Underground Press* (New York: Pantheon Books, 1985). For an examination of the events leading up to the violence of the Democratic Convention, see David Farber, "'Welcome to Chicago,'" *Chicago History* 17, nos. 1 and 2 (spring–summer 1988): 62–77; and Farber's book-length treatment, *Chicago '68* (Chicago: University of Chicago Press, 1988). *Democracy Is in the Streets: From Port Huron to the Siege of Chicago* by James Miller (Cambridge, Mass.: Harvard University Press, 1994) offers a history of the people and events that shaped the New Left in the 1960s. For the Conspiracy 7 trial itself, you can do no better than Tom Hayden, *Trial* (New York: Holt, Rinehart and Winston, 1970). The peace movement in Chicago is discussed in Bradford Lyttle, *The Chicago Anti-Vietnam War Movement* (Chicago: Midwest Pacifist Center, 1988).

LIFE IN THE NEIGHBORHOODS

Back Streets and Alleys: Urban Playgrounds to a Generation

Highly recommended neighborhood guides include Dominic A. Pacyga and Ellen Skerrett, *Chicago: City of Neighborhoods* (Chicago: Loyola University Press, 1986); and Glen E. Holt and Dominic A. Pacyga, *Chicago: A Historical Guide to the Neighborhoods, The Loop and South Side* (Chicago: Chicago Historical Society, 1979).

Going to the Baths

Ira Berkow offers a fascinating and evocative portrait of the customs and characters of Maxwell Street in *Maxwell Street: Survival in a Bazaar* (Garden City, N.Y.: Doubleday, 1977).

Chinatown

Not much is available on Chinatown, especially by insiders. For a brief history by a Chinese American, see Harry Ying Cheng Kiang, *Chicago's Chinatown* (Lincolnwood, Ill.: Institute of China Studies, 1992). Dominic Pacyga and Ellen Skerrett examine the history of Chicago by exploring its neighborhoods in *Chicago, City of Neighborhoods.* In *Chinatown: A*

Portrait of a Closed Society (New York: Harper Collins, 1992), Gwen Kinkead examines New York's Chinatown, but it could just as easily apply to Chicago.

Opium Dens

A terrific examination of opium addiction in Chicago is Dick Griffin, "Opium Addiction in Chicago: 'The Noblest and the Best Brought Low,'" *Chicago History* 6, no. 2 (summer 1977): 107–16.

In the Blink of a Camera's Eye

Paul W. Petraitis examines the work of one neighborhood photographer in "Henry Ralph Koopman II: The Life and Times of a Neighborhood Photographer," *Chicago History* 7, no. 3 (fall 1978): 161–77.

Black Hearses and White Horses:
The Role of the Undertaker

Thomas J. Jablonsky*, Pride in the Jungle: Community and Everyday Life in Back of the Yards Chicago* (Baltimore: Johns Hopkins University Press, 1993) focuses on the period between the world wars and traces the community's emergence as a distinctive neighborhood with a strong sense of place. A similar study is Robert A. Slayton, *Back of the Yards: The Making of a Local Democracy* (Chicago: University of Chicago Press, 1986).

Days and Nights in "Bronzeville"

For those wishing to study African-American migration to the North, see James R. Grossman, *Land of Hope: Chicago, Black Southerners, and the Great Migration* (Chicago: University of Chicago Press, 1989). The classic study of African-American life in Chicago is Drake St. Clair and Horace R. Cayton, *Black Metropolis: A Study of Negro Life in a Northern City.* Revised and enlarged with an introduction by Richard Wright and a new foreword by William Julius Wilson (Harcourt, Brace, Jovanovich, 1945, 1970; Chicago: University of Chicago Press, 1993). See also Allan H. Spear, *Black Chicago: The Making of a Negro Ghetto, 1890–1920* (Chicago: University of Chicago Press, 1967); and Arna Bontemps and Jack Conroy, *Anyplace But Here* (Hill and Wang, 1966). Dempsey J. Travis offers a personal perspective of growing up black in Chicago in *An Autobiography of Black Chicago* (Chicago: Urban Research Institute, 1981) and *An Autobiography of Black*

Jazz (Chicago: Urban Research Institute, 1983). The heyday of Chicago jazz is examined by William Howland Kenney in *Chicago Jazz: A Cultural History, 1904–1930* (New York: Oxford University Press, 1993).

In Every Dream a Bungalow

A fine article on Chicago's love affair with the bungalow is Daniel J. Prosser, "Chicago and the Bungalow Boom of the 1920s," *Chicago History* 10, no. 2 (summer 1981): 86–95.

LAW AND DISORDER

The German Beer Riots of 1855 (or "Real" Americans Drink Whiskey)

For a general history of Germans in Chicago, see Rudolf A. Hofmeister, *The Germans of Chicago* (Chicago: University of Illinois Press, 1976). Richard Wilson Renner addresses the German beer riots of 1855 in "In a Perfect Ferment: Chicago, the Know-Nothings, and the Riot for Lager Beer," *Chicago History* 5, no. 3 (fall 1976): 161–70. German working-class culture is examined in *German Workers in Chicago: A Documentary History of Working-Class Culture from 1850 to World War I,* edited by Hartmut Keil and John B. Jentz (Urbana, Ill.: University of Illinois Press, 1988).

The Eye That Never Sleeps

Histories of the Pinkertons include James D. Horan, *The Pinkertons: The Detective Dynasty That Made History* (New York: Crown Publishers, 1967); Frank T. Morn, *The Eye That Never Sleeps: A History of the Pinkerton National Detective Agency* (Bloomington, Ind.: Indiana University Press, 1982); and Sigmund A. Lavine, *Allan Pinkerton: America's First Private Eye* (New York: Dodd, Mead and Company, 1963).

Nightmare on Sixty-third Street

For an informative history of Chicago during the 1890s, see Robert I. Goler and Susan E. Hirsch, *A City Comes of Age: Chicago in the 1890s* (Chicago: Chicago Historical Society, 1990); and Richard Lindberg, *Chicago Ragtime: Another Look at Chicago, 1880–1920* (South Bend, Ind.: Icarus Press, 1985). A chapter on the notorious H. H. Holmes murder case appears in *Chicago Murders,* edited by Sewell Peaslee Wright (New York: Duell, Sloan, and Pearce, 1945). See also David Franke, *The Torture Doctor* (New York: Hawthorn Books, 1975). A contemporary perspective is offered in Harold Schecter's *Depraved: The Shocking True Story of America's First Serial Killer* (New York: Pocket Books, 1994).

Streets on Fire: The Chicago Race Riots of 1919

The classic study of the riots is Carl Sandburg, *The Chicago Race Riots, July 1919* (New York: Harcourt, Brace, 1919). William M. Tuttle offers a sociological approach in *Race Riot: Chicago in the Red Summer of 1919* (New York: Atheneum, 1970).

Shutting Down the Levee

The story of Red Top appears in Finis Farr, *Chicago: A Personal History of America's Most American City* (New Rochelle, N.Y.: Arlington House, 1973). See also William T. Stead, *If Christ Came to Chicago* (Chicago: Laird and Lee, 1894). Richard Lindberg presents a lengthy and fascinating portrait of the Levee in the chapter "Levee Low Life," *Chicago Ragtime,* 119–68.

The Gangster and the Songbird

For a somber history of Chicago's underworld, see Virgil W. Peterson, *Barbarians in Our Midst: A History of Chicago Crime and Politics* (Boston: Little, Brown & Co., 1952).

"Scarface" Takes Over Cicero

For biographical information on Capone, see John Kobler, *Capone: The Life and World of Al Capone* (New York: G. P. Putnam's Sons, 1971) and Fred D. Pasly, *Al Capone: The Biography of a Self-Made Man* (New York: Ives Washburn, 1930). A more recent biography is *Capone: The Man and the Era* by Laurence Bergreen (New York: Simon and Schuster, 1994). Capone's nemesis, Eliot Ness, told his own story with the help of Oscar Fraley in *The Untouchables* (New York: Award Books, 1969).

"Texas" Guinan: The Magic Touch of a Sassy Prohibition Baby

The only full-length biography available is Louise Berliner, *Texas Guinan: Queen of the Nightclubs* (Austin, Tex.: University of Texas Press, 1993).

Whispering in the Dark: The Secret World of Speakeasies

The speakeasy era is examined in John H. Lyle, *The Dry and Lawless Years* (Englewood Cliffs, N.J.: Prentice Hall, 1960). For a thoughtful account of the role of the saloon in American life, see Perry Duis, *The Saloon: Public Drinking in Chicago and Boston, 1880–1920* (Urbana, Ill.: University of Illinois Press, 1983).

THE SPIRITUAL LIFE

The Perilous Journey of Father Jacques Marquette

For biographies of Marquette and Jolliet, see Joseph P. Donnelly, *Jacques Marquette* (Chicago: Loyola University Press, 1985); and Virginia S. Eifert, *Louis Jolliet: Explorer of Rivers* (New York: Dodd, Mead & Co., 1961). Gilbert J. Garraghan in *The Jesuits of the Middle United States,* 3 vols. (Chicago: Loyola University Press, 1984) offers a thorough history of Jesuit life in the Midwest. A history of early Chicago is Milo Quaife, *Checagou: From Indian Wigwam to Modern City 1673–1835* (Chicago: University of Chicago Press, 1933).

Ministry for All: The Fourth Presbyterian Church

The story of the Fourth Presbyterian Church is often complex and tricky. Marilee Munger Scroggs proves an able navigator in *A Light in the City: The Fourth Presbyterian Church of Chicago* (Chicago: Fourth Presbyterian Church of Chicago, 1990). See also Elam Davies, *One Hundred Years: The Fourth Presbyterian Church of Chicago* (Chicago: Fourth Presbyterian Church, 1971); and George A. Lane and Algimantas Kezys, *Chicago Churches and Synagogues: An Architectural Pilgrimage* (Chicago: Loyola University Press, 1981).

Dwight Moody and the Business of Saving Souls

For biographies of Moody, see Richard K. Curtis, *They Called Him Mister Moody* (Garden City, N.Y.: Doubleday, 1962); Paul D. Moody, *My Father: An Intimate Portrait of Dwight Moody* (Boston: Little, Brown & Co., 1938); and John C. Pollock, *Moody: A Biographical Portrait of the Pacesetter in Modern Mass Evangelism* (New York: Macmillan, 1963). A history of the Moody Bible Institute is the subject of Gene A. Getz, *MBI: The Story of the Moody Bible Institute* (Chicago: Moody Press, 1969).

The Building of a Great Temple along the North Shore

Michael H. Ebner offers a thoughtful and enlightening history of the North Shore in *Creating Chicago's North Shore: A Suburban History* (Chicago: University of Chicago Press, 1988). See also Robert McClory, "New Time Religion," *Chicago Reader,* September 2, 1983, 8–9, 22–25. For a history of Wilmette, Illinois, see George D. Bushnell, *Wilmette: A History* (Wilmette, Ill.: Wilmette Bicentennial Commission, 1976).

A Red Hat for Cardinal Mundelein

For a biography of Cardinal Mundelein, see Edward R. Kantowicz, *Corporation Sole: Cardinal Mundelein and Chicago Catholicism* (Notre Dame, Ind.: University of Notre Dame Press, 1983). *Catholicism, Chicago Style* (Chicago: Loyola University Press, 1993) is a series of essays by Ellen Skerrett, Edward R. Kantowicz, and Steven M. Avella on the importance of the Catholic Church in Chicago neighborhood history.

POLITICAL BEDFELLOWS

The Day the Mayor Fired the Police Department

Don Fehrenbacher offers a profile of the controversial mayor in *Chicago Giant: A Biography of "Long John" Wentworth* (Madison, Wis.: American History Research Center, 1957).

The First Ward Ball

The always-entertaining Bathhouse and Hinky Dink are in top form in Herman Kogan and Lloyd Wendt, *Lords of the Levee: The Story of Bathhouse John and Hinky Dink* (Indianapolis, Ind.: Bobbs-Merrill Co., 1943).

The Shooting of the Mayor

For a portrait of Carter Harrison, see Claudius O. Johnson, *Carter Henry Harrison I: Political Leader* (Chicago: University of Chicago Press, 1928).

"Big Bill" and the King

Douglas Bukowski tackles the bigger-than-life politician in "Big Bill Thompson: The 'Model' Politician," in *The Mayors: The Chicago Political Tradition,* Paul M. Green and Melvin G. Holli, eds. (Carbondale, Ill.: Southern Illinois University Press, 1987). See also Lloyd Wendt and Herman Kogan, *Big Bill of Chicago* (Indianapolis, Ind.: Bobbs-Merrill Co., 1953).

A Martyr Comes Home to Rest

The definitive biography of Cermak is Alex Gottfried, *Boss Cermak of Chicago: A Study of Political Leadership* (Seattle: University of Washington, 1962). See also Paul M. Green, "Anton J. Cermak: The Man and His Machine" in *The Mayors: The Chicago Political Tradition,* Paul M. Green and Melvin G. Holli, eds. (Carbondale, Ill.: Southern Illinois University Press, 1987).

DISASTERS AND EVENTS

Shipwreck of the *Lady Elgin*

For a description of the shipwreck of the *Lady Elgin* and other tales, see Dwight Boyer, *Ghost Ships of the Great Lakes* (New York: Dodd, Mead, 1968); and Boyer, *True Tales of the Great Lakes* (New York: Dodd, Mead, 1971). See also Walter Havighurst, *The Great Lakes Reader* (New York: Macmillan, 1978); and William Ratigan, *Great Lakes Shipwrecks and Survivals* (Grand Rapids, Mich.: William B. Eerdmans Publishing, 1978).

The *Eastland:* Tragedy in the Chicago River

Ann D. Gordon examines the aftermath of the *Eastland* disaster in "Investigating the *Eastland* Accident," *Chicago History* 10, no. 2 (summer 1981): 74–85. For a complete history, see George W. Hilton, *Eastland: Legacy of the Titanic* (Stanford, Calif.: Stanford University Press, 1995).

The Iroquois Fire

For a personal perspective of the fire, see Ruth Thompson McGibeny, "The Iroquois Theatre Fire," *Chicago History* 3, no. 3 (winter 1974–75): 177–80.

The Dawn of the Atomic Age

Several biographies of Enrico Fermi are available. They include Pierre deLatil, *Enrico Fermi: The Man and His Theories* (New York: P. S. Eriksson, 1964); Emilio Segre, *Enrico Fermi, Physicist* (Chicago: University of Chicago Press, 1970); and Laura Fermi, *Atoms in the Family—My Life with Enrico Fermi* (Chicago: University of Chicago Press, 1954).

THE ARTS

The Celluloid Dream Factory

Charles A. Jahant discusses Chicago's heyday as motion picture capital in "Chicago: Center of the Silent Film Industry," *Chicago History* 3, no. 1 (spring–summer 1974): 45–53.

The Glory Days of Yiddish Theater

For a history of the Jews in Chicago, see H. L. Meites, *History of the Jews of Chicago* (Chicago: Chicago Jewish Historical Society and Wellington Publishing, 1990). This revised edition is a facsimile of the original 1924 edition and contains a new introduction by James R. Grossman. Ira Berkow is a fine writer who creates finely etched portraits of Maxwell Street in *Maxwell Street: Survival in a Bazaar* (Garden City, N.Y.: Doubleday, 1977). See also Philip P. Bregstone, *Chicago and Its Jews: A Cultural History* (Privately published, 1933); Morris A. Gutstein, *A Priceless Heritage, The Epic Growth of Nineteenth Century Chicago Jewry* (New York: Bloch Publishing Co., 1953); and Sentinel Publishing Co., *The Sentinel's History of Chicago Jewry, 1911–1961* (Chicago: Sentinel Publishing Co., 1961). For an evocative description of Jewish neighborhood history, see Carolyn Eastwood, *Chicago's Jewish Street Peddlers* and Beatrice Michaels Shapiro, *Memories of Lawndale* (Chicago: Chicago Jewish Historical Society, 1991); and Irving Cutler, "The Jews of Chicago: From Shtetl to Suburb" in *Ethnic Chicago,* edited by Melvin G. Holli and Peter d'A. Jones (Grand Rapids, Mich.: William B. Eerdmans Publishing, 1984). For a book-length treatment by Cutler, see *The Jews of Chicago* (Champaign, Ill.: University of Illinois Press, 1995).

The Night *Salome* Shocked the Town

Robert L. Brubaker discusses the history of opera in Chicago in "130 Years of Opera in Chicago," *Chicago History* 8, no. 3 (fall 1979): 156–59. See also Ronald L. Davis, *Opera in Chicago* (New York: Appleton-Century, 1966). Mary Garden presents the story of her own life (with Louis Biancolli) in *Mary Garden's Story* (New York: Simon & Schuster, 1951).

The Little Theater Movement

For a look at the little theater movement and the many personalities involved, see Maurice Browne, *Too Late to Lament* (Bloomington, Ind.: Indiana University Press, 1956); Douglas Clayton, "Yesterday's City: Temple of a Living Art," *Chicago History* 22, no. 3 (November 1993): 52–64; Alice Gerstenberg, *Unquenched Fire* (Boston: Small, Maynard and Co., 1912); and Anna Morgan, *My Chicago* (Chicago: R. F. Semour, 1918). For an examination of contemporary off-Loop theater, see Special Collections Department of the Chicago Public Library, *Resetting the Stage: Theater Beyond the Loop 1960–1990* (Chicago: Chicago Public Library, 1990). Thomas J. Schlereth in "A Robin Egg's Renaissance: Chicago Culture, 1893–1933," *Chicago History* 8, no. 3 (fall 1979): 144–55 looks at Chicago culture from a broader perspective, while in "Staging the Avant-Garde" (*Chicago History* 17, nos. 1 and 2 [spring-summer 1988]: 46–61), Stuart J. Hecht describes the role of Hull-House in perpetuating the little theater tradition and its considerable influence on the Chicago theater renaissance of the 1970s and beyond.

The Little Theatre was housed in the Fine Arts Building, a magnificent structure with a renowned history of its own (see Commission on Chicago Historical and Architectural Landmarks, "Fine Arts Building," 1984). Many artists rented studios on its tenth floor, including sculptor Lorado Taft and cartoonist John T. McCutcheon. A fine appreciation of its role in the artistic life of the city is offered by Perry R. Duis in two articles: "'Where is Athens Now? The Fine Arts Building 1898 to 1918," *Chicago History* 6, no. 2 (summer 1977): 66–78; and "'All Else Passes—Art Alone Endures,' The Fine Arts Building, 1918–1930," *Chicago History* 7, no. 1 (spring 1978): 40–51.

In the late 1890s, Chicago was a major center of the burgeoning Arts and Crafts movement, an artistic movement originating in England that sought to create beauty in the design of ordinary products. The Chicago Arts and Crafts Society was founded in 1897 with a membership of 126, which included artists, architects, designers, metalworkers, and writers. Many of the movement's local artisans rented space in the Fine Arts Building. Sharon S. Darling describes the various small shops, studios, and galleries and explores Chicago's neglected role in the movement in "Arts and Crafts Shops in the Fine Arts Building," *Chicago History* 6, no. 2 (summer 1977): 79–85.

Home of the Blues

Many books have been written on the blues. An excellent history is Mike Rowe, *Chicago Breakdown* (New York: Drake Publishers, 1975). Also recommended is Peter Guralnick, *Feel Like Going Home: Portraits in Blues and Rock 'n' Roll* (New York: Vintage Books, 1981). For an up-to-date history of the blues, see Francis Davis, *The History of the Blues: The Roots, the Music, the People from Charley Patton to Robert Cray* (New York: Hyperion, 1995). Blues landmarks are discussed by Dave Hoekstra in "Blue Byways," *Chicago Sun-Times,* May 28, 1995, 15.

VISITORS AND OTHER STRANGERS

Rudy, Oscar, and Sarah's Adventures in the Windy City

To get an outsider's perspective of Chicago, consider Bessie Louise Pierce, *As Others See Chicago: Impressions of Visitors, 1673–1933* (Chicago: University of Chicago Press, 1933).

A City Falls under Houdini's Spell

The standard biography of Houdini, Milbourne Christopher's, *Houdini: The Untold Story* (New York: Thomas Y. Crowell Company, 1969), has been superseded by Ruth Brandon, *The Life and Many Deaths of Harry Houdini* (New York: Random House, 1994). See also *Houdini: His Life and Art* by The Amazing Randi and Bert Randolph Sugar (New York: Grosset and Dunlap, 1976).

SPORTS, FAIRS, AND RECREATION

The Grand Illusion: The World's Columbian Exposition of 1893

The best overall description of the Exposition employing both word and image is Stanley Appelbaum, *The Chicago World's Fair of 1893: A Photographic Record* (New York: Dover Publications, 1980). See also R. Reid Badger, *The Great American Fair: The World's Columbian Exposition and American Culture* (Chicago: Nelson-Hall, 1979); and David F. Burg, *Chicago's White City of 1893* (Lexington, Ky.: University of Kentucky Press, 1976). For a description of the popular Ferris wheel, see Sisley Barnes, "George Ferris' Wheel: The Great Attraction of the Midway Plaisance," *Chicago History* 6, no. 3 (fall 1977): 177–82.

One of the most imposing structures of the fair was the Norway Building. Modeled after an early Christian Norwegian church or stave church (*stavkirke*) from the twelfth century, it was built near Trondheim, Norway, for display at the fair. When the fair ended, the building was moved to the Lake Geneva, Wisconsin, estate of C. K. G. Billings. The property was later purchased by the William Wrigley family. In 1935 Isak Dahle, a Chicago insurance executive who had grown up in the Norwegian community of Mount Horeb, Wisconsin, had the building dismantled and moved to nearby Blue Mounds, Wisconsin. It is now part of the Little Norway pioneer homestead, which Dahle had founded as a tribute to his Norwegian ancestors. For a description of the Norway Building, see Odd S. Lovoll, *A Century of Urban Life: The Norwegians in Chicago Before 1830* (Norwegian-American Historical Association, 1988), 188.

Several recent titles have dared to yield some deeper sociological meanings of the fair. They include James Gilbert, *Perfect Cities: Chicago's Utopias of 1893* (Chicago: University of Chicago Press, 1991); and Neil Harris, Wim de Wit, James Gilbert, and Robert W. Rydell, *Grand Illusions:*

Chicago's World's Fair of 1893 (Chicago: Chicago Historical Society, 1993). For an examination of the Century of Progress of 1933, see Robert W. Rydell, *World of Fairs: The Century of Progress Expositions* (Chicago: University of Chicago Press, 1993).

Amos Alonzo Stagg: A Man for All Seasons

For biographical details on Amos Alonzo Stagg, see Ellis Lucia, *Mr. Football, Amos Alonzo Stagg* (New York: A. S. Barnes, 1970), as well as Stagg's autobiography, *Touchdown* (New York: Longmans, Green & Co., 1927), as told to Wesley Winans Stout. For background information on the University of Chicago and the beginning of its football program, see Thomas Wakefield Goodspeed, *The Story of the University of Chicago, 1890–1925* (Chicago: University of Chicago Press, 1925); and Richard J. Storr, *Harper's University, The Beginnings* (Chicago: University of Chicago Press, 1966).

The "Friendly Confines" of an Earlier Field of Dreams

For a history of the Chicago Cubs, see Jim Enright, *Chicago Cubs* (New York: Macmillan, 1975). Jim Langford offers Cubs history from a personal perspective in *The Game Is Never Over: An Appreciative History of the Chicago Cubs* (South Bend, Ind.: Icarus Press, 1982). For a history of Chicago's other professional baseball team, see Richard C. Lindberg, *Stealing First in a Two-Team Town: The White Sox from Comiskey to Reinsdorf* (Champaign, Ill.: Sagamore Publishing, 1994).

Against All Odds: The Bears Wage a Comeback

The history of the Bears is chronicled in George Vass, *Halas and the Chicago Bears* (Chicago: Henry Regnery Co., 1971). A more recent contribution is the coffee-table book *The Bears: A 75-Year Celebration* (Dallas, Tex.: Taylor Publishing, 1994), by Richard Whittingham.

Riverview: The Closing of a Chicago Landmark

For a history of the popular amusement park, see Al Griffin, *"Step Right Up, Folks!"* (Chicago: Henry Regnery, 1974) and Joseph Sander, "Riverview: Wonderland on Western Avenue," *Chicago Magazine*, November 1983. Strictly for fun is Chuck Wlodarczyk, *Riverview Gone But Not Forgotten: A Photo History 1904–1967* (Chicago: Riverview Publications, 1977).

INDEX

Other titles in the Chicago series from Loyola Press

Reclaiming Our Schools
The Struggle for Chicago School Reform
by Maribeth Vander Weele
Shocking account of one city's struggle to rid itself of educational corruption and bureaucratic waste. Award-winning education reporter for the Chicago Sun-Times, Vander Weele relates, from an insider's point of view, the extraordinary efforts of the Chicago school reform movement to improve a system once called the worst in America.
Hardcover, 366 pp., $21.95 ISBN 0-8294-0812-6 1994
Pbk perfect, 366 pp., $12.95 ISBN 0-8294-0773-1 1994

Catholicism, Chicago Style
by Ellen Skerrett, Edward R. Kantowicz, and Steven M. Avella
Catholicism, Chicago Style marks the 150th anniversary year of the Archdiocese of Chicago. Includes eight historical essays reflecting the distinctive characteristics of Catholicism in Chicago. Contains 79 black-and-white photographs.
Hardcover, 194 pp., $35.00 ISBN 0-8294-0774-X 1993
Pbk perfect, 194 pp., $21.95 ISBN 0-8294-0799-5 1993

Chicago Portraits
Biographies of 250 Famous Chicagoans
by June Skinner Sawyers
Foreword by Bill Kurtis
Detailed biographies of prominent figures from Chicago's past, including Richard J. Daley, Bill Veeck, and Jane Addams. Each entry, which is accompanied by a black-and-white photograph, contains facts about the individual's childhood, education, career, and accomplishments.
Hardcover, 322 pp., $27.95 ISBN 0-8294-0701-4 1991
Pbk perfect, 322 pp., $22.95 ISBN 0-8294-0700-6 1991

Streetwise Chicago
A History of Chicago Street Names
by Don Hayner and Tom McNamee
Filled with delightful and surprising stories of the history of every street name in Chicago. Accented by historical photographs and illustrations.

Hardcover, 153 pp., $22.50 ISBN 0-8294-0597-6 1988
Pbk perfect, 153 pp., $14.95 ISBN 0-8294-0596-8 1988

Chicago: City of Neighborhoods
Histories and Tours
by Dominic A. Pacyga and Ellen Skerrett
Recounts the origins, growth, and development of 49 of Chicago's 77 neighborhoods. Contains histories, a walking guide to the Loop, 14 driving tours of the neighborhoods, maps, and photographs.
Pbk perfect, 582 pp., $22.95 ISBN 0-8294-0497-X 1986

Chicago Stained Glass
by Erne R. and Florence Frueh
photographs by Erne R. Frueh and George A. Lane, S.J.
The first book completely devoted to Chicago's vast and still largely undiscovered stained glass treasures. Lavishly illustrated with more than 80 color plates.
Hardcover, 160 pp., $19.95 ISBN 0-8294-0435-X 1983

Chicago Churches and Synagogues
An Architectural Pilgrimage
by George A. Lane, S.J.
photographs by George A. Lane, S.J., and Algimantas Kezys
Detailed descriptions of 125 architecturally significant churches and synagogues. Outlines the history of each building and the congregations who worshiped there. More than 225 black-and-white photos and 20 color plates.
Hardcover, 255 pp., $25.00 ISBN 0-8294-0373-6 1981

Wild Onion Books
an imprint of Loyola Press
3441 North Ashland Avenue
Chicago, Illinois 60657
FOUNDED IN 1912
Call toll-free (800) 621-1008 or (312) 281-1818 in Illinois